The Hebrew Bible

The
Hebrew Bible

Dan Cohn-Sherbok

CASSELL

For Lavinia

Cassell
Wellington House, 125 Strand, London WC2R 0BB
215 Park Avenue South, New York, NY 10003

First published 1996

British Library Cataloguing in Publication Data
A catalogue record for this book is available from the British Library.
ISBN 0 304 33702 1 Hardback
    0 304 33703 X Paperback

Library of Congress Cataloging-in-Publication Data
Cohn-Sherbok, Dan.
    The Hebrew Bible / Dan Cohn-Sherbok.
      p.   cm.
    Includes bibliographical references and index.
    ISBN 0-304-33702-1. — ISBN 0-304-33703-X (pbk.)
    1. Bible. O.T. — Introductions.   I. Title.
    BS1140.2b.C643   1996
    221.6'1—dc20   95-41003
                                                     CIP

Cover illustration: *Habakkuk and the Angel*
This depicts the prophet Habakkuk who was miraculously transported to Babylon to feed the prophet Daniel. This Apocryphal image symbolizes God's love for his chosen people.

Typeset by BookEns Ltd, Royston, Herts.
Printed and bound in Great Britain by Biddles Ltd,
Guildford and Kings Lynn

Contents

CONTENTS

Preface

For 2000 years the Hebrew Scriptures have been a source of inspiration for both Jews and Christians. Yet the Hebrew Bible is not uniform in character; rather, it is composed of a number of separate books incorporating history, theology, philosophy, prayer, religious poetry and wisdom. Because of its variegated nature, the Hebrew Bible is not easy to understand – indeed, anyone who begins to read Scripture from the beginning would in all likelihood quickly become baffled and bored. The purpose of this survey is hence to provide an introduction to its contents.

Designed for students, Bible study groups as well as general readers, this guide begins with a time-scale of the ancient Near East; its purpose is to highlight the major events and personalities of the biblical narrative. This is supplemented by a map of the ancient world as well as the Holy Land. The book then continues with an account of the place of the Hebrew Scriptures in Jewish life and thought from the early rabbinic period to the present day. This is followed by an outline of each of the thirty-six books of the Jewish canon, following the order of the Jewish canon rather than the more familiar Protestant canon. A brief presentation of their contents illustrated by quotations from Scripture follows – in each case the presentation proceeds according to the structure of the book itself. The volume concludes with a list of further reading for those who seek to gain a greater understanding of the Hebrew Scriptures; this is composed of commentaries as well as studies of each individual book.

The survey is thus intended as a first point of entry into this fascinating and rich religious and cultural heritage – it is hoped that readers will be sufficiently stimulated by this guide to deepen their understanding of the biblical text. As the Jewish sage Ben Bag Bag declared with regard to the *Torah*: 'Turn it and turn it over again, for everything is in it.'

Acknowledgements

I would like to acknowledge my indebtedness to a number of important books from which I have obtained information: R.E. Brown, J.A. Fitzmyer, R.E. Murphy, *The New Jerome Bible Handbook* (London, Geoffrey Chapman, 1992); A. McGrath, *NIV Bible Commentary* (London, Hodder and Stoughton, 1988); R.B. Dillard, T. Longman III, *An Introduction to the Old Testament* (Leicester, Apollos, 1995).

Scripture quotations are from the Revised Standard Version of the Bible, copyright 1946, 1952, 1971 by the Division of Christian Education of the National Council of the Churches of Christ in the USA. Used by permission.

Chronology

JEWISH HISTORY		WORLD HISTORY
Patriarchs	c. 19th–16th century BCE	
Joseph	c. 19th–16th century BCE	
Exodus	c. 1250–1230 BCE	Rameses II 1290–1224 BCE
Joshua	c. 1230–1190 BCE	
Judges	c. 1200–1050 BCE	
Saul	c. 1050–1010 BCE	
David	1010–970 BCE	
Solomon	970–930 BCE	

Divided Kingdom: Israel		Prophets	
Jeroboam	930–909 BCE		
Nadab	909–908 BCE		
Baasha	908–885 BCE		
Elah	885–884 BCE		
Zimri	884 BCE		
Omri	884–873 BCE		
Ahab	873–853 BCE	Elijah	
Ahaziah	853–852 BCE		
Joram	852–841 BCE	Elisha	
Jehu	841–813 BCE		
Jehoahaz	813–798 BCE		
Jehoash	798–781 BCE		
Jeroboam II	781–753 BCE	Amos	
Zechariah	753–752 BCE		
Shallum	752 BCE		
Menahem	752–741 BCE	Hosea	
Pekahiah	741–739 BCE		Tiglath Pileser III 747–727 BCE
Pekah	739–731 BCE		
Hoshea	732–722 BCE		
Fall of Israel	722 BCE		Shalmaneser V 727–722 BCE of Assyria

CHRONOLOGY

Divided Kingdom: Judah		*Prophets*	
Rehoboam	930–913 BCE		
Abijah	913–910 BCE		
Asa	910–869 BCE		
Jehoshaphat	869–848 BCE		
Jehoram	848–841 BCE		
Ahaziah	841 BCE		
Athaliah	841–835 BCE		
Joash	835–796 BCE		
Amaziah	796–767 BCE		
Uzziah	792–740 BCE		Tiglath Pileser III 747–727 BCE
Jotham	739–731 BCE	Isaiah	
Ahaz	735–715 BCE	Micah	Shalmaneser V 727–722 BCE of Assyria
Hezekiah	715–686 BCE		Sennacherib 705–681 BCE of Assyria
Manasseh	686–641 BCE		
Amon	641–639 BCE		
Josiah	640–609 BCE	Jeremiah Zephaniah Nahum	
Jehoahaz	609 BCE	Habakkuk	Nebuchadnezzar 605 BCE of Babylon
Jehoiakim	609–598 BCE		
Jehoiachin	597 BCE		
Zedekiah	597–586 BCE	Ezekiel Obadiah	
Cyrus' Decree	538 BCE		Cyrus of Persia 539–530 BCE
		Second Isaiah Third Isaiah Haggai Zechariah Malachi	
Nehemiah in Jerusalem	445 BCE	Nehemiah	
Ezra in Jerusalem	428 BCE	Ezra	
Israel under Ptolemies	328–198 BCE		
Israel under Seleucids	198–166 BCE		Antiochus Epiphanes 175–163 BCE

Temple rededicated	165 BCE
Jewish independence	142 BCE
Herod the Great	40 BCE – 4 CE
Rebellion against Rome	66 – 70 CE

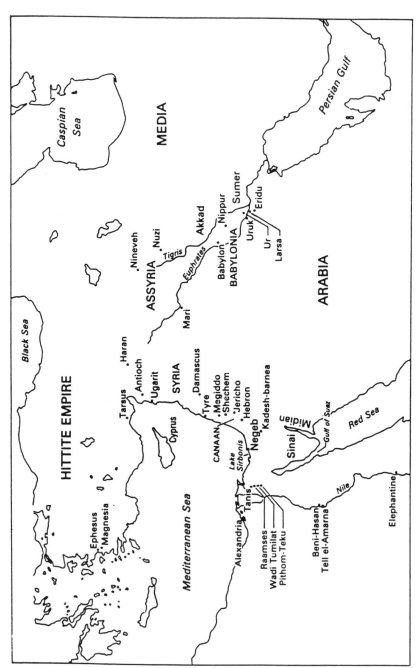

Map 1 *The ancient Near East*

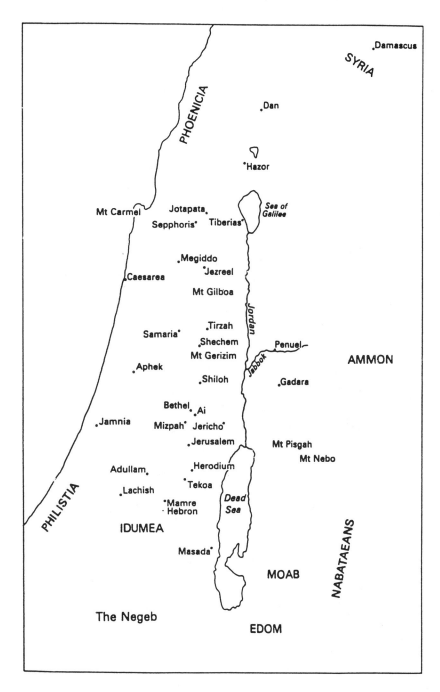

Damascus

SYRIA

PHOENICIA

Dan

Hazor

Mt Carmel   Jotapata   Sea of
Sepphoris   Tiberias   Galilee

Megiddo
Jezreel
Caesarea   Mt Gilboa

Jordan

Tirzah
Samaria   Shechem   Penuel
Mt Gerizim   Jabbok   AMMON
Aphek   Shiloh   Gadara

Bethel   Ai
Jamnia   Mizpah   Jericho
Jerusalem   Mt Pisgah
Mt Nebo
Adullam   Herodium
Tekoa
Lachish   Dead
Mamre   Sea
Hebron

IDUMEA

Masada   NABATAEANS

MOAB

The Negeb

EDOM

Map 2   *Ancient Israel*

Introduction

The Jewish faith is a revealed religion. Its basis is the Bible. The Hebrew name for the canon of Scripture is *Tanakh*: the Hebrew term is an abbreviation of the principal letters of the words standing for its three divisions: *Torah* (teaching); *Neviim* (prophets); *Ketuvim* (writings). The *Torah* consists of Genesis, Exodus, Leviticus, Numbers and Deuteronomy; according to tradition these five books were revealed by God to Moses on Mount Sinai. The second division of the Hebrew Bible – Prophets – is divided into two parts. The first – Former Prophets – contains the books of Joshua, Judges, 1 and 2 Samuel and 1 and 2 Kings. The second part – Latter Prophets – is composed of the major prophets (Isaiah, Jeremiah and Ezekiel) and the minor prophets (Hosea, Joel, Amos, Obadiah, Jonah, Micah, Nahum, Habakkuk, Zephaniah, Haggai, Zechariah and Malachi). The third division consists of a variety of divinely inspired books: Psalms, Proverbs, Job, Song of Songs, Ruth, Lamentations, Ecclesiastes, Esther, Daniel, Ezra, Nehemiah and 1 and 2 Chronicles.

During the Second Temple period and afterwards, a large number of other books were written by Jews in Hebrew, Aramaic and Greek which were not included in the biblical canon. None the less, these texts did gain canonical status in the Roman Catholic and Eastern Orthodox Churches. Known as the Apocrypha, they had an important impact on Christian thought. The most substantial is the Wisdom of Jesus Son of Sirah (also known as Ben Sira or Ecclesiasticus). Other works include: the Wisdom of Solomon, 1 and 2 Maccabees, Tobit and Judith. Additional literary sources of the Second Temple period are known as the Pseudepigrapha – these non-canonical books consist of such works as the Testament of the Twelve Patriarchs, 1 and 2 Enoch and Jubilees.

The books of the Hebrew Bible in the Jewish canon, Protestant canon, and Roman Catholic and Orthodox canons are arranged in the following order:

Jewish Canon	Protestant Canon	Roman Catholic and Orthodox Canon
Torah	*Pentateuch*	*Pentateuch*
1. Genesis	1. Genesis	1. Genesis
2. Exodus	2. Exodus	2. Exodus
3. Leviticus	3. Leviticus	3. Leviticus
4. Numbers	4. Numbers	4. Numbers
5. Deuteronomy	5. Deuteronomy	5. Deuteronomy
Prophets	*Historical Books*	*Historical Books*
The Former Prophets	6. Joshua	6. Joshua
	7. Judges	7. Judges
6. Joshua	8. Ruth	8. Ruth
7. Judges	9–10. 1, 2 Samuel	9–10. 1, 2 Samuel
8. 1, 2 Samuel	11–12. 1, 2 Kings	11–12. 1, 2 Kings
9. 1, 2 Kings	13–14. 1, 2 Chronicles	13–14. 1, 2 Chronicles
The Latter Prophets	15. Ezra	15. Ezra
	16. Nehemiah	16. Nehemiah
10. Isaiah	17. Esther	17. Tobit
11. Jeremiah		18. Judith
12. Ezekiel		19. Esther
13. Hosea		20–21. 1, 2 Maccabees
14. Joel	*Poetical and Wisdom Books*	*Poetical and Wisdom Books*
15. Amos		
17. Jonah	19. Psalms	23. Psalms
18. Micah	20. Proverbs	24. Proverbs
19. Nahum	21. Ecclesiastes	25. Ecclesiastes
20. Habakkuk	22. Song of Songs	26. Song of Songs
21. Zephaniah		27. Wisdom of Solomon
22. Haggai		
23. Zechariah		28. Ecclesiasticus
24. Malachi	*Prophetic Books*	*Prophetic Books*
Writings	23. Isaiah	29. Isaiah
25. Psalms	24. Jeremiah	30. Jeremiah
26. Proverbs	25. Lamentations	31. Lamentations
27. Job	26. Ezekiel	32. Baruch
28. Song of Songs	27. Daniel	33. Ezekiel

29. Ruth	28. Hosea	34. Daniel
30. Lamentations	29. Joel	35. Hosea
31. Ecclesiastes	30. Amos	36. Joel
32. Esther	31. Obadiah	37. Amos
33. Daniel	32. Jonah	38. Obadiah
34. Ezra	33. Micah	39. Jonah
35. Nehemiah	34. Nahum	40. Micah
36. 1, 2 Chronicles	35. Habakkuk	41. Nahum
	36. Zephaniah	42. Habakkuk
	37. Haggai	43. Zephaniah
	38. Zechariah	44. Haggai
	39. Malachi	45. Zechariah
		46. Malachi

In rabbinic literature a distinction is drawn between the revelation of the Pentateuch (*Torah* in the narrow sense) and the prophetic writings. This is frequently expressed by saying that the *Torah* was given directly by God, whereas the prophetic books were given by means of prophecy. The remaining books of the Bible (Hagiographa) were conveyed by means of the holy spirit rather than through prophecy. None the less all these writings constitute the canon of Scripture.

According to the rabbis, the expositions and elaborations of the Written Law (*Torah She-Bi-Ketav*) were also revealed by God to Moses on Mount Sinai; subsequently they were passed from generation to generation, and through this process additional legislation was incorporated. This process is referred to as 'The Oral Torah' (*Torah She-Be-Al Peh*). Thus traditional Judaism affirms that God's revelation is twofold and binding for all time. Committed to this belief, Orthodox Jews pray in the synagogue that God will guide them to do his will as recorded in their sacred literature:

O our Father, merciful Father, ever compassionate, have mercy upon us. O put it into our hearts to understand and to discern, to mark, learn and teach, to heed, to do and to fulfil in love all the words of instruction in thy *Torah*. Enlighten our eyes in thy *Torah*, and let our hearts cling to thy commandments, and make us single-hearted to love and fear thy name, so that we never be put to shame.

In the Middle Ages this traditional belief was continually affirmed. Thus the twelfth-century Jewish philosopher, Moses Maimonides declared that the belief in *Torah MiSinai* (*Torah* from Sinai) is a fundamental principle of the Jewish faith:

> The *Torah* was revealed from heaven. This implies our belief that the whole of the *Torah* found in our hands this day is the *Torah* that was handed down by *Moses*, and that it is all of divine origin. By this I mean that the whole of the *Torah* came unto him from before God in a manner which is metaphorically called 'speaking'; but the real nature of that communication is unknown to everybody except to Moses to whom it came.
>
> > (*in* L. Jacobs, *Principles of the Jewish Faith*,
> > Jason Aronson, North Vale, NJ, 1988, p. 216)

Like Maimonides, the thirteenth-century philosopher Nahmanides in his *Commentary to the Pentateuch* argued that Moses wrote the Five Books of Moses at God's dictation. It is likely, he observed, that Moses wrote Genesis and part of Exodus when he descended from Mount Sinai. At the end of the forty years in the wilderness he completed the rest of the Pentateuch. Nahmanides observed that this view follows the rabbinic tradition that the *Torah* was given scroll by scroll. For Nahmanides, Moses was like a scribe who copied an older work. Underlying this conception is the mystical idea of a primordial *Torah* which contains the words describing events long before they happened. This entire record was in heaven before the creation of the world. In addition, Nahmanides maintained that the secrets of the *Torah* were revealed to Moses and are referred to in the *Torah* by the use of special letters, the numerical values of words and letters, and the adornment of Hebrew characters.

Paralleling Nahmanides' mystical interpretation of the *Torah*, the medieval mystical work, the *Zohar*, asserts that the *Torah* contains mysteries beyond human comprehension. As the *Zohar* explains:

> Said R. Simeon: 'Alas for the man who regards the *Torah* as a book of mere tales and everyday matters! If that were so, even we could compose a *Torah* dealing with everyday affairs, and of even greater excellence. Nay, even the princes of the world possess books of greater worth which we could use as a model for composing such *Torah*. The *Torah*, however, contains in all its words supernal truths and sublime mysteries ... Thus had the *Torah* not clothed herself in garments of this world, the world could not endure it. The stories of the *Torah* are thus only her outer garments, and whoever looks upon that garment as being the *Torah* itself, woe to that man — such a one has no portion in the next world.'
>
> > (*Ibid.*, p. 225)

In the modern period, however, it has become increasingly difficult to sustain the traditional Jewish concept of divine revelation in the light of scholarly investigation and discovery. As early as the sixteenth century, scholars pointed out that the Five Books of Moses appear to be composed from different sources. In the middle of the nineteenth century sustained investigation by two German scholars, Karl Heinrich Graf and Julius Wellhausen, concluded that the Five Books of Moses are composed of four main documents which once existed separately but were later combined by a series of editors or redactors. The first document, 'J', dating from the ninth century BCE, attributes the most anthropomorphic character to God, referred to by the four Hebrew letters YHWH. The second source, 'E', stemming from the eighth century BCE, is less anthropomorphic and utilizes the divine name *Elohim*. In the seventh century BCE the 'D' source was written, concentrating on religious purity and the priesthood. Finally, the 'P' source from the fifth century BCE, which has a more transcendental view of God, emphasizes the importance of the sacrificial cult.

By utilizing this framework, Graf and Wellhausen maintained that it is possible to account for the manifold problems and discrepancies in the biblical text. The Graf-Wellhausen hypothesis was subsequently modified by other scholars. Some preferred not to speak of separate sources but of circles of tradition. On this view, J, E, D, and P represent oral traditions rather than written documents. Further, these scholars stress that the separate traditions themselves contain early material; thus it is a mistake to think they originated in their entirety at particular periods. Other scholars reject the theory of separate sources altogether; they argue that oral traditions were modified throughout the history of ancient Israel and only eventually were compiled into a single narrative. Yet despite these different theories there is a general recognition among modern biblical critics — including Reform, Conservative and Reconstructionist Jews — that the Pentateuch was not written by Moses. Rather, it is seen as a collection of traditions originating at different times in ancient Israel.

In addition to the findings of biblical scholarship, textual studies of ancient manuscripts highlight the improbability of the traditional Jewish view of Scripture. According to the Jewish heritage, the Hebrew text of the Five Books of Moses used in synagogues today (the Masoretic text) is the same as that given to Moses. Yet it is widely accepted among scholars that the script of contemporary

Torah scrolls is not the same as that which was current in ancient Israel from the time of the monarchy until the sixth century BCE. It was only later, possibly under Aramaic influence, that the square script was adopted as the standard for Hebrew writing. Furthermore, the fact that the ancient translations of the Hebrew Bible into languages such as Syriac and Greek contain variant readings from the Masoretic text suggests that the Hebrew text of the Pentateuch now in use is not entirely free from error.

A final aspect of modern studies which bears on the question of Mosaic authorship concerns the influence of the ancient Near East on the Bible. According to Orthodox Judaism, the Five Books of Moses were essentially created out of nothing. But there are strong parallels in the Jewish Bible to laws, stories and myths found throughout the ancient Near East. It is unlikely that this is simply a coincidence – the similarities offer compelling evidence that the Pentateuch emerged in a specific social and cultural context. The authors of the biblical period shared much the same world view as their neighbours and no doubt transformed this framework to fit their own religious ideas. In this light, most modern biblical scholars would find it impossible to reconcile the traditional conception of Mosaic authorship of the Five Books of Moses with the discoveries of modern biblical criticism and scientific discovery.

For Orthodox Jews, however, such investigations are irrelevant. Orthodox Judaism remains committed to the view that the Written as well as the Oral *Torah* were imparted by God to Moses on Mount Sinai. This act of revelation serves as the basis for the entire legal system as well as doctrinal beliefs about God. Yet despite such an adherence to tradition, many modern Orthodox Jews pay only lip service to such a conviction. The gap between traditional belief and contemporary views of the *Torah* is even greater in the non-Orthodox branches of Judaism. Here – among Reform, Conservative and Reconstructionist Jews – there is a general acceptance of the findings of biblical scholarship. Such a non-fundamentalist approach, which takes account of recent scholarly developments in the field of biblical studies, rules out the traditional belief in the infallibility of Scripture and thereby provides a rationale for changing the law and reinterpreting the theology of the Hebrew Scriptures in the light of contemporary knowledge. In the modern period, therefore, there has been a shift away from the fundamentalism of the past – none the less non-Orthodox Jews join ranks with the Orthodox in continuing to regard the Jewish Bible as fundamental to the faith. As the liturgy used in all synagogues proclaims: 'It is a tree of life to those who hold fast to it.'

TORAH

1. Genesis

1. History of the nation (1: 1–11: 26)
   1. Creation of the cosmos (1: 1–2: 3)
   2. Creation of Adam and Eve and their offspring (2: 4–4: 26)
      a. Adam and Eve (2: 4–3: 24)
      b. Cain and Abel (4: 1–16)
      c. Cain's descendants (4: 17–24)
      d. Seth (4: 25–26)
   3. Generations before the flood (5: 1–6: 8)
      a. Adam to Noah (5: 1–32)
      b. Divine beings and women (6: 1–8)
   4. The flood (6: 9–9: 29)
      a. Flood (6: 9–9: 17)
      b. Sons of Noah (9: 18–29)
   5. The world and Babel (10: 1–11.19)
      a. Noah's descendants (10: 1–31)
      b. Tower of Babel (10: 32–11: 9)
      c. Shem to Terah (11: 10–26)

2. Ancestors of Israel (11: 27–50: 26)
   1. Abraham and Sarah (11: 27–25: 18)
      a. Terah in Haran (11: 27–32)
      b. Abraham's journey to Canaan (12: 1–9)
      c. Abraham and Sarah in Egypt (12: 10–13: 1)
      d. Abraham and Lot (13: 2–18)
      e. Abraham and the kings (14: 1–24)
      f. God's promise to Abraham (15: 1–21)
      g. Abraham and Hagar (16: 1–16)
      h. God's covenant with Abraham (17: 1–27)
      i. Abraham, Lot and Sodom (18: 1–19: 38)
      j. Abraham and Abimelech (20: 1–18)
      k. Birth of Isaac and expulsion of Hagar and Ishmael
         (21: 1–21)

      l. Treaty with Abimelech (21: 22–34)
      m. God's test of Abraham (22: 1–19)
      n. Ancestors of Nahor (22: 20–24)
      o. Burial site for Sarah (23: 1–20)
      p. Isaac's wife (24: 1–67)
      q. Abraham's descendants (25: 1–18)

2. Isaac and Jacob (25: 19–36: 43)
      a. Birth of Esau and Jacob (25: 19–34)
      b. Isaac stories (26: 1–35)
      c. Jacob's blessing (27: 1–45)
      d. Jacob to Paddan-aram (27: 46–28: 9)
      e. Jacob's vision at Bethel (28: 10–22)
      f. Jacob's marriages (29: 1–30)
      g. Jacob's children (29: 31–30: 24)
      h. Jacob and Laban (30: 25–43)
      i. Jacob's escape (31: 1–54)
      j. Preparation for confronting Esau (32: 1–22)
      k. Jacob wrestles with God (32: 23–33)
      l. Jacob and Esau (33: 1–20)
      m. Rape of Dinah (34: 1–21)
      n. Jacob at Bethel (35: 1–15)
      o. Various events (35: 16–29)
      p. Esau's descendants (36: 1–43)

3. Story of Joseph (37: 1–50: 26)
      a. Joseph into Egypt (37: 1–36)
      b. Judah and Tamar (38: 1–30)
      c. Joseph's temptation (39: 1–23)
      d. Joseph and prisoner's dreams (40: 1–23)
      e. Joseph and Pharaoh's dreams (41: 1–57)
      f. Joseph and his brothers (42: 1–38)
      g. Journey to Egypt (43: 1–45: 28)
      h. Jacob's journey to Egypt (46: 1–30)
      i. Pharaoh (46: 31–47: 28)
      j. Jacob adopts Joseph's sons (47: 29–48: 22)
      k. Jacob's testament (49: 1–28)
      l. Death of Jacob and Joseph (49: 29–50: 26)

The Book of Genesis, the first book of the *Torah*, traces the history of the world from creation through God's call to Abraham, Isaac, Jacob and their descendants. The Hebrew title, *Bereshit* (in the beginning) is based on the initial words of the book; the English title

Genesis refers to the opening theme of the book – creation – and is derived via the Latin translation of the title of the book in the Greek translation (Septuagint). The book itself divides naturally into two parts: (a) the history of early humankind (1–11); and (b) the story of the patriarchs and their descendants (12–50). In theory the time span for this book is 2307 years, a sum derived by combining the ages of the fathers of humanity at the birth of their successors with the years that elapsed between the birth of Abraham and the death of Joseph. The themes elaborated in Genesis include: creation, the first man and woman, the origin of evil, the moral law, the unity of humankind, divine election, and the covenant.

Genesis begins with an account of the creation of the universe – a depiction which differs in numerous ways from the myths of the ancient Near East. Unlike the Babylonian creation poem, *Emunah Elish*, creation in the Jewish Bible is presented as a manifestation of the divine will. Here God is described as forming the cosmos without any struggle, and all created entities are depicted as having no divine aspect. God is utterly transcendent, ruling over his creation: light, the firmament of heaven, the dry land with its vegetation, and the seas. These entities, which were formed on the first three days, provide an abode for the objects created on the following three days: sun, moon and stars, fish, birds and animals. According to Genesis, humankind was created in God's image to have dominion over the earth. The creation narrative concludes with God's resting from his work on the seventh day.

The Garden of Eden story (2: 5–3: 24) provides a different picture of the process of creation. In this account the history of Adam and Eve is described in detail: Adam was placed into an idyllic setting together with wild animals and birds; later a female partner, Eve, was fashioned from his rib. God then allowed this couple to eat from all the trees of the garden except from the tree of the knowledge of good and evil. When tempted by the serpent, however, they disobeyed God's command and ate the forbidden fruit. As a punishment they were banished from the garden, and condemned to suffer hardship and death.

The theme of human freedom is developed by the account of Cain and Abel (4: 1–16). Cain, the farmer, was jealous of his brother Abel whose offering to God was accepted in preference to his own. Full of rage, he murdered his brother. When confronted by God, Cain disclaimed any knowledge. 'Am I my brother's keeper?,' he asked. Condemned to wander the earth, Cain was denounced for his immorality. This narrative is followed by a series of genealogical lists – yet as humankind turned out so badly, God resolved to destroy all living things by means of a flood. But he spared Noah together with his family because he was deemed to be righteous among his generation. Subsequently, however, God stated he would never destroy humanity again and established a covenant through Noah, symbolized by the rainbow.

This primeval narrative focuses on the offspring of Noah who populated the earth. Chapter 11 goes on to explain the human quest to achieve fame through the construction of a tower reaching to heaven. God, however, disapproved of this plan and confounded people's speech:

> And the Lord came down to see the city and the tower, which the sons of men had built. And the Lord said, 'Behold, they are one people, and they have all one language; and this is only the beginning of what they will do; and nothing that they propose to do will now be impossible for them. Come, let us go down, and there confuse their language, that they may not understand one another's speech.' (11: 5–7)

The remaining chapters of Genesis trace the history of the Jewish nation, beginning with the patriarch Abraham. According to Scripture, Abraham was the father of the Jewish nation. Originally known as Abram, he came from Ur of the Chaldeans – a Sumerian city of Mesopotamia near the head of the Persian Gulf. Together with his father Terah, his wife Sarai, and his nephew Lot, he travelled to Haran, a trading centre in northern Syria. There his father died, and God called upon him to go to Canaan: 'Go from your country and your kindred and your father's house to the land I will show you. And I will make of you a great nation' (12: 1–2). During a famine in Canaan, he went first to Egypt and then proceeded to the Negeb, finally settling in the plain near Hebron. Here he experienced a revelation which confirmed that his deliverance from Ur was an act of providence: 'I am the Lord who brought you from Ur of the Chaldeans, to give you this land to possess' (15: 7).

Since Sarai had not given birth to children, Abram had relations with her servant girl, Hagar, who bore Ishmael. But when Abram was ninety-nine and Sarai ninety, God granted them a son, Isaac. It was then that Abram was given his new name Abraham ('the father of a multitude'), and Sarai was renamed Sarah ('princess'). When Isaac was born, Abraham sent Hagar and Ishmael away at Sarah's request. During this time God made a covenant with Abraham symbolized by an act of circumcision: 'You shall be circumcised in the flesh of your foreskins, and it shall be a sign of the covenant between me and you' (17: 11). Later God tested Abraham's dedication by ordering him to sacrifice Isaac, only telling him at the last moment to refrain. When Isaac became older, Abraham sent a servant to his kinsfolk in Hebron to find a wife, and the messenger returned with Rebecca. After many years, God answered Isaac's prayers for a son, and twins — Esau and Jacob — were born. Jacob bought his brother's birthright for food, and with his mother's help secured Isaac's blessing thereby incurring Esau's wrath. Fleeing from his brother, Jacob travelled northwards towards Haran; en route he had a vision of a ladder rising to heaven and heard God speak to him promising that his offspring would inherit the land and fill the earth.

After arriving in Haran, Jacob worked for twenty years as a shepherd for his uncle Laban. There he married Laban's daughters Rachel and Leah, and they and their maids (Bilhah and Zilpah) bore twelve sons and a daughter. When he eventually returned to Canaan Jacob wrestled with a mysterious stranger in the gorge of the Jabbok river, a tributary of the Jordan, where God bestowed upon him the new name 'Israel':

> When the man saw that he did not prevail against Jacob, he touched the hollow of his thigh; and Jacob's thigh was put out of joint as he wrestled with him. Then he said, 'Let me go, for the day is breaking.' But Jacob said, 'I will not let you go, unless you bless me.' And he said to him, 'What is your name?' And he said, 'Jacob.' Then he said, 'Your name shall no more be called Jacob, but Israel, for you have striven with God and with men, and have prevailed.' (32: 25–28)

Jacob was welcomed by Esau in Edom, but then the brothers parted. Jacob lived in Canaan until one of his sons, Joseph, invited him to settle in Egypt where he died at the age of 147.

For some time scholars have attempted to relate the patriarchal stories to biblical times. In particular they have emphasized, on the basis of ancient documents found at the Mesopotamian sites of Mari and Nuzi, that the accounts of the Hebrew patriarchs accurately reflect the conditions of the Middle Bronze Age period (2000–1500 BCE). Names like Abraham, Isaac and Jacob, for example, have been found in numerous texts — they appear to have been especially popular among the Amorites. Other names from Genesis as well (such as Terah and Ishmael) were also widely used. Furthermore, these ancient documents illustrate that the wanderings of the patriarchs mirror what is known of life in the early part of the second millennium BCE. The legal documents found at Nuzi also help to explain patriarchal customs. Though these Mari and Nuzi texts do not specially refer to the patriarchs themselves, we can see that the Genesis legends are largely in accord with the laws and customs of the second millennium BCE. Thus there is good reason to believe that the Genesis narrative preserved a broadly accurate picture of the earliest ancestors of the Jewish people.

The history of the three patriarchs is followed by the cycle of stories about Jacob's son Joseph. As a young boy, Joseph was presented with a special coat (or a long-sleeved robe) of many colours as a sign that he was his father's favourite. When he was in Shechem helping his brothers tend his family flocks, he angered them by recounting dreams in which they bowed down before him. They reacted by plotting his death, but one of the brothers (Reuben) persuaded them to wait, and another (Judah) suggested that they should sell him as a slave rather than kill him. Eventually Joseph was taken to Egypt; his brothers dipped his coat in a kid's blood and declared to their father that he had been mauled by a wild animal. In Egypt Joseph served in the house of Potiphar but was falsely accused by Potiphar's wife of rape and incarcerated in prison. Some time later he was set free by the chief minister of the land. After a famine, he made the country rich and later encountered his brothers who came before him to buy grain. Movingly he revealed to them his true identity, and God's providential care: 'I am your brother, Joseph,' he declared, 'whom you sold into Egypt. And now do not be distressed, or angry with yourselves, because you sold me here; for God sent me before you to preserve life' (45: 4–5). Joseph died when he was 110, and his family remained and flourished in Egypt.

As far as Joseph is concerned, scholars point out that the Joseph legends consist of a collection of stories which were woven together into a complex form. Yet it is recognized that Semitic-speaking groups had for centuries been emigrating into Egypt to escape the adverse conditions in the north as well as to find food and engage in trade. Some scholars have pointed out that if the story of Joseph took place in the time of the Hyksos empire in Egypt (1720–1580/ 1567 BCE), it is possible that these non-Egyptian Semitic-speaking rulers were more likely to appoint an alien like Joseph to a position of authority. Other scholars, however, date the Joseph story much later; they suggest that the ancient Hebrews may have migrated to Egypt during the reign of the Pharaoh Seti I (1304–1290), the son of

Rameses I. On this account the pharaoh who 'did not know Joseph' may have been Rameses II (1290–1224 BCE) who appears to have built the cities of Pithom and Rameses where it is recorded that the Jewish people worked as slaves.

2. Exodus

    c. Covenant law (20: 22–26)
      i. The shrine (20: 22–26)
      ii. Hebrew slaves (21: 1–11)
      iii. Capital crimes (21: 12–17)
      iv. Harm or death of humans and animals caused by neglect (21: 18–36)
      v. Burglary and theft (22: 1–4)
      vi. Burning another's fields (22: 5–6)
      vii. Deposited property (22: 7–15)
      viii. Seduction of a young woman (22: 16–17)
      ix. Social and cultic issues (22: 18–23: 19)
      x. Blessings (23: 20–33)
    d. Ratification of the covenant (24: 1–18)
2. The Sanctuary (25: 1–31: 18)
    a. Material (25: 1–9)
    b. Ark (25: 10–22)
    c. Table (25: 23–30)
    d. Lampstand (25: 31–40)
    e. Tabernacle (26: 1–37)
    f. Altar (27: 1–8)
    g. Court (27: 9–19)
    h. Lamp (27: 20–21)
    i. Priestly garments (28: 1–43)
    j. Consecration of priests (29: 1–46)
    k. Additional laws (30: 1–31: 17)
      i. Altar of incense (30: 1–10)
      ii. Ransom during a census (30: 11–16)
      iii. Bronze laver (30: 17–21)
      iv. Anointing oil (30: 22–33)
      v. Incense (30: 34–38)
      vi. Artisans (31: 1–11)
      vii. Sabbath (31: 12–17)
    l. Tablets of the law (31: 18)
3. Renewal of the covenant (32: 1–34: 35)
    a. The nation makes new gods (32: 1–6)
    b. God decides to destroy the people (32: 7–14)
    c. The people lament (33: 1–6)
    d. The tent of meeting outside the camp (33: 7–11)
    e. Appearance of God (33: 12–23)
    f. Rededication of the covenant (34: 1–35)
4. Building the tabernacle and God's glory (35: 1–40: 38)

    a. The Tabernacle (35: 1–39: 43)
    b. Dedication (40: 1–38)

The biblical narrative continues with an account of the deliverance of the Jews from Egyptian bondage. The Book of Exodus relates that a son had been born to Amram of the House of Levi and his wife Jochebed. When he was three months old, his parents concealed him among the reeds growing on the banks of the Nile to save him from Pharaoh's decree. Pharaoh's daughter found the child and adopted him as her son, Moses. When he became older, he attacked and killed a taskmaster who was oppressing a Hebrew slave, and fled to the desert. There he dwelt with Jethro (a priest of Midian) and married his daughter, Zipporah. Eventually God revealed himself to Moses out of a burning bush, commanding that he deliver the chosen people from Pharaoh's harsh bondage:

> I am the God of your father, the God of Abraham, the God of Isaac, and the God of Jacob ... I have seen the affliction of my people who are in Egypt, and have heard their cry because of their taskmasters; I know their sufferings ... Come, I will send you to Pharaoh that you may bring forth my people, the sons of Israel, out of Egypt. (3: 6–7, 10)

To persuade Pharaoh that he should let the Jewish people go, God inflicted a series of plagues on the Egyptians (blood, frogs, lice, flies, pestilence, skin disease, hail, locusts, darkness) culminating in the slaying of every Egyptian first-born son. The first-born of the Israelites were spared as each family slaughtered a lamb and smeared its blood on the doorposts. Seeing this, the Angel of Death passed over the household. After this final plague, Pharaoh released the Israelites, and they fled without even waiting for their bread to rise. However, the perils were not over; Pharaoh changed his mind and sent his forces in pursuit. When the Israelites came to an expanse of water, it seemed they were trapped. Miraculously it was converted to dry land by a strong wind so they were able to escape. The Egyptians, however, were drowned as they chased after them:

> The Egyptians pursued, and went in after them into the midst of the sea, all Pharaoh's horses, his chariots, and his horsemen ... The waters returned and covered the chariots and the horsemen and all the host of Pharaoh that had followed them into the sea; not so much as one of them remained. (14: 23, 28)

The band of free people entered the wilderness of Sinai where Moses performed miracles to provide them with food and water. In the desert God miraculously sent quails and manna to sustain his people:

> In the evening quails came up and covered the camp; and in the morning dew lay round about the camp. And when the dew had gone up, there was on the face of the wilderness a fine, flake-like thing, fine as hoarfrost on the ground. When the people of Israel saw it, they said to one another, 'What is it?' For they did not know what it was. And Moses said to them, 'It is the bread which the Lord has given you to eat.' (16: 13–15)

After travelling for about ninety days, they encamped before Mount Sinai. God called Moses up to the top of the mountain and told him that if his people would listen to him and keep his covenant, they would become God's special people. They were commanded to wash and purify themselves for two days; on the third day they came to the foot of the mountain amongst thunder, lightning and the sound of a ram's horn to hear God's voice. Alone Moses climbed the mountain again where he remained for forty days. At the end of this period, he returned with two tablets of stone on which were inscribed the Ten Commandments:

> 1. I am the Lord your God, who brought you out of the land of Egypt, out of the house of bondage. You shall have no other gods before me.
> 2. You shall not make for yourself a graven image, or any likeness of anything that is in heaven above, or that is in the earth beneath, or that is in the water under the earth; you shall not bow down to them or serve them; for I the Lord your God am a jealous God, visiting the iniquity of the fathers upon the children to the third and the fourth generation of those who hate me, but showing steadfast love to thousands of those who love me and keep my commandments.
> 3. You shall not take the name of the Lord your God in vain; for the Lord will not hold him guiltless who takes his name in vain.
> 4. Remember the sabbath day, to keep it holy. Six days you shall labour and do all your work; but the seventh day is a sabbath to the Lord your God; in it you shall not do any work, you, or your son, or your daughter, your manservant, or your maidservant, or your cattle or the sojourner who is within your gates; for in six days the Lord made heaven and earth, the sea, and all that is in them, and rested the seventh day; therefore the Lord blessed the sabbath day and hallowed it.

5. Honour your father and your mother, that your days may be long in the land which the Lord your God gives you.

6. You shall not kill.

7. You shall not commit adultery.

8. You shall not steal.

9. You shall not bear false witness against your neighbour.

10. You shall not covet your neighbour's house; you shall not covet your neighbour's wife, or his manservant, or his maidservant, or his ox, or his ass, or anything that is your neighbour's. (20: 2–17)

On his return, however, Moses found the people had forsaken him and their God:

> When the people saw that Moses delayed to come down from the mountain, the people gathered themselves together to Aaron, and said to him, 'Up, make us gods, who shall go before us ... And Aaron said to them, 'Take off the rings of gold which are in the ears of your wives, your sons, and your daughters, and bring them to me' ... And he received the gold at their hand, and fashioned it with a graving tool, and made a molten calf; and they said, 'These are your gods, O Israel, who brought you up out of the land of Egypt!' (32: 1–2, 4)

In anger Moses smashed the tablets of stone, only later carving new ones.

The Book of Exodus continues with a detailed account of the construction of the tabernacle, a portable shrine constructed by Moses following God's instructions. This structure travelled with the Israelites in the desert and was placed in the centre of the camp in an open courtyard 1000 cubits by 50 cubits in size. The fence surrounding the tabernacle consisted of wooden pillars from which a cloth curtain was suspended. Located in the eastern half of the courtyard, the tabernacle measured 30 cubits by 10 cubits; at its end stood the holy of holies, which was separated by a veil hanging on five wooden pillars on which were woven images of the cherubim. Inside the holy of holies was the ark of the covenant, the table on which the shewbread was placed, the incense altar, and the *menorah* (candelabrum). In the courtyard there was also an outer altar on which sacrifices were offered, as well as a brass laver for priests. The Book of Exodus concludes with a depiction of God's presence in the tabernacle following its construction:

> Then the cloud covered the tent of meeting, and the glory of the Lord filled the tabernacle. And Moses was not able to enter the tent of

meeting, because the cloud abode upon it, and the glory of the Lord filled the tabernacle. (40: 34–35)

From a geographical standpoint, there is considerable uncertainty about the details of the narrative account of the Exodus. Some scholars have suggested that the crossing of the Red Sea (or Reed Sea) took place, not at the head of the Gulf of Suez which is a long way from the Israelites' point of departure, but at one of the lakes now joined by the Suez Canal. Other suggestions include the head of the Gulf of Aqaba or alternatively Lake Sirbonis. The mountain where God revealed himself to Moses has traditionally been identified with Jebel Musa in the south of Sinai, but it has been objected that such a location would have taken the Israelites dangerously near the route the Egyptians used to reach copper and turquoise mines in that area. Another suggestion is that the occurrences on the mountain suggest volcanic activity: since no mountain in the Sinai peninsula is volcanic, it has been advanced that the site was in north-western Arabia, east of the Gulf of Aqaba. The Bible thus does not enable us to trace the route of the Jews in the wilderness. Regarding the date of the Exodus, 1 Kings 6: 1 states that it took place 480 years before Solomon founded the temple (in the fourth year of his reign). Assuming Solomon came to the throne in 961 BCE, the Exodus would have taken place in 1438 BCE. But, if the Israelites laboured at Pithom and Rameses as Scripture relates, the Exodus would have taken place much later. Thus it can be seen that from a historical viewpoint, the Exodus narrative poses a number of serious historical difficulties.

3. Leviticus

1. Sacrificial laws (1: 1–7: 38)
    1. Types of sacrifice (1: 1–5: 26)
        a. Holocaust (1: 1–17)
        b. Cereal offerings (2: 1–16)
        c. Peace offerings (3: 1–17)
        d. Sin offerings (4: 1–5: 13)
        e. Guilt offerings (5: 14–26)
    2. Priest and sacrifice (6: 1–7: 38)
        a. Daily holocaust (6: 1–6)
        b. Daily cereal offering (6: 7–16)
        c. Sin offerings (6: 17–23)
        d. Guilt offerings (7: 1–10)
        e. Peace offerings (7: 11–21; 28–34)
        f. Blood and fat prohibitions (7: 22–27)
        g. Conclusion (7: 35–38)

2. Ordination (8: 1–10: 20)
    1. Aaron and his sons (8: 1–13)
    2. Ordination sacrifices (8: 14–36)
    3. Octave of the ordination (9: 1–24)
    4. Sin of Aaron's sons (10: 1–20)

3. Legal purity (11: 1–15: 33)
    1. Clean and unclean animals (11: 1–47)
    2. Childbirth (12: 1–8)
    3. Leprosy (13: 1–14: 57)
        a. Humans (13: 1–46)
        b. Clothing (13: 47–59)
        c. Purification (14: 1–32)
        d. Buildings (14: 33–57)
    4. Sexual uncleanliness (15: 1–33)

4. Day of Atonement (16: 1–34)

5. Law of holiness (17: 1–26: 46)
    1. Sacredness of blood (17: 1–16)
    2. Sacredness of sex (18: 1–30)
    3. Rules of conduct (19: 1–37)
    4. Punishments (20: 1–27)
    5. Sanctity of priests (21: 1–24)
    6. Sacrificial rules (22: 1–33)
    7. Liturgical year (23: 1–44)
        a. Passover and unleavened bread (23: 4–14)
        b. Shavuot (23: 15–22)
        c. New Year (23: 23–25)
        d. Day of Atonement (23: 26–32)
        e. Sukkot (23: 33–36, 29–43)
    8. Additional laws (24: 1–23)
    9. Holy years (25: 1–55)
        a. Sabbatical year (25: 1–7)
        b. Jubilee year (25: 8–55)
    10. Sanctions (26: 1–46)

6. Redemption of votive offerings (27: 1–34)

The Book of Leviticus is called *Vayikra* (and he called), the first Hebrew word of the book. The name 'Leviticus' is derived from the Greek translation of the Five Books of Moses (Septuagint) via the Latin translation (Vulgate) meaning 'pertaining to the Levites'. In rabbinic literature it is referred to as *Torat Kohanim* (the priests' manual). Following on from Exodus, Leviticus is an independent entity providing a detailed picture of cultic practice. While the book does contain laws relating to the priests, it also covers a wide range of observances. As far as biblical and rabbinic regulations are concerned, nearly half of the 613 scriptural commandments and about the same proportion of rules in the *Talmud* are based on this book. Historically Leviticus was the first book taught to Jewish school children.

Leviticus begins with a general introduction to the sacrificial system; here Moses is commanded to explain the nature of animal sacrifice:

> The Lord called Moses and spoke to him from the tent of meeting saying, 'Speak to the people of Israel, and say to them, When any man of you brings an offering to the Lord, you shall bring your offering of cattle from the herd or from the flock.' (1: 1–2)

The next verses encapsulate the central elements of the sacrificial system – laying on of hands, acceptance, expiation, slaughter, handling of blood, and entrance to the tent of meeting. Leviticus stresses that the person who makes a sacrifice is responsible for the preparation of the animal; the priest, however, undertakes the blood rite and the burning of the animal. Here it is emphasized that only male, unblemished and eligible species of the herd, flock or birds are to be used.

Chapter 2 deals with the cereal offerings of various types – the purpose of this sacrifice is to stress that an individual's offering to God should be the product of his labour. Continuing the discussion of animal sacrifice, chapter 3 outlines the nature of peace offerings, sacrifices usually prompted by a joyous occasion. The rules for this sacrifice are similar to those of the holocaust offering, but their portions were assigned to the priests as well as God. In chapter 4 Moses is commanded to explain the laws regarding sin offerings: the purpose of these sacrifices is to remove any impurity affecting the sanctuary due to an inadvertent violation of the commandments. The procedure for the sin offering is of two types: (1) In the first case the blood is brought into the sanctuary by the high priest and the flesh is burned outside the camp; (2) the second case deals with sins requiring cheaper animals scaled to the status of the offender where the blood is not brought into the sanctuary and the flesh is eaten by the priest rather than burned.

The first part of chapter 5 covers borderline cases requiring the guilt offering. Here the sin is not simply the contraction of impurity but its prolongation:

> Or if any one touches an unclean thing, whether the carcass of an unclean beast or a carcass of unclean cattle or a carcass of unclean swarming things, and it is hidden from him, and he has become unclean, he shall be guilty. Or if he touches human uncleanness, of whatever sort the uncleanness may be with which one becomes unclean, and it is hidden from him, when he comes to know it he shall be guilty. Or if any one utters with his lips a rash oath to do evil or to do good, any sort of rash oath that men swear, and it is hidden from him, when he comes to know it he shall in any of these be guilty. (5: 2–4)

In such cases the person is to bring an offering to the priest so that he can make expiation for him. Chapter 5 continues with a discussion of the reproach offering which is enjoined for trespassing on divine or human property.

Chapters 6 and 7 contain supplementary instructions concerning sacrifices – subjects considered include: the altar fire, the manner and place of eating the cereal offering, the daily cereal offerings, safeguards in sanctifying the sin offering, the ritual for the reparation offerings, the priestly share in holocaust and cereal offerings, the holocaust offering, the prohibition against consuming suet and blood, and the priestly share of the peace offering. Chapter 6 summarizes these topics:

> This is the law of the burnt offering, of the cereal offering, of the sin offering, of the guilt offering, of the consecration, and of the peace offerings, which the Lord commanded to Moses on Mount Sinai, on the day that he commanded the people of Israel to bring their offerings to the Lord, in the wilderness of Sinai. (7: 37–38)

The ordination service in the tabernacle is discussed in detail in chapters 8 to 10, beginning with the installation of the priests. On the eighth day following the week of consecration, the priests began their official duties of offering up sacrifices for the people – this discussion is interrupted by an account of Nadab and Abihu who offered unholy fire before the Lord and were killed. Chapter 10 continues with a discussion of the consumption of the initiatory offerings by the priests. The laws of impurity are then outlined in chapters 11 to 16 beginning in chapter 11 with the impurities of land animals, fish, birds and winged insects, contact with carcasses, and swarming things. This chapter concludes with a general summation in verse 46:

> This is the law pertaining to beast and bird and every living creature that moves through the waters and every creature that swarms upon the earth, to make a distinction between the unclean and the clean and between the living creature that may be eaten and the living creature that may not be eaten.

Chapter 13 continues with a discussion of the impurity of skin disease. According to Scripture leprosy is here understood as a non-contagious eruption of dull white spots. The beginning of the chapter diagnoses the various symptoms of this condition and specifies that the sufferer should be removed outside the camp; the remainder of the chapter describes the deterioration of garments due to mildew or fungus. The next chapter continues this discussion by focusing on diseases that infect houses due to the spread of saltpetre or moss; in such cases quarantine procedures are deployed. The ritual for dealing with physical leprosy is also included in chapter 14 – it involves three separate ceremonies which are to take place on the first, sixth and eighth days. In chapter 15 the impurity of genital discharges is divided into two sections: first, Scripture states that natural discharges of men and women can be removed simply by bathing:

> And if a man has an emission of semen, he shall bathe his whole body in water, and be unclean until the evening. And every garment and every skin on which the semen comes shall be washed with water. (15: 16–17)

Pathological discharges on the other hand, require ritual sacrifice:

> And on the eighth day she shall take two turtledoves or two young pigeons, and bring them to the priest, to the door of the tent of meeting. And the priest shall offer one for a sin offering and the other for a burnt offering. (15: 29–30)

Chapter 16 deals with the impurities of the sanctuary and the nation: the first part focuses on the sanctuary itself; the second outlines the means whereby the expiation of the people can take place through the transference of their sins to a goat:

> Then he shall kill the goat of the sin offering which is for the people, and bring its blood within the veil ... thus he shall make atonement for the holy place, because of the uncleannesses of the people of Israel, and because of their transgressions. (16: 15–16)

The remainder of the book of Leviticus – chapters 17 to 26 – consists of an independent source referred to as the 'Holiness Code'. This collection of material begins in chapter 17 with the theme of killing for food; here Scripture lays down a fundamental principle of the sacrificial system – the prohibition of eating blood:

> If any man of the house of Israel or of the strangers that sojourn among them eats any blood, I will set my face against that person who eats blood ... For the life of the flesh is in the blood. (17: 10–11)

The next three chapters concentrate directly on the concept of holiness. Beginning with a series of laws concerning forbidden sexual relationships, chapter 19 specifies that the Jewish people are to imitate God: 'And the Lord said to Moses, "Say to all the congregation of the people of Israel, You shall be holy; for I the Lord your God am holy"' (19: 1).

What does such imitation involve? The answer of Leviticus 19 is that human beings must follow both ritual and moral commands. In this chapter no distinction is made between obligations to God and laws concerning human relationships. Chapter 20 continues this discussion by specifying the punishment for sin. Here the Jewish Bible stresses that the nation must avoid becoming like other peoples: 'And you shall not walk in the customs of the nation which I am casting out before you' (20: 23).

In chapters 21 to 22 the rules for priests are specified. The priest, ranking highest in holiness, is able to enter the sanctuary and regulate the sacrificial cult. For this reason special mention is made of the holiness of the priestly class and the proper procedure to be followed.

The next chapters deal with the major festivals of the Jewish nation:

1. Of primary importance is the Sabbath; it is to be observed as a holy day of rest: 'Six days shall work be done; but on the seventh day is a sabbath of solemn rest, a holy convocation; you shall do no work; it is a sabbath to the Lord in all your dwellings' (23: 3).
2. The Passover which commemorates the exodus from Egypt is to be celebrated for seven days beginning on the fourteenth day of the first month. This festival recounts the haste in which the ancient Israelites fled from their Egyptian oppressors.
3. The Feast of First Fruits is celebrated on the tenth day of the first month to acknowledge God's goodness in making the land fertile.
4. The Feast of Weeks is celebrated on the sixth day of the seventh month — it is essentially a harvest festival offering thanks to God for providing food.
5. The Feast of Trumpets is celebrated on the first day of the seventh month — it is a form of the New Year Festival, subsequently known as *Rosh Ha-Shanah*.
6. The Day of Atonement is observed on the tenth day of the seventh month; it is concerned with ritual cleansing of priests and the people from sin.
7. The Feast of Tabernacles is celebrated for seven days beginning

on the fifteenth day of the seventh month; it commemorates the wanderings of the ancient Israelites in the desert.

8. The Sabbath Year is to take place every seventh year to allow the land to rest.

9. The Jubilee Year takes place after a period of seven Sabbath Years. During this period all debts are to be cancelled and all slaves freed.

The Book of Leviticus concludes with a discussion of reward for obedience and punishment for transgression. The obligation for Israel to be holy and observe the divine commandments is here reiterated.

4. Numbers

1. Ancient Israelite community before the departure from Mount Sinai (1: 1–10: 10).
    1. Census (1: 1–4: 49)
        a. First census (1: 1–47)
        b. Role of the Levites (1: 48–54)
        c. The camp and the march (2: 1–34)
        d. Priestly hierarchy (3: 1–51)
        e. Levites (4: 1–49)
    2. Purity of the camp and community (5: 1–6.27)
        a. Impure (5.1–4)
        b. Restitution for offences against neighbours (5: 5–10)
        c. Woman suspected of adultery (5: 11–31)
        d. Nazirite vow (6: 1–21)
        e. Priestly blessing (6: 22–27)
    3. Cultic preparations for departure (7: 1–10: 10)
        a. Offerings for tribal representation (7: 1–89)
        b. Lampstand (8: 1–4)
        c. Purification of the Levites (8: 5–26)
        d. Passover (9: 1–14)
        e. Cloud (9: 15–23)
        f. Trumpets (10: 1–10)

2. Journey from Sinai to the plains of Moab (10: 11–21: 35)
    1. From Sinai to the desert of Paran (10: 11–12: 16)
        a. Departure from Sinai (10: 11–28)
        b. Habad and the Ark (10: 29–36)
        c. Taberah (11: 1–3)
        d. Quail, seventy elders, Eldad and Medad (11: 4–35)
        e. Miriam and Aaron rebel against Moses (12: 1–16)
    2. Threshold of the Promised Land (13: 1–15: 41)
        a. Exploration of the Promised Land (13: 1–14: 45)
        b. Cultic laws (15: 1–41)

3. Revolt of Korah, Dathan and Abiram and priestly status (16: 1–19: 22)
   a. Revolt of Korah, Dathan and Abiram (16: 1–35)
   b. Covering of the altar (17: 1–5)
   c. Intercession of Aaron (17: 6–15)
   d. Aaron's staff (17: 16–28)
   e. Dues of priests and Levites (18: 1–32)
   f. Red heifer and water of purification (19: 1–22)
4. From Kadesh to the plains of Moab (20: 1–21: 35)
   a. Waters of Meribah (20: 1–13)
   b. Kingdom of Edom (20: 14–21)
   c. Death of Aaron (20: 22–29)
   d. Battle with the Canaanites (21: 1–3)
   e. Fiery serpents (21: 4–9)
   f. Journey through Transjordan (21: 10–20)
   g. Defeat of Sihon and Og (21: 21–35)

3. The plains of Moab and preparation for the journey to the Promised Land (22: 1–36: 13)
   1. Balaam (22: 1–24: 25)
      a. Balak sends for Balaam (22: 1–21)
      b. Balaam's ass (22: 21–35)
      c. Balaam and Balak (22: 36–40)
      d. Oracle at Bamoth Baal (22: 41–23: 12)
      e. Oracle at Mount Pisgah (23: 13–26)
      f. Oracle on Peor (23: 27–24: 9)
      g. Oracle of Balaam (24: 10–11)
      h. Further oracles (24: 20–25)
   2. Apostasy at Baal Peor (25: 1–18)
   3. Preparation for conquest and division of land (25: 19–36: 13)
      a. Second census (25: 19–26: 65)
      b. Daughters of Zelophehad (27: 1–11)
      c. Joshua (27: 12–23)
      d. Ritual calendar (28: 1–30: 1)
      e. Woman's vows (30: 2–17)
      f. War against Midian (31: 1–54)
      g. Gad and Reuben (32: 1–42)
      h. Desert hierarchy (33: 1–49)
      i. Division of the land of Canaan (33: 50–35: 34)
      j. Daughters of Zelophehad (36: 1–13)

In Hebrew the Book of Numbers is referred to as *Bamidbar* (in the wilderness), the first significant word in the book. The English title is derived from its census figures. Continuing the narrative of the Pentateuch, Numbers narrates the history of the Jewish nation from the preparations for the departure from Sinai, culminating with the stay in Shittim in Moab. It is divided into three major sections: (1) Sojourn in Sinai (1: 1–10: 10); (2) Journey from Sinai to the plains of Moab (10: 11–21: 35); and (3) Dwelling in Moab (22: 1–36: 13).

The book begins with an account of the numbers of the tribes – this census was taken so that Israel's military capacity could be ascertained. According to Scripture, 603,550 men were available for service; this implies that the total population of the Israelites was approximately two million. Yet this calculation poses a serious difficulty since in 3: 42 the number of first-born is 22,273 suggesting that a much lower number is required. Numbers continues in chapters 3 to 4 with an account of the Levites – unlike other tribes they were assigned specifically religious duties such as those outlined in the Book of Leviticus. Through their ministrations it was believed that the community would be kept holy.

The next section of the book sets out regulations designed to ensure the religious and moral purity of the nation. Here the Lord commands Moses to instruct the priests how to bless the people:

> The Lord said to Moses, 'Say to Aaron and his sons, Thus you shall bless the people of Israel: you shall say to them,
> The Lord bless you and keep you;
> The Lord make his face to shine upon you, and be gracious to you:
> The Lord lift up his countenance upon you, and give you peace.' (6: 22–26)

Chapter 6 contains detailed prescriptions concerning the Nazirite. Such individuals were consecrated to serve God by separating themselves from normal activities by taking a vow which was sealed through sacrifice and rituals performed by a priest. The requirements for a Nazirite vow including abstaining from wine, refraining from cutting one's hair, and avoiding touching dead bodies:

> And the Lord said to Moses, 'Say to the people of Israel, When either a man or a woman makes a special vow, the vow of a Nazirite, to separate himself to the Lord, he shall separate himself from wine and strong drink ... All the days of his vow of separation no razor shall come upon his head ... All the days that he separates himself to the Lord he shall not go near a dead body.' (6: 1–3, 5, 6)

33

In chapter 7 the earlier account of the setting up of the tabernacle is continued; this is followed by a list of regulations concerning Passover, with special mention of those who have become unclean through contact with a dead body.

After sojourning eleven months at Mount Sinai, the ancient Israelites set out for the Promised Land. Despite the people's enthusiasm, the nation soon began to grumble, evoking God's displeasure: 'And the people complained in the hearing of the Lord about their misfortunes; and when the Lord heard it, his anger was kindled, and the fire of the Lord burned among them, and consumed some outlying parts of the camp' (11: 1). Discontented with their lot, they reminisced about the delicacies of Egyptian life they had left behind, rebelling against the manna that the Lord had sent: 'O that we had meat to eat! We remember the fish we ate in Egypt for nothing, the cucumbers, the melons, the leeks, the onions, and the garlic' (11: 4–5). In response God provided the Israelites with quail. This narrative continues with an account of the quarrel between Moses and his brother Aaron and sister Miriam who resented his marriage with a Chushite woman; as a punishment, God made Miriam leprous.

From the wilderness of Paran northeast of Sinai, God commanded Moses to send spies to Canaan:

> Go up into the Negeb yonder, and go up into the hill country, and see what the land is, and whether the people who dwell in it are strong or weak, whether they are few or many, and whether the land that they dwell in is good or bad, and whether the cities that they dwell in are camps or strongholds, and whether the land is rich or poor, and whether there is wood in it or not. (13: 17–20)

After the spies entered Canaan through the Desert of Zin, they penetrated as far as Hebron. After forty days they returned to Moses, declaring: 'We came to the land to which you sent us; it flows with milk and honey, and this is its fruit. Yet the people who dwell in the land are strong, and the cities are fortified and very large' (13: 27–28).

Continuing to long for the life they had left behind, the people announced that they wished to return to Egypt. Joshua and Caleb, however, pleaded with the nation, emphasizing that the Lord would be with them. Yet in opposition to God's intentions, the Israelites continued to rebel against Moses; angered by such ingratitude, the Lord resolved to punish them despite Moses' intercession:

But truly, as I live, and as all the earth shall be filled with the glory of the Lord, none of the men who have seen my glory and my signs which I wrought in Egypt and in the wilderness, and yet have put me to the proof these ten times and have not hearkened to my voice, shall see the land which I swore to give to their fathers. (14: 20–23)

Distraught by God's decree that they will be condemned to wander in the desert for forty years, the people attempted to conquer the land without God's assistance – only to be defeated by the Amalekites and the Canaanites.

Numbers continues with a description of another rebellion against Moses. A group of Levites led by Korah accused Moses of setting himself above the nation. Adding their voices to this complaint, Dathan and Abiram claimed that Moses had failed to lead them into a land flowing with milk and honey. As a punishment for such disloyalty, these rebels and their families were killed in an earthquake:

The ground under them split asunder; and the earth opened its mouth and swallowed them up, with their households and all the men that belonged to Korah and all their goods. So they and all that belonged to them went down alive into Sheol; and the earth closed over them. (16: 31–33)

The death of Korah, Dathan and Abiram none the less generated new discontent quelled only by the budding of Aaron's staff, a symbol of God's approval of his faithful servant.

For forty years the nation travelled through the wilderness, and the Book of Numbers resumes the narrative with the deaths of Miriam and Aaron: only Moses remained of the old Israel. The people still grumbled about the hardships they endured and a water shortage fuelled their discontent. In response, Moses was commanded to speak to a rock so that it would produce water. Instead he disobeyed and struck the rock with his staff. Such disobedience angered God, and he resolved not to allow either Moses or Aaron to enter the Promised Land.

At this stage Moses sought permission to pass through Edom on his way to Moab. Not surprisingly the king of Edom was distressed about this plan, refused Moses' request, and gathered a large army. Confronted by such a challenge, Israel avoided entering Edom, skirting its borders instead. At Mount Hor Aaron died and was mourned by the nation. At this period a marauding Canaanite king attacked Israel, but was defeated. Despite this success, Moses decided to circumvent the Edomite nation, constructing a bronze snake which he erected on a pole to cure the people of snakebites.

Avoiding Edomite territory, the Israelites followed the course of Arnon, a dried-up riverbed on the eastern shore of the Dead Sea. Moses then sought permission from Sihon, King of the Amonites, for permission to travel through his territory; like the king of Edom he refused and sent an army to stop the Israelites. After vanquishing these enemies, Israel took possession of territory north of Moab stretching as far as the Jabbok river. From this point, the nation prepared to cross the plains of Moab in order to enter Canaan. Fearing their intentions Balak, king of Moab, sought to persuade Balaam – a pagan prophet – to put a curse on this invading force. On his way to Moab, however, an angel of the Lord blocked Baalam's path. Although he was unable to see this divine messenger, his donkey recognized the presence of the angel and refused to move. Eventually, the Lord opened Baalam's eyes:

> Then the Lord opened the eyes of Baalam, and he saw the angel of the Lord standing in the way, with his sword drawn in his hand; and he bowed his head, and fell on his face. And the angel of the Lord said to him, 'Why have you struck your ass these three times? Behold, I have come forth to withstand you, because your way is perverse before me; and the ass saw me, and turned aside before me these three times. If she had not turned aside from me, surely just now I would have slain you and let her live.' (22: 31–33)

To the fury of Balak, Baalam then delivered four oracles blessing Israel and predicting victory over the Moabites:

> I see him, but not now;
> I behold him, but not nigh:
> a star shall come forth out of Jacob,
> and a sceptre shall arise out of Israel;
> it shall crush the forehead of Moab. (24: 17)

Despite such predictions, Israel was beset with sin; waiting at Shittim to cross over the Jordan to Jericho, Israelite men were seduced into participation in Canaanite fertility cults involving illicit sexual relations.

A second census was then undertaken, thirty-eight years after the first census. Its purpose was to determine Israel's military might. A new generation had arisen; only Moses, Joshua and Caleb remained of those who set out from Egypt. But who was to be the leader of this invading army? Neither Moses nor Aaron was permitted to enter the Promised Land – Moses was allowed only to see it from a mountain range across the Jordan. Instead the Lord selected Joshua:

> And the Lord said to Moses, 'Take Joshua the son of Nun, a man in whom is the spirit, and lay your hand upon him ... You shall invest him with some of your authority, that all the congregation of the people of Israel may obey.' (27: 18,20)

The Book of Numbers concludes with God's command to drive out all the inhabitants of the Promised Land; as he declared to Abraham, Isaac and Jacob, it was to be Israel's inheritance:

> And the Lord said to Moses in the plains of Moab by the Jordan at Jericho, 'Say to the people of Israel, When you pass over the Jordan into the land of Canaan, then you shall drive out all the inhabitants of the land from before you, and destroy all their figured stones, and destroy all their molten images, and demolish all their high places; and you shall take possession of the land and settle in it, for I have given the land to you to possess it.' (33: 50–53)

5. Deuteronomy

1. Moses' first address (1: 1–4: 49)
   1. Introduction (1: 1–5)
   2. Command to occupy the Promised Land (1: 6–8)
   3. Tribal and judicial organization (1: 9–18)
   4. Sojourn at Kadesh (1: 19–46)
   5. Journey through Edom, Moab, and Ammon (2: 1–25)
   6. Victory over Heshbon and Bashan (2: 26–3: 11)
   7. Settlement of the Transjordanian tribes (3: 12–22)
   8. Moses' prayer (3: 23–29)
   9. Introduction to the revelation of the law (4: 1–14)
   10. Idolatry (4: 15–31)
   11. Israel's vocation (4: 32–40)
   12. Cities of refuge (4: 41–43)
   13. Conclusion (4: 44–49)

2. Moses' second address (5: 1–11: 32)
   1. Summons (5: 1–5)
   2. Ten Commandments (5: 6–21)
   3. God and Moses at Sinai (5: 22–6: 3)
   4. Law for life in the Promised Land (6: 4–25)
   5. Command to destroy the people and cults of Canaan (7: 1–11)
   6. Obedience to God and prosperity in the land (7: 12–26)
   7. God's past mercies and admonition against pride (8: 1–20)
   8. God's gift of the land (9: 1–6)
   9. The golden calf (9: 7–24)
   10. Moses' intercession and the second covenant (9: 25–10: 11)
   11. Election and duties (10: 12–11: 1)
   12. Moses' exhortation (11: 2–25)
   13. Blessing and curse (11: 26–32)

3. The legal code (12: 1–26: 15)
   1. Sanctuary law (12: 1–27)

The Book of Deuteronomy is referred to in Hebrew as *Devarim* (words), the second word of the first verse of the book. The name Deuteronomy is derived from the Latin *Deuteronomium* – it is based on the Greek translation of the Hebrew expression *Mishneh Ha-Torah* (second law). This designation was used since the Book of Deuteronomy repeats the law and history found in other parts of the *Torah*. The book itself contains Moses' review of events after the giving of the law on Mount Sinai; his ethical exhortations; a summary of divine legislation; his final speeches; his farewell song and blessing; and an account of his death.

Deuteronomy commences with the ancient Israelites encamped

on the plains of Moab after forty years of wandering in the desert. Only Moses, Joshua and Caleb remained of those who fled from Eygpt. Moses began his first speech by reminding the nation that they were chosen by God to be his special people. As related previously, he sent spies out from the camp at Kadesh to explore Canaan, returning with favourable reports of what they discovered. None the less, the Israelites rebelled against the Lord. Because of their sinfulness, the people were condemned to wander around the hill country of Seir, south of the Dead Sea; eventually, however, God declared: 'You have been going about this mountain country long enough; turn northward' (2: 3).

As Moses explained, the Israelites then marched northwards conquering all those who stood in their path. This narrative was intended to remind the nation of all that God did for them and encourage them for the future. Moses then related how he divided the land east of the Jordan and distributed it among the tribes of Reuben and Gad. Yet, as Moses recounted, he himself was destined only to see the Promised Land from a distance. As God told him: 'Go up to the top of Pisgah, and lift up your eyes westward and northward and southward and eastward, and behold it with your eyes, for you shall not go over this Jordan' (3: 27).

Encouraging all the people to remember these events, Moses went on to explain that the nation was to observe the divine commandments as outlined from chapters 4 to 28. This law code opens with a declaration that what follows is the law that was given by Moses to Israel as they waited in the Moabite region near Beth Peor. The covenant, Moses emphasized, was not made solely with Abraham, Isaac, and Jacob, but with their descendants: 'The Lord our God made a covenant with us in Horeb. Not with our fathers did the Lord make this covenant, but with us, who are all of us here alive this day' (5: 2–3).

This declaration was followed by a second formulation of the Decalogue (5: 6–21).

Chapter 6 continues with the proclamation that the Jewish people are to love the Lord with all their hearts — this is the first paragraph of the *Shema* — the most important of all Jewish prayers:

Hear, O Israel: The Lord our God is one Lord; and you shall love the Lord your God with all your heart, and with all your soul, and with all your might. And these words which I command you this day shall be upon your heart; and you shall teach them diligently to your children, and shall talk of them when you sit in your house, and when you walk by the way, and when you lie down, and when you rise. And you shall bind them as a sign upon your hand, and they shall be as frontlets between your eyes. And you shall write them on the doorposts of your house and on your gates. (6: 4–9)

On the basis of this declaration, Jews feel obligated to put on *tephillin* (phylacteries), two small leather boxes containing passages from the *Torah* (Exodus 13: 1–10; Exodus 11–16; Deuteronomy 6: 4–9; Deuteronomy 13–21); they are bound by leather straps to the arm and the head, and are worn on weekdays in the morning service (but not on Sabbaths and festivals). In addition, in compliance with this commandment, Jews affix *mezuzahs* to the doorpost of rooms in a Jewish house; inside these containers are scrolls on which are inscribed Deuteronomy 6: 4–9 and 11: 13–21.

Emphasizing that Canaan was God's gift to his people, Moses reassured the nation that the Lord would be with them in their struggle against the inhabitants of the land. Israel's victory would not be due to their own might, but to God's presence. In presenting this message, Moses stressed that God chose Israel because he loved them and was faithful to his promise to the patriarchs:

It was not because you were more in number than any other people that the Lord set his love upon you and chose you, for you were the fewest of all peoples; but it is because the Lord loves you, and is keeping the oath which he swore to your fathers, that the Lord has brought you out with a mighty hand, and redeemed you from the house of bondage, from the hand of Pharaoh king of Egypt. (7: 7–8)

Further, it was because of such divine love that Israel was chastened in the desert. God only disciplines those whom he loves – his decree that Israel wander in the desert for forty years was thus a symbol of his love and care. Before entering Canaan, the people needed to learn that 'man does not live by bread alone, but that man lives by everything that proceeds out of the mouth of the Lord' (8: 3). Such a lesson was designed to enable those who were entering the Promised Land to remain faithful to God and obey his commandments. As a recompense for such faithfulness, Israel would be rewarded with the land across the Jordan river. Yet Moses stated that such a benefaction would not be due to Israel's merit; given their sinfulness in making the golden calf, they rendered themselves unworthy of divine benefit. None the less God decided to bless his people assuming that they remain loyal.

In chapter 11, the theme of love and obedience is repeated. The very existence of Israel depends upon their faithfulness – without God, all will be lost:

> You shall therefore love the Lord your God, and keep his charge, his statutes, his ordinances, and his commandments always ... that you may be strong, and go in and take possession of the land which you are going over to possess, and that you may live long in the land which the Lord swore to your fathers to give to them and to their descendants, a land flowing with milk and honey. (11: 1, 8–9)

Israel is hence confronted with a choice: either they can obey God's decrees and be blessed, or disobey them and be cursed. Pleading with his people to be faithful, Moses declared that they would thereby inherit the riches promised to their ancestors:

> Behold, I set before you this day a blessing and a curse: the blessing if you obey the commandments of the Lord your God, which I command you this day, and the curse, if you do not obey the commandments of the Lord your God. (11: 26–28)

Such obedience, Moses stated, involves right worship. Israel must not be led astray by embracing pagan rites; instead, the nation must maintain its separateness, resisting every temptation to worship other gods. Any prophet or dreamer who urges fellow Jews to engage in idolatry is to be put to death:

> If a prophet arises among you, or a dreamer of dreams, and gives you a sign or a wonder, and the sign or wonder which he tells you comes to pass, and if he says, 'Let us go after other gods,' which you have not known, 'and let us serve them,' you shall not listen to the words of that prophet or to that dreamer of dreams; ... But that prophet or that dreamer of dreams shall be put to death. (13: 1–3, 5)

Chapters 12 to 26 are a summary of the legal code restating and extending the list of commandments previously specified in Exodus and Leviticus. Here such subjects as sanctuary law, observances relating to clean and unclean animals, regulations concerning the festivals, criminal laws, procedures governing war, humanitarian and cultic practices, and precepts concerning first-fruits are discussed in detail. This section concludes with an assurance that by obeying God's decree, the nation will be blessed: however, God declared that the punishment for disobedience will be severe:

> But if you will not obey the voice of the Lord your God or be careful to do all his commandments and his statutes ... The Lord will send upon you curses, confusion, and frustration, in all that you undertake to do, until you are destroyed and perish quickly, on account of the evil of your doings, because you have forsaken me. (28: 15, 20)

Following this warning Moses and Israel renewed the covenant in a solemn ceremony; here Moses again reminded the people of all that God had done for them:

> And Moses summoned all Israel and said to them: 'You have seen all that the Lord did before your eyes in the land of Egypt, to Pharaoh and to all his servants and to all his land, the great trials which your eyes saw, the signs, and those great wonders; but to this day the Lord has not given you a mind to understand, or eyes to see, or ears to hear. I have led you forty years in the wilderness; your clothes have not worn out upon you, and your sandals have not worn off your feet; you have not eaten bread, and you have not drunk wine or strong drink; that you may know that I am the Lord your God. And when you came to this place, Sihon the king of Heshbon and Og the king of Bashan came out against us to battle, but we defeated them; we took their land and gave it for an inheritance to the Reubenites, the Gadites, and the half-tribe of Manassites. (29: 2–8)

In the light of God's concern for his chosen people, the nation must remain loyal to him if it is to prosper in the land. As Moses explained, Joshua will now take his place to lead the people into Canaan. In the presence of all the people Moses reassured Joshua of God's continuing presence. Yet despite all his warnings, Moses was convinced the nation would be attracted to other gods. To ensure that the people would be reminded of his teaching, Moses was instructed to write down the words of the law in a book to be placed in the ark of the covenant.

Deuteronomy then continues with the Song of Moses, glorifying God. At the beginning of this hymn the Lord is praised for his greatness:

> Give ear, O heavens, and I will speak;
> and let the earth hear the words of my mouth.

> May my teaching drop as the rain,
> my speech distil as the dew,
> as the gentle rain upon the tender grass,
> and as the shower upon the herb.
> For I will proclaim the name of the Lord.
> Ascribe greatness to our God! (32: 1–3)

In the verses which follow the tribes are blessed: here Moses spoke of his hopes for each of the tribes just as in Genesis 49: 1–28 Jacob blessed his sons.

The Book of Deuteronomy concludes with an account of Moses' death; after blessing the tribes, Moses ascended Mount Nebo where he gazed at the Promised Land. On his death he was buried in Moab:

> And Moses went up from the plains of Moab to Mount Nebo, to the top of Pisgah, which is opposite Jericho. And the Lord showed him all the land ... And the Lord said to him, 'This is the land of which I swore to Abraham, to Isaac, and to Jacob, "I will give it to your descendants." I have let you see it with your eyes, but you shall not go over there.' So Moses the servant of the Lord died there in the land of Moab. (34: 1, 4–5)

PROPHETS

Former Prophets

6. Joshua

The Book of Joshua is named after Joshua, son of Nun, who led the conquest of the land. Previously he accompanied Moses at Mount Sinai and was put in charge of security at the tent of meeting. In addition, he was one of the twelve spies sent out from Kadesh; together with Caleb he opposed the report of the other ten. Because of their trust in God, Joshua and Caleb were the only two privileged to enter the Promised Land. In the Book of Deuteronomy, Moses appointed Joshua as his successor, charging him to conquer the land and apportion it among the tribes.

Following the death of Moses, a new chapter began in the history of the nation. After wandering in the desert for forty years, the Israelites were permitted to cross over into the land promised to their ancestors. At the beginning of the book, Joshua was formally commissioned by God to lead the Israelites across the Jordan:

After the death of Moses, the servant of the Lord, the Lord said to Joshua the son of Nun, Moses' minister, 'Moses my servant is dead; now therefore arise, go over this Jordan, you and all this people, into the land which I am giving to them, to the people of Israel. Every place that the sole of your foot will tread upon I have given to you, as I promised to Moses ... Be strong and of good courage; for you shall cause this people to inherit the land which I swore to their fathers to give them.' (1: 1–3, 6)

Anxious to begin this conquest, Joshua took only three days to prepare for the invasion of Canaan. Speaking to the nation he reminded them of God's promises and the people's responsibility to keep the covenant. Concerning the tribes of Reuben and Gad and the half-tribe of Manasseh, he reminded them that they would be compelled to take part in the conquest of Canaan before they would be permitted to return to the eastern side of the Jordan to rejoin their families.

The conquest of the Promised Land begins in chapter 2 with an account of Rahab and the spies. Following the precedent set by Moses, Joshua sent out two spies to report concerning the inhabitants of Canaan. En route they entered the house of a harlot, Rahab, who offered them shelter. Declaring that she believed the Lord had given the land to the Israelites, she asked that they deal kindly with her during the invasion. The spies agreed and instructed her to hang a scarlet cord in her window so that the Israelites would recognize her house. After escaping, the spies reported back to Joshua stating that the inhabitants of the land were terrified of the Israelite forces. Encouraged by this report, Joshua issued orders to cross the Jordan with the ark of the covenant. After marking the site of the crossing with twelve stones, Joshua undertook to circumcise all Israelite men. During the period of wandering this rite had not been performed; now it was to be carried out before battle. Following this ceremony, the people celebrated the Passover.

Chapters 5 to 12 provide a detailed account of the conquest of the land, commencing with the onslaught of Jericho. After receiving a vision of a heavenly figure, Joshua prepared to attack the city. For six days the men marched around Jericho blowing shofars until the city was vanquished and all inhabitants were slaughtered except Rahab and her family:

And at the seventh time, when the priests had blown the trumpets, Joshua said to the people, 'Shout; for the Lord has given you the city ...' So the people shouted, and the trumpets were blown. As soon as the people heard the sound of the trumpet, the people raised a great shout, and the wall fell down flat, so that the people went up into the city ... Then they utterly destroyed all in the city, both men and women, young and old, oxen, sheep, and asses, with the edge of the sword. (6: 16, 20–21)

Despite this success, the people sinned by stealing booty from Jericho which was to have been dedicated to God. The Lord expressed his displeasure by allowing the Israelites to fail in their attempt to subdue the city of Ai; eventually Achan – the person responsible for this theft – was discovered and put to death. After this purging of guilt, Joshua set out again to conquer the city. This invasion was successful and its inhabitants killed, leaving only the cattle and the spoil of the city which the Israelites confiscated. Following these victories, Joshua built an altar on Mount Ebal to the Lord where he reminded the nation of its covenantal obligations. Here he 'read all the words of the law, the blessing and the curse, according to all that is written in the book of the law. There was not a word of all that Moses commanded which Joshua did not read before all the assembly of Israel, and the women, and the little ones, and the sojourners who lived among them' (8: 34–35).

The Book of Joshua continues with a depiction of the conquest of the land west of the Jordan. The first section of this narrative deals with the Gibeonites who lived north of Jerusalem. Aware of the impending danger posed by the Israelite army, the Gibeonites pretending they came from a distant place outside of Canaan sent emissaries to the Israelite camp in order to establish a peace treaty. When their deceit was discovered, however, Joshua insisted they act as hewers of wood and drawers of water for the congregation. In the second section Joshua confronted a coalition of kings from the southern regions of Canaan. Initially the armies of five Amorite cities assaulted Gibeon; acceding to a request from the Gibeonites, the Israelite army routed these forces. During the battle, Joshua caused the sun and moon to stand still in the sky:

> Then spoke Joshua to the Lord in the day when the Lord gave the Amorites over to the men of Israel; and he said in the sight of Israel,
> 'Sun, stand thou still at Gibeon,
> and thou Moon in the valley of Aijalon,'
> And the sun stood still, and the moon stayed,
> until the nation took vengeance on their enemies. (10: 12–13)

After this victory the five kings were tracked down and slaughtered:

> And when they brought those kings out to Joshua, Joshua summoned all the men of Israel, and said to the chiefs of the men of war who had gone with him, 'Come near, put your feet upon the necks of these kings.' ... And afterward Joshua smote them and put them to death, and

he hung them on five trees. And they hung upon the trees until evening; but at the time of the going down of the sun, Joshua commanded, and they took them down from the trees, and threw them into the cave where they had hidden themselves. (10: 24, 26–27)

Chapter 11 continues the narrative of Joshua's victory with an account of the conquest of northern Canaan. After defeating the cities there, he returned to the south to destroy the city of Hazor and then conquered the Anakites. This description of the conquest of Canaan is followed by a long list of those defeated in the campaign.

From chapters 13 to 19, the Book of Joshua provides a detailed chronicle of the allocation of Canaan to the Israelite tribes, beginning with a description of the lands yet to be conquered; this is followed by a depiction of the land east of the Jordan which had been allocated to the tribes of Reuben and Gad and the half-tribe of Manasseh. The narrative then proceeds with the areas west of the Jordan which were distributed to the remaining tribes. The next chapters deal with the six cities of refuge and the towns reserved for the Levites. Finally with the conquest of the Promised Land complete, the eastern tribes returned to their families who had settled on the east bank of the Jordan. Due to a misunderstanding a feud took place between these tribes and those on the west bank. Eventually, however, the issue was resolved.

The Book of Joshua concludes with Joshua's farewell speech to the leaders of the nation. Ten years had passed since Joshua's victory over the Canaanites. As an old man he reminded the people of the need to remain loyal to the covenant, emphasizing the dangers of religious syncreticism. In response, the Israelites affirmed their commitment:

Then the people answered, 'Far be it from us that we should forsake the Lord, to serve other gods; for it is the Lord our God who brought us and our fathers up from the land of Egypt, out of the house of bondage, and who did those great signs in our sight, and preserved us in all the way we went, and among all the peoples through whom we passed; and the Lord drove out before us all the peoples, the Amorites who lived in the land; therefore we also will serve the Lord, for he is our God.' (24: 16–18)

To ensure the nation's loyalty Joshua made a covenant with the people and set up a stone under an oak in the sanctuary, at Shechem. 'Behold,' he declared, 'this stone shall be a witness against us; for it has heard all the words of the Lord which he spoke to us; therefore it shall be a witness against you, lest you deal falsely with your God' (24: 27).

7. Judges

The Book of Judges is named after the leaders of the nation during the period following the death of Joshua to the institution of the monarchy. The individuals were charismatic leaders upon whom God's spirit rested; they led the tribes in campaigns against foreign oppressors. In this respect the Book of Judges places the history of Israel in a wider context than the Book of Joshua which focuses on the conflict between Israel and the inhabitants of the Promised Land. During this later stage in the history of the nation, the Israelites constituted a settled people who increasingly identified with the individual tribes and clans rather than with the community as a whole.

The events of the first chapter of the book took place after Joshua's death. Despite the Israelites' victorious campaign, large sections of the land still remained in the hands of the Canaanites – the first assault on this area was made by an army from Judah who were largely successful, capturing the Philistine cities of Gaza, Ashkelon and Ekron and the surrounding territories. Because of their location, each of these cities was of strategic importance. Subsequently other tribes were victorious in battle, including the house of Joseph (the tribe of Ephraim and the half-tribe of Manasseh which settled on the west side of the Jordan). Yet repeatedly the Book of Judges stresses that the Israelites were incapable of driving out all the inhabitants of the land – a failure which provoked God's wrath:

> Now the angel of the Lord went up from Gilgal to Bochim. And he said,
> 'I brought you up from Egypt, and brought you into the land which I

swore to give to your fathers. I said, "I will never break my covenant with you, and you shall make no covenant with the inhabitants of this land; you shall break down their altars." But you have not obeyed my command. What is this you have done? So now I say, I will not drive them out before you; but they shall become adversaries to you, and their gods shall be a snare to you.' (2: 1–3)

Chapter 2 continues with the events following Joshua's death. Scripture records that a new generation arose which did not know the Lord and was unaware of what he had done for Israel. As a consequence the Israelites worshipped the Canaanite gods Baal and Asheroth; such apostasy included cultic prostitution as well as child sacrifice. Through such disobedience the nation lost God's favour and thereby became vulnerable to attack. In desperation God resolved to test his people:

Because this people have transgressed my covenant which I have commanded their fathers, and have not obeyed my voice, I will not henceforth drive out before them any of the nations that Joshua left when he died, that by them I may test Israel, whether they will take care to walk in the way of the Lord as their fathers did, or not. (2: 20–22)

Faced with this challenge the people persisted in their idolatrous ways, as Scripture relates: 'And the people of Israel did what was evil in the sight of the Lord, forgetting the Lord their God, and serving the Baals and the Asheroth' (3: 7). As a result of such disloyalty, the nation was overwhelmed by a Canaanite king — only when they repented of their sinfulness were they delivered. This pattern of disobedience and deliverance was repeated with a Moabite king and later with Jabin, king of Canaan. In this case, the prophetess Deborah was victorious over Sisera, the commander of Jabin's forces. Sisera himself was killed by Jael, the wife of Heber the Kenite, who struck him with a tent peg when he sought refuge in her tent. Rejoicing in this victory Deborah sang a song of triumph, one of the oldest poems in the Hebrew Bible:

Most blessed of women be Jael,
the wife of Heber the Kenite,
of tent-dwelling women most blessed.
He asked water and she gave him milk,
she brought him curds in a lordly bowl.
She put her hand to the tent peg
and her right hand to the workmen's mallet;

she struck Sisera a blow,
she crushed his head,
she shattered and pierced his temple.
He sank, he fell,
he lay still at her feet;
at her feet he sank, he fell;
where he sank, there he fell dead ...
So perish all thine enemies,
O Lord!
But thy friends be like the sun as he rises in his might. (5: 24–27, 31)

The Book of Judges continues with the story of Gideon. Because of their waywardness, Israel was oppressed by the Midianites. Despairing of their fate, the Israelites called on God for assistance. In response God sent Gideon who initially purged his father's shrine to Baal, replacing it with an altar dedicated to the Lord. Eventually Gideon vanquished the Midianites; Scripture emphasizes that this triumph was not due to Israel's strength but the result of God's will. Because of this victory, the people sought to make Gideon king, but he refused. Only the Lord, he believed, should rule over Israel:

Then the men of Israel said to Gideon, 'Rule over us, you and your son and your grandson also; for you have delivered us out of the hand of Midian.' Gideon said to them, 'I will not rule over you, and my son will not rule over you; the Lord will rule over you.' (8: 22)

After the death of Gideon the Israelites returned to Baal worship, and his son Abimelech attempted to establish himself as king. In the following chapters the same pattern of disobedience and deliverance continues. After a period of tranquillity under the judges Tola and Jair, the people returned to pagan worship – an act of apostasy which led to attack from the Philistines to the west and the Ammonites to the east. In despair the Israelites again cried out to God for protection. In response the Lord sent Jephthah the Gileadite to defeat the Ammonites as well as the Ephraimites. These conquests were followed by a period of relative stability; however, the Israelites eventually began to follow other gods and as a result were overwhelmed by the Philistines.

Scripture relates that at this stage in Israelite history an angel appeared to the wife of Manoah of the tribe of the Danites announcing that she would give birth to a son who would deliver the Israelite nation from its oppressors. This boy Samson, the angel explained, would be a Nazirite: 'No razor shall come upon his head, for the boy shall be a Nazirite to God from birth; and he shall begin to deliver Israel from the hand of the Philistines' (13: 5). After a series of exploits in which Samson demonstrated his great might, he fell in love with Delilah. To discover the source of his strength the Philistines bribed her with silver. After several attempts to entice Samson to tell her the secret of his strength, Samson eventually complied:

> And she said to him, 'How can you say, "I love you," when your heart is not with me? You have mocked me these three times, and you have not told me wherein your great strength lies.' And when she pressed him hard with her words day after day, and urged him, his soul was vexed to death. And he told her all his mind, and said to her, 'A razor has never come upon my head; for I have been a Nazirite to God from my mother's womb. If I be shaved, then my strength will leave me, and I shall become weak, and be like any other man.' (16: 15–17)

Betraying her lover, Delilah related what Samson told her to the Philistine officers. As he slept on her lap they shaved off his hair, seized him, gouged out his eyes, and bound him. Yet once his hair began to grow, Samson avenged his enemies. When the lords of the Philistines gathered to offer a sacrifice to Dagon their god, Samson prayed for strength:

> Then Samson called to the Lord and said, 'O Lord God, remember me, I pray thee, and strengthen me, I pray thee, only this once, O God that I may be avenged upon the Philistines for one of my two eyes.' And Samson grasped the two middle pillars upon which the house rested, and he leaned his weight upon them, his right hand on the one and his left hand on the other. And Samson said, 'Let me die with the Philistines.' Then he bowed with all his might; and the house fell upon the lords and upon all the people that were in it. (16: 28–30)

The epilogue to the Book of Judges states that Israel was in danger of disintegrating into spiritual anarchy. According to an account in chapters 17 and 18, a man named Micah established a local shrine in Ephraim dedicated to local gods presided over by a Levite; such apostasy subsequently spread to the tribe of Dan. A second incident in chapter 19 concerns members of the tribe of Dan who attempted to molest a male traveller in Gibeah before raping a woman instead who died from shock. Appalled by this evil act, the men of Israel were determined to take revenge on the inhabitants of Gibeah. However, the tribe of Benjamin defended their city and its inhabitants even though this led to the destruction of their army and the devastation of their habitations. The Book of Judges thus concludes with a vivid portrayal of the degeneration of the country. As Judges 21: 25 relates, 'In those days there was no king in Israel; every man did what was right in his own eyes.'

8. 1 and 2 Samuel

1. The judgeship of Samuel (1 Samuel 1: 1–7: 17)
   1. Samuel's background (1: 1–4: 1)
      a. Birth (1: 1–2: 11)
      b. Samuel and the sons of Eli (2: 12–3: 18)
      c. Samuel announces the doom of Eli's house (3: 19–4: 1)
   2. Departure of the ark (4: 1–7: 1)
      a. Capture of the ark (4: 1–22)
      b. The ark among the Philistines (5: 1–12)
      c. The return of the ark (6: 1–7: 1)
   3. Samuel as judge (7: 2–17)

2. Saul as king (1 Samuel 8: 1–12: 25)
   1. Desire for a king (8: 1–22)
   2. Anointing of Saul (9: 1–10: 16)
   3. Announcement of Saul as king (10: 17–27)
   4. Defeat of the Ammonites (11: 1–15)
   5. Samuel's teaching about kingship (12: 1–25)

3. The early kingdom (1 Samuel 13: 1–2 Samuel 5: 10)
   1. Rejection of first king (13: 1–15: 35)
      a. First account of rejection (13: 1–15)
      b. Battle at Michmash (13: 15–14: 52)
      c. Second description of rejection (15: 1–35)
   2. Second king (1 Samuel 16: 1–2 Samuel 5: 10)
      a. Anointing of David (16: 1–13)
      b. David's exploits (16: 14–18: 5)
      c. David's rise and Saul's decline (18: 6–31: 13)
         i. Conflict between David and Saul (18: 6–16)
         ii. Struggle between David and Saul (18: 17–21: 1)
         iii. Open conflict (21: 2–27: 12)
         iv. Saul's defeat (28: 1–31: 13)
      d. David as leader (2 Samuel 1: 1–5: 10)

      b. David's testament (23: 1–7)
3. Administration (23: 8–24: 25)
      a. David's soldiers (23: 8–39)
      b. Plague and census (24: 1–25)

According to the Book of Judges, Israel underwent a process of religious degeneration after the conquest of the Promised Land – the saga of Israel's history continues with the Books of 1 and 2 Samuel. Originally these books were unified, but only later divided into two parts. Together they trace the development of kingship in ancient Israel: with Joshua's death the age of Moses was superseded by a new period in the life of the nation. The emergence of the monarchy under Saul and the subsequent age of David are the central theme of these two books.

1 Samuel begins with an account of Elkanah and his wives, Hannah and Peninah. Deeply distressed by her barrenness Hannah prayed for a child, promising that she would dedicate him to God as a Nazirite. When a local priest Eli heard of her plight, he assured her that the Lord would be merciful. Eventually she conceived and gave birth to Samuel. As she promised, Hannah dedicated the child to God and in gratitude she offered up a hymn of praise to God:

> My heart exults in the Lord;
> my strength is exalted in the Lord.
> My mouth derides my enemies,
> because I rejoice in thy salvation.
> There is none holy like the Lord,
> there is none besides thee;
> there is no rock like our God. (1 Samuel 2: 1–2)

As intended, Samuel served in the household of Eli and assisted in the sanctuary at Shiloh. Distancing himself from the immoral practices of Eli's sons, Samuel remained faithful to God. Eventually a messenger of God visited Eli, condemned his family, and proclaimed that the Lord would raise up a future priest. Subsequently Samuel as a young man was called by the Lord as he lay near the ark. Mistaken in believing it was Eli calling him, Samuel woke up the old man, who, realizing it was the Lord who was calling, urged Samuel to reply. God then revealed that the house of Eli was doomed; as Samuel grew, he was increasingly recognized as a prophet.

Chapter 4 relates that the Israelites were defeated in their most recent battle with the Philistines. Acknowledging that this conquest was due to their unfaithfulness, the people resolved to carry the ark with them into battle. But in the ensuing conflict, the Philistines vanquished the Israelite army, captured the ark, and killed Eli's sons. Hearing this report, Eli was overcome, fell off his chair, and died of a broken neck; his daughter-in-law also died through premature labour. Before her death, however, she chose the name *Ichobod* (no glory) for her son since, as she remarked, God's glory had departed from his people. Discouraged by later defeat, however, the Philistines resolved that the ark be transferred back to Israel. Determined that the nation return to God, Samuel demanded that the people recommit themselves to the Lord; they must, he believed, rid themselves of their *Baals* and *Asheroth*. Once this was accomplished, Samuel made a sacrifice to God and then led the Israelites in victory over the Philistines.

The following chapters recount Israel's quest for a king. After judging the people for several years, Samuel appointed his sons as judges. But their failings gave rise to widespread discontent and the desire for kingship. Hearing this plea, God was despondent: the Lord was their king. Why should they need another? Through Samuel the Lord warned the people of the dangers of kingly rule:

> These will be the ways of the king who will reign over you; he will take your sons and appoint them to his chariots and be his horsemen, and to run before his chariots; and he will appoint for himself commanders of thousands and commanders of fifties, and some to plough his ground and to reap his harvest, and to make his implements of war and the equipment of his chariots. He will take your daughters to be perfumers and cooks and bakers. He will take the best of your fields and vineyards and olive orchards and give them to his servants. (1 Samuel 8: 11–14)

Despite such words of caution, the people insisted on having a monarch:

> But the people refused to listen to the voice of Samuel; and they said, 'No! but we will have a king over us, that we also may be like all the nations, and that our king may govern us and go out before us and fight our battles.' (1 Samuel 8: 19–20)

Reluctantly the Lord acceded to the people's demand, and Samuel was told to await the arrival of a young man from the tribe of Benjamin and anoint him as king: he would be the one to deliver the nation from its oppressors. In accordance with God's wish, Samuel anointed Saul as king and shortly afterwards Saul received the spirit of God: 'When they came to Gibeah, behold, a band of prophets met him; and the spirit of God came mightily upon him, and he prophesied among them' (1 Samuel 10: 10). At Gilgal, Saul was publically recognized as leader of the nation. In a farewell speech, Samuel then reminded Israel of all that God had accomplished and warned them again of the dangers of kingly rule.

Saul's reign begins in chapter 13 with an attack by his son Jonathan against a Philistine outpost – this account gave rise to consternation in Philistia. As a result the Philistines counterattacked causing the Israelite army to dissipate in the face of this offensive. After seven days Saul offered a sacrifice to God which should have been made by Samuel, evoking Samuel's fury. Because of Philistia's mastery over iron, the Israelites were severely disadvantaged, yet Israel was able to prevail and in their confusion the Philistines used their iron weapons against one another. Scripture emphasizes that this victory was due to the Lord's intervention rather than to Saul or Jonathan. Here Saul's deficiencies were highlighted. Saul is portrayed as increasingly disobedient, refusing to obey Samuel's instruction that he rid the land of Amalekites. In desperation Samuel declared that the Lord no longer regarded Saul with favour. In response to Saul's plea for forgiveness, Samuel declared: 'I will not return with you; for you have rejected the word of the Lord, and the Lord has rejected you from being king over Israel' (1 Samuel 15: 26). The Lord then revealed to Samuel that one of the eight sons of the Bethlehemite Jesse would become the future king of Israel – in obedience to God's decree, Samuel anointed David with oil.

In time David entered the court as a musician whose task was to soothe the king. While in his service David demonstrated his bravery in a conflict with the Philistines. Confronted by the Philistine giant Goliath, David volunteered to face him in combat. Armed with only a sling, he emerged triumphant:

When the Philistine arose and came and drew near to meet David, David ran quickly toward the battle line to meet the Philistine. And David put his hand in his bag and took out a stone, and slung it, and struck the Philistine on his forehead; and the stone sank into his forehead, and he fell on his face to the ground.

So David prevailed over the Philistine with a sling and with a stone, and struck the Philistine, and killed him; there was no sword in the hand of David. Then David ran and stood over the Philistine, and took his sword and drew it out of its sheath, and killed him, and cut off his head with it. (1 Samuel 17: 48–51)

On their return from battle, the women celebrated David's victory. Jealous of David, Saul was enraged and sought to bring about his death in a further confrontation with the Philistines. This plan failed, however, when David returned from battle bearing two hundred foreskins of the Philistines, thereby winning Saul's daughter Michal in marriage. In desperation Saul decided to have David killed, but Saul's son Jonathan alerted David to his father's plot. Fleeing from the king, David sought refuge with Samuel at Ramah. Eventually Saul repented, but David continued to be suspicious of the king's intentions. In the midst of this feud Samuel died, giving rise to considerable uncertainty about the future leadership of the nation. Fearing for his life, David fled to the territory of the Philistines where he believed he could be safe – with six hundred men he settled in Ziglag. In a state of uncertainty Saul disguised himself and consulted the witch of Endor to learn of his fate from the spirit of Samuel:

Then Samuel said to Saul, 'Why have you disturbed me by bringing me up?' Saul answered, 'I am in great distress; for the Philistines are warring against me, and God has turned away from me and answers me no more, either by prophets or by dreams; therefore I have summoned you to tell me what I shall do.' And Samuel said, 'Why then do you ask me, since the Lord has turned from you and become your enemy? ... the Lord will give Israel also with you into the hand of the Philistines; and tomorrow you and your sons shall be with me.' (1 Samuel 28: 15–16, 19)

As the narrative unfolds, this prophecy was fulfilled. At Mount Gilboa the Philistines killed Saul's sons including Jonathan, and Saul was wounded by an arrow, eventually committing suicide.

2 Samuel continues with the report of this defeat. Hearing news of the battle, David was overcome. In a moving lament, he mourned for Saul and Jonathan:

Thy glory, O Israel, is slain upon thy high places!
How are the mighty fallen! ...
Saul and Jonathan, beloved and lovely!
In life and in death they were not divided;
they were swifter than eagles,
they were stronger than lions. (2 Samuel 1: 19, 23)

In Hebron David was publically recognized as king over Judah, however, Saul's family was bitterly opposed to his accession to the throne. In opposition to David, one of Saul's sons Ish-bosheth was proclaimed king without divine authority. Initially there was a minor clash between these two factions at Gibeon where David's followers emerged victorious. When Abner, the commander who had installed Ish-bosheth as king, defected to David's camp he was killed by Joab, one of David's generals. These events brought about the collapse of Saul's party, leading to the murder of Ish-bosheth. With the end of this rebellion, David was appointed king over all Israel:

> Then all the tribes of Israel came to David at Hebron, and said, 'Behold, we are your bone and flesh. In times past, when Saul was king over us, it was you who led out and brought in Israel; and the Lord said to you, "You shall be shepherd of my people Israel, and you shall be prince over Israel."' So all the elders of Israel came to the king at Hebron; and King David made a covenant with them at Hebron before the Lord, and they anointed David king over Israel. (2 Samuel 5: 1–3)

Once David became king, he attacked the Jebusite city of Jerusalem which he designated as his capital. After defeating the Philistines, David arranged for the ark to be transferred to Jerusalem and placed in a tent. Through the prophet Nathan it was foretold that David's descendants would construct a house for the Lord and that his throne would be established forever. God's faithfulness to David was reflected in subsequent victories in which a series of Israel's enemies were defeated. Yet God's favour began to wane as David succumbed to temptation.

When Joab led the army against the Ammonites, David remained behind in Jerusalem. From his palace he spied Bathsheba (the wife of Uriah the Hittite) bathing. After seducing her, she became pregnant. David then summoned Uriah home in the hope that he might sleep with his wife and thereby remove the suspicion of pregnancy. When this plan failed, David resolved to bring about Uriah's death by sending him to the front. Once Uriah died in battle David married Bathsheba, but as Scripture records 'the thing that David had done displeased the Lord' (2 Samuel 11: 27). Confronting David the prophet Nathan rebuked him by telling a parable about a rich man who had many sheep yet slaughtered the lamb belonging to a poor man and served it to his guests; Nathan accused David of a similar act in bringing about Uriah's death. As a punishment, Nathan explained, God would not allow the child of this adulterous relationship to live. None the less, Bathsheba eventually gave birth to another son, Solomon.

2 Samuel recounts other events indicative of the moral disintegration of David's reign. After Amnon, one of David's sons, raped Tamar (his daughter of another wife), Tamar's brother Absalom killed Amnon and subsequently rebelled against his father, the king. Fearful of this rebellion, David fled Jerusalem while instructing a member of his inner circle (Hushai the Arkite) to insinuate himself with Absalom's party and report back to him. Believing that Hushai and Ahithophel had joined with him against David, Absalom sought their advice. Ahithopel encouraged Absalom to send out 12,000 troops to kill the king; Hushai, however, urged him to mobilize the entire nation, allowing David time to escape. When Ahithopel discovered that his advice was ignored, he took his own life. In the ensuing battle between the opposing forces, Absalom got stuck in a tree and was killed by Joab and his companions. To Joab's dismay, David was distraught over his son's death. In the period that followed, David returned to Jerusalem but his reign was beset by tension between the men of Judah and those in the north. 2 Samuel concludes with a hymn of praise and David's last words:

The Spirit of the Lord speaks by me,
his word is upon my tongue.
The God of Israel has spoken,
the Rock of Israel has said to me:
When one rules justly over men,
ruling in the fear of God,
he dawns on them like the morning light,
like the sun shining forth upon a cloudless morning,
like rain that makes grass to sprout from the earth.
Yea, does not my house stand so with God?
For he has made with me an everlasting covenant. (2 Samuel 23: 2–5)

9. 1 and 2 Kings

      c. Dedication of the temple (8: 1–9: 9)
         i. Ark brought to the temple (8: 1–13)
        ii. Solomon's speech (8: 14–61)
       iii. Offerings and feast (8: 62–66)
       iv. Covenant (9: 1–9)
      d. Details about Solomon (9: 10–25)
   6. God's gifts to Solomon (9: 26–10: 29)
      a. Solomon's gold (9: 26)
      b. Solomon and the Queen of Sheba (10: 1–13)
      c. Splendour of Solomon (10: 14–29)
   7. Solomon breaks God's covenant (11: 1–43)
      a. Solomon takes strange wives (11: 1–13)
      b. Adversaries against Solomon (11: 14–40)
         i. Hadad (11: 14–22)
        ii. Rezen (11: 23–25)
       iii. Jeroboam (11: 26–40)
      c. Death of Solomon (11: 41–43)

2. History of Israel and Judah (1 Kings 12: 1–2 Kings 17: 41)
   1. Jeroboam I (12: 1–14: 33)
      a. Revolt of the ten tribes (12: 1–20)
      b. God forbids Rehoboam to go to war (12: 21–24)
      c. Calf worship at Dan and Bethel (12: 25–33)
      d. Man of God from Judah (13: 1–10)
      e. The lying prophet (13: 11–19)
      f. Man of God killed by a lion (13: 20–32)
      g. Jeroboam's apostasy (13: 33)
   2. Early kings of Judah and Israel (14: 1–16: 34)
      a. End of Jeroboam's kingship (14: 1–20)
      b. Early kings of Judah (14: 21–15: 24)
         i. Rehoboam (14: 21–31)
        ii. Abijah (15: 1–8)
       iii. Asa (15: 9–24)
      c. Early kings of Israel (15: 25–16: 34)
         i. Nadab (15: 25–32)
        ii. Baasna (15: 33–16: 7)
       iii. Elah (16: 8–14)
       iv. Zimri (16: 15–22)
       v. Omri (16: 23–28)
      vi. Ahab (16: 29–34)
   3. Elijah (17: 1–19: 21)
      a. Elijah and the drought (17: 1–24)

b. Elijah causes rain (18: 1–46)
   i. Obadiah seeks water (18: 1–6)
   ii. Elijah and the servant (18: 7–16)
   iii. Elijah and Ahab (18: 17–20)
   iv. Contest on Mount Carmel (18: 21–40)
   v. Rain (18: 41–43)
c. Elijah flees to Horeb (19: 1–21)

4. Ahab's downfall (1–22: 40)
  a. Syria attacks Israel (20: 1–43)
    i. Ben-Hadad's tribute (20: 1–11)
    ii. Battle of Samaria (20: 12–21)
    iii. Battle of Aphek (20: 22–30)
    iv. Ben-Hadad pleas for his life (20: 31–34)
  b. Naboth's vineyard (21: 1–29)
    i. Naboth's murder (21: 1–16)
    ii. Prophecy (21: 17–29)
  c. Israel attacks Syria (22: 1–38)
    i. Preparations for war (22: 1–4)
    ii. Prophetic narrative (22: 5–28)
    iii. Ahab's plan (22: 29–30)
    iv. Battle (22: 31–34)
    v. Death of Ahab (22: 35–40)
    vi. Events after the war (22: 39–40)

5. Kings of Judah and Israel (1 Kings 22: 41–2 Kings 1: 18)
  a. Jehoshaphat (22: 41–51)
  b. Ahaziah (1 Kings 22: 52–2 Kings 1: 18)

6. Elisha (2: 1–8: 29)
  a. Elisha follows Elijah (2: 1–15)
  b. Jehoram (3: 1–27)
  c. Ten stories (4: 1–8: 15)
    i. Widow's plight (4: 1–7)
    ii. Shunammite woman (4: 8–37)
    iii. Elijah and food poisoning (4: 38–41)
    iv. Elijah and bread (4: 42–44)
    v. Elijah and leprosy (5: 1–27)
    vi. Axe recovered (6: 1–7)
    vii. Elijah as a military resource (6: 8–23)
    viii. Deliverance of Samaria (6: 24–7: 20)
    ix. Property recovered (8: 1–6)
    x. Elisha and Hazael (8: 7–15)
  d. Jehoram (8: 16–24)

e. Ahaziah (8: 25–29)
7. Jehu to the fall of Samaria (9: 1–17: 41)
   a. Jehu (9: 1–10: 36)
   b. Athaliah (11: 1–20)
   c. Joash (12: 1–21)
   d. Jehoahaz (13: 1–9)
   e. Jehoash (13: 10–25)
   f. Amaziah (14: 1–22)
   g. Jeroboam II (14: 23–29)
   h. Azeriah (15: 1–7)
   i. Zechariah and Shallum (15: 8–16)
   j. Menahem (15: 17–22)
   k. Pekahiah and Pekah (15: 23–31)
   l. Jetham (15: 32–38)
   m. Ahaz (16: 1–20)
   n. Hoshea (17: 1–14)

3. Judah (2 Kings 18: 1–25: 30)
   1. Hezekiah (18: 1–20: 21)
      a. Hezekiah's reign (18: 1–12)
      b. Assyrian threat (18: 13–19: 37)
      c. Narrative and conclusion (20: 1–26)
   2. Manasseh and Amon (21: 1–26)
   3. Josiah (22: 1–23: 30)
   4. Jehoahaz (23: 31–24: 7)
   5. Jehoiachin and Zedekiah (24: 8–25: 30)

Like 1 and 2 Samuel, 1 and 2 Kings were originally one book only later divided into two by translators. These books follow directly from 1 and 2 Samuel. Thus the Books of 1 and 2 Samuel and 1 and 2 Kings provide a panoramic account of the history of the nation from the establishment of the monarchy until the Babylonian exile. A major feature of 1 and 2 Kings is the division of the country into two kingdoms after Solomon's reign. The northern kingdom eventually fell to the Assyrians in 722–721 BCE; the southern kingdom met a similar fate in 586 BCE when it was conquered by the Babylonians. The first twelve chapters of 1 Kings outline the succession and reign of Solomon. After his death, his son Rehoboam became king and sought the allegiance of the northern tribes. When he went to Shechem from Jerusalem to meet them, they stated the terms by which they would accept the monarchy. Rehoboam refused to listen and arrogantly declared: 'My father made your yoke heavy, but I will add to your yoke; my father chastised you with whips, but I will chastise you with scorpions' (1 Kings 12: 14). As a consequence of Rehoboam's policies the northern tribes revolted against him and chose Jeroboam I as their monarch: 'And when all Israel heard that Jeroboam had returned, they sent and called him to the assembly and made him king over all Israel' (1 Kings 12: 20). Shechem initially served as Jeroboam's administrative centre, but he later made Tirzah his capital. No major battle appears to have taken place between the northern kingdom (Israel) and the southern kingdom (Judah), but border clashes resulted from Judah's retention of the territory of Benjamin.

As the kingdoms divided, the aggressor who threatened the nation was Shoshenk I, the first pharaoh of the Twenty-Second Dynasty who invaded the land and forced Rehoboam to pay tribute. In the north the external danger was matched by an internal threat. The tribes keenly felt the loss of the temple and desired to make pilgrimage to Jerusalem. To stem such disloyalty, Jeroboam I set up alternative shrines at the old centres of Canaanite worship, Dan and Bethel. There he placed golden bulls in an attempt to reconcile the faith of Israel with features of Canaanite belief, a policy which he believed to be necessary since there was a sizeable Canaanite population within his territory: the Canaanite elements would have no difficulty in associating these idols with their own god Baal who was often represented as a bull; the Israelites could regard them as thrones for their God.

Jeroboam I's successor was his son Nadab who was followed by Baasha. Like Jeroboam I, he encouraged a mixture of Canaanite and Israelite religions, or as Scripture asserts, he 'made Israel to sin' (1 Kings 15: 34). When he died, his son Elah attempted to succeed him, but was assassinated and Zimri the army commander usurped the throne. Zimri's reign lasted only seven days; he was followed by another general Omri and his son Ahab. Under the rule of these two later kings, the position of the northern kingdom was greatly strengthened. They ended the conflict with Judah, and the alliance of the kingdoms was sealed by the marriage of Ahab's daughter, Athaliah, to Jehoram, the son of Jehoshaphat, king of Judah. Israel also made peace with the powerful kingdom of Phoenicia and Ahab himself married the Phoenician princess, Jezebel. Further, Omri gained control over Moab. To solidify his position, Omri built a new administrative centre and shrine in Samaria. Like Jeroboam, Ahab incorporated Canaanite religious features. He provided for the worship of Baal, and thereby incurred the condemnation of Scripture:

> And Ahab the son of Omri did evil in the sight of the Lord more than all that were before him. And as if it had been a light thing for him to walk in the sins of Jeroboam ... and went and served Baal and worshipped him. (1 Kings 16: 30–31)

Such idolatrous practice was encouraged by Jezebel who wanted Baal to become the god of Israel. To combat this threat, the prophet Elijah was determined to prove that the God of Israel was supreme. Thus he challenged 450 prophets of Baal and 400 prophets of Asherah to a contest on Mount Carmel, near Phoenician territory. This had once been the site of an altar to the Israelite God, but it had been displaced by a shrine to Baal. There he and the Canaanite prophets prepared sacrifices and prayed to their respective gods to send fire from heaven to ignite the offerings. Although the prophets of Baal and Asherah cried aloud in ecstatic frenzy and cut themselves with swords, no answer was forthcoming. But Elijah's supplication was successful:

> Then the fire of the Lord fell, and consumed the burnt offering, and the wood and the stones, and the dust, and licked up the water that was in the trench. And when the people saw it, they fell on their faces; and they said, 'The Lord, he is God; the Lord, he is God.' (1 Kings 18: 38–39)

Despite Elijah's victory, Jezebel encouraged Ahab to follow Phoenician customs. She regarded the life and property of every subject as belonging to the king, and so had no hesitation in having the Israelite Naboth killed in order that Ahab could take possession of his property. But Elijah denounced the foreign queen, just as Nathan had previously rebuked David for similar unscrupulousness.

Ahab was succeeded by his two sons, Ahaziah and Joram, but it was not long before those loyal to the faith of Israel rebelled. These devotees, inspired by the prophet Elisha, Elijah's successor, chose an army officer Jehu to be the next king of Israel. During a battle between Israel and Syria, Joram was wounded and returned to recuperate in Jezreel. Jehu followed him there where he discovered Ahaziah, king of Judah, who was paying a visit. Jehu assassinated both kings as well as Jezebel, the queen mother, and appealed to the city rulers of Samaria to pay allegiance to him. This they did by presenting him with the heads of seventy members of Ahab's family.

But Jehu was less successful politically. Since he had killed the Phoenician princess Jezebel, he could no longer rely on the support of a Phoenician alliance. And by killing the king of Judah, he also lost the loyalty of the southern kingdom. In Judah Athaliah, Ahab's sister, seized control and murdered all claimants for the throne except for one child, Joash, who was rescued by the priest Jehoiada. Athaliah reigned for six years, but was deposed in a coup led by Jehoiada. Joash was then installed as king.

During this period the Syrians had been engaged in war with the Assyrian king Shalmaneser III who was intent on expanding his empire. After Jehu came to power, Shalmaneser invaded Syria and besieged Damascus; Phoenicia and Israel were forced to pay tribute to avoid being conquered by Assyria. At the end of Shalmaneser's III's reign, a revolt took place in Nineveh which weakened the Assyrian empire and gave the king of Damascus, Hazael, an opportunity to invade Israel. Under Jehu's son Jehoahaz, Israel became almost a province of Syria. The entire country east of the Jordan was occupied, and the Syrians continued to attack Judah. But Jehoash offered Hazael treasure from the temple to dissuade him from invading Jerusalem.

By the time Jehu's grandson Jehoash became king, Assyria had grown in power under Shalmaneser's grandson, Adad-Nirari III. According to Assyrian records, Israel was forced to pay tribute to Assyria along with the Edomites and Philistines. Damascus was devastated by the Assyrian advance. The Assyrian attack on Syria gave Jehoash the opportunity to recover Israel's lost territory; Amaziah the king of Judah similarly captured his land from the Edomites. At this stage Amaziah declared war also on the northern kingdom, but Judah was defeated and Jehoash raided Jerusalem. As a consequence, Amaziah lost favour and was assassinated, to be succeeded by his son Uzziah.

Under Uzziah in Judah and Jeroboam II in Israel, the nation prospered for the next forty years. Uzziah repaired the fortifications in Jerusalem, reorganized the army, and equipped it with new weapons. He also instituted new agricultural methods and reopened parts of Solomon's copper refineries on the Gulf of Aqabah. In the northern kingdom Jeroboam II constructed new buildings and engaged in international trade. As the nation grew richer, the people became more religious – they believed their wealth was a sign of God's favour. Yet some dissenters thought that the quest for riches was incompatible with God's covenant.

Towards the end of Jeroboam II's reign, Amos, a shepherd from Tekoa who firmly differentiated himself from the official cultic prophets, expressed his dissatisfaction; he proclaimed that Israelite society had become morally corrupt. His later contemporary, the prophet Hosea, echoed Amos's dire predictions. Israel had gone astray and would be punished. Yet through personal tragedy Hosea was able to offer words of consolation and hope. It was not long before these prophecies of destruction were fulfilled. The Assyrian king Tiglath Pileser III embarked on a policy of expansion during the reign of Menahem, king of Israel. Menahem's son Pekahiah held his throne for two years by paying tribute to the Assyrian king, but was overthrown by his rival Pekah. The new Israelite king formed an alliance with the king of Syria against the Assyrians. Together they attempted to persuade Jotham, king of Judah, to join them; when he refused, they declared war on Judah. In the face of this danger, the southern prophet Isaiah declared to Ahaz, Jotham's successor, that this threat would come to naught: both Israel and Syria would collapse. But Ahaz was unconvinced. He attempted to placate the Assyrians and went to Damascus to pay homage to Tiglath Pileser III. He returned with the plans for an altar to be erected in the temple as a sign of Judah's submission.

In the northern kingdom, Pekah's position was weakened as the Assyrians pressed forward, and he was assassinated by Hoshea who surrendered to the Assyrians. When Shalmaneser V replaced Tiglath Pileser III, Egyptian forces were powerless to help, and Shalmaneser V conquered Israel's capital, Samaria, after a siege of two years.

With the collapse of the northern kingdom, Judah was under threat. To avoid a similar fate in the south, King Ahaz continued to pay tribute to Assyria and to encourage the nation to worship Assyrian gods. However, the prophet Isaiah was deeply concerned about such idolatrous practices. He believed that the collapse of Israel was God's punishment for sinfulness, and he foresaw a similar fate for Judah. A contemporary of Isaiah, the prophet Micah, also criticized the people for their iniquity and foretold destruction. Ahaz refused to listen to these words, trusting in his own political alliances.

By the time Hezekiah succeeded Ahaz, the Assyrian king, Sargon II, had turned his attentions to problems in other parts of the empire. This gave Egypt and Philistia an opportunity to join ranks to throw off Assyrian domination. Seeking the help of Judah, the Philistine ambassadors tried to secure Hezekiah's support. But the prophet Isaiah warned that such an alliance would be of no avail. Fortunately

Hezekiah heeded Isaiah's prediction – Assyria quickly conquered the Philistine and Egyptian nations. After this conquest Hezekiah attempted to establish his independence from Assyrian domination by reforming the religious practices of the people. As well as removing the altar to Assyrian gods in the temple which his father Ahaz had erected, he tried to close down local shrines in order to centralize the cult in Jerusalem. Further, he sent a message to those who remained in the former northern kingdom urging them to come south to worship. Hezekiah also prepared his kingdom for an Assyrian onslaught: he created new defences, restructured the army, established new store cities, and rationalized the civil service.

After the death of Sargon II, the kings of Babylon and Egypt asked Hezekiah to help overthrow the Assyrians; Isaiah cautioned against joining such an alliance, but Hezekiah took no notice. Sargon's successor Sennacherib quickly acted to suppress this revolt. He subdued Babylon, Phoenicia and Philistia, and then moved against Judah in 701 BCE. The next step in the Assyrian campaign was the assault on Jerusalem. 2 Kings contains an account of a siege of Jerusalem which ended in failure: the Assyrian army camped outside the city, but just as their victory seemed imminent the Assyrians withdrew.

Following the invasion of Judah, Sennacherib was murdered. He was succeeded by Esarhaddon who was a successful ruler. When he died the empire was divided between his two sons: Ashur-bani-pal who reigned in Nineveh, and Shamash-Shanakin who had head-quarters in Babylon. During this period Assyria was victorious against the Egyptians and became the dominant force in Mesopotamia. Under Ashur-bani-pal Nineveh emerged as a cultural centre. In the kingdom of Judah, Hezekiah's successor Manasseh was completely under Assyrian domination. The nation's faith was neglected, and pagan ceremonies again became prevalent. Like Ahaz, Manasseh was forced to worship Assyrian gods as a sign of submission, and his son and successor Amon continued his father's policies.

Despite its prominence, Assyria came under increasing threat from the kingdom of Lydia in the north-west, the Medes in the east and the Scythians in the north. This weakening of the Assyrian empire brought about a nationalistic revival in Judah. The prophet Jeremiah warned that the southern kingdom would eventually be devastated by foreign powers. The new king, Josiah, believed he could restore Judah to its former glory through territorial expansion and religious reform. During his reign there was found in the temple a forgotten book which asserted that a single God should be worshipped in a central place by a united people. In a solemn ceremony, the people pledged their allegiance to God:

And the king stood by the pillar and made a covenant before the Lord, to walk after the Lord and to keep his commandments and his testimonies and his statutes, with all his heart and all his soul, to perform the words of this covenant that were written in this book; and all the people joined in the covenant. (2 Kings 23: 3)

While these events took place in Judah, the Babylonians advanced against Syria and captured all its main cities. Some years after Josiah's reform, the Assyrians made a final attempt to regain the town of Harran. Embroiling himself in this struggle, Josiah tried to halt the Egyptian army which had been summoned by the Assyrians to come to their aid. In the ensuing battle Josiah was mortally wounded, and Judah came under the domination of Egypt. Eventually, however, the Assyrian empire collapsed and the Babylonians succeeded in conquering the Egyptians at Carchemish in 605 BCE. At this King Jehoiakim who had been put in power by the Egyptians transferred his allegiance to King Nebuchadnezzar III of Babylon. During the reign of Jehoiakim Jeremiah continued to prophesy disaster. His contemporary the prophet Habakkuk echoed the prediction that God would use foreign nations as instruments of his wrath.

When Babylon was defeated by Egypt several years later, Jehoiakim decided the time was ripe for rebellion. Nebuchadnezzar, however, quickly responded by invading the country and conquering Jerusalem. In this siege Jehoiakim was killed and replaced by his son Jehoiachin who was captured. Along with other important citizens he was led into captivity, and the treasures of the palace and temple were plundered. A new king, Zedekiah was placed on the throne by Nebuchadnezzar. After a siege of eighteen months, Jerusalem was conquered in 586 BCE; all the main buildings were destroyed and Zedekiah was exiled to Babylon.

PROPHETS

Latter Prophets

10. Isaiah

1. Introduction (1: 1–31)
   1. Inscription (1: 1)
   2. God's complaint (1: 2–3)
   3. Jerusalem criticized (1: 4–9)
   4. Worship and justice (1: 10–17)
   5. Choice (1: 18–20)
   6. Judgement on Jerusalem (1: 21–4)
   7. Crime and punishment (1: 29–31)

2. Judah and Israel (Part I) (2: 1–5: 30)
   1. Zion (2: 1–5)
   2. Day of Judgement (2: 6–22)
   3. Deterioration of leadership (3: 1–12)
   4. God criticizes leaders (3: 13–15)
   5. Women of Jerusalem (3: 16–4: 1)
   6. Jerusalem protected (4: 2–6)
   7. Song of God's vineyard (5: 1–7)
   8. Woes (5: 8–24)
   9. God's outstretched hand (5: 25–30)

3. Isaiah's recollections (6: 1–9: 6)
   1. The call (6: 1–13)
   2. Ahaz (7: 1–9)
   3. Sign of Immanuel (7: 10–17)
   4. Fragments (7: 18–25)
   5. Maher-shalal–hash-baz (8: 1–4)
   6. Waters of Shiloah (8: 5–8)
   7. Plans of nations (8: 9–10)
   8. Isaiah conspires with God (8: 11–15)
   9. A waiting for God (8: 16–18)
   10. Additions (8: 19–22)

11. Prince of Peace (8: 23–9: 6)

4. Judah and Israel (Part 2) (9: 7–12: 6)
   1. God's outstretched hand (9: 7–20)
   2. Woe against rulers (10: 1–4)
   3. Woe against Assyria (10: 5–15)
   4. Completions (10: 16–27)
   5. Advance of the fee (10: 27–34)
   6. Future king (11: 1–9)
   7. Additions (11: 10–16)
   8. Song of thanksgiving (12: 1–6)

5. Oracles (13: 1–23: 18)
   1. Oracle against Babylon (13: 1–22)
   2. Restoration of the Gentiles and Israel (14: 1–2)
   3. Song against the king of Babylon (14: 3–23)
   4. God's plan for Assyria (14: 24–27)
   5. Warning to Philistia (14: 28–32)
   6. Moab (15: 1–16: 14)
   7. Syria and Israel (17: 1–11)
   8. Assault and deliverance (17: 12–14)
   9. Egyptian embassy (18: 1–7)
   10. Egypt (19: 1–25)
   11. Isaiah as a sign of Egypt (20: 1–6)
   12. Fall of Babylon (21: 1–10)
   13. Dumah, Dedan and Kedar (21: 11–17)
   14. Valley of vision (22: 1–14)
   15. Shebna and Eliakim (22: 15–25)
   16. Tyre (23: 1–18)

6. Apocalypse (24: 1–27: 13)
   1. Judgement for sin (24: 1–20)
   2. God's triumph (24: 21–27: 1)
      a. God's kingship (24: 21–23)
      b. Hymn to God (25: 1–5)
      c. Banquet on Mount Zion (25: 6–10)
      d. Moab (25: 10–12)
      e. Prayer for deliverance (26: 1–27: 1)
   3. Vineyard and city (27: 2–13)

7. Oracles and promises of future salvation (28: 1–33: 24)
   1. Against Samaria (28: 1–6)
   2. Against the ruling classes of Jerusalem (28: 7–22)

3. Ariel (29: 1–8)
4. Against the people's unknowing (29: 9–16)
5. Salvation (29: 17–21)
6. Jacob's future (29: 22–24)
7. Rebellious sons (30: 1–5)
8. Beasts of the south (30: 6–7)
9. Perils of rejecting God (30: 8–17)
10. Those who wait for God (30: 18–26)
11. Defeat of Assyria (30: 27–33)
12. Against reliance on Egypt (31: 1–3)
13. Against Assyria (31: 4–9)
14. Ideal kingdom (32: 1–8)
15. Complacent women (32: 9–14)
16. Reversal (32: 15–20)
17. Prayer and prophecy (33: 1–24)

8. Judgement on Edom and joy for the saved (34: 1–35: 10)
1. Judgement (34: 1–17)
2. Flowering of the desert (35: 1–10)

9. Isaiah and Hezekiah (36: 1–39: 8)
1. Sennacherib (36: 1–37: 38)
2. Hezekiah's sickness (38: 1–22)
3. Embassy from Merodach-baladan (39: 1–8)

10. Book of comfort (40: 1–55: 13)
1. Introduction (40: 1–31)
   a. The messenger of the Lord (40: 1–11)
   b. Dispute with Israel (40: 12–31)
2. New exodus (41: 1–48: 22)
   a. The servant hears (41: 1–44: 23)
      i. Israel's salvation (41: 1–42: 13)
         1. Justice (41: 1–20)
         2. Military and peaceful ways of justice (41: 21–42: 13)
      ii. Redeemer (42: 14–44: 23)
         1. Blind and deaf servant (42: 14–43: 21)
         2. God as saviour (43: 22–44: 23)
   b. Cyrus (44: 24–47: 15)
      i. Commissioning (44: 24–45: 13)
         1. World events (44: 24–28)
         2. Commissioning of Cyrus (45: 1–8)
         3. Dispute with Israel (45: 9–13)

        ii.   God's decree (45: 14–25)
        iii. Trial (46: 1–13)
        iv. Taunt against Babylon (47: 1–15)
     c. Conclusion (48: 1–22)
        i.   Eternal God (48: 1–16)
        ii.   Promise (48: 17–19)
        iii. Hymn (48: 20–22)
  3. Comfort of Zion (49: 1–54: 17)
     a. Sorrow to redemption (49: 1–51: 18)
        i.   Commissioning of the prophet (49: 1–7)
        ii.   Announcement of new exodus (49: 8–13)
        iii. Announcement of salvation (49: 14–26)
        iv. Confidence of the prophet (50: 1–11)
        v.   Promise of salvation (51: 1–8)
     b. Comfort for mourners (51: 9–52: 12)
        i.   Lament and comfort (51: 9–52: 6)
        ii.   Messenger of salvation (52: 7–10)
        iii. New exodus (52: 11–12)
     c. Thanksgiving for servant (52: 13–53: 12)
     d. Zion (54: 1–17)
  4. Conclusion (55: 1–13)

11. New temple and leadership (56: 1–66: 24)
  1. Gentiles included in Israel's blessing (56: 1–8)
  2. Struggle for leadership (56: 9–59: 21)
     a. False leaders and the faithful (56: 9–57: 13)
     b. Comfort for the faithful (57: 14–21)
     c. True and false fasting (58: 1–14)
     d. Accusation, lament and triumph (59: 1–21)
  3. New Zion (60: 1–62: 12)
     a. Glory (60: 1–22)
     b. Anointing of the prophet (61: 1–3)
     c. Glory of the new Zion (61: 4–62: 9)
     d. Reflection (62: 10–12)
  4. Sorrow to a new heaven and earth (63: 1–66: 16)
     a. Solitary victor (63: 1–6)
     b. Confessions (63: 7–64: 11)
     c. True and false servants (65: 1–25)
     d. New temple (66: 1–16)
  5. Foreigners in God's house (66: 17–24)

Traditionally it was assumed that the Book of Isaiah was the work of one person. Today, however, most scholars maintain that there were three Isaiahs: First Isaiah, who composed chapters 1 to 39, lived in the latter half of the seventh century BCE; Second Isaiah in all likelihood lived about 150 years later during the Babylonian exile and wrote chapters 40 to 54; Third Isaiah, who was responsible for chapters 55 to 66 also lived after the exile. The Book of Isaiah thus reflects the religious and political situation from the period prior to the collapse of the northern kingdom to the exile in Babylonia.

First Isaiah

The Book of Isaiah begins by explaining that what follows is an account of the prophecies of Isaiah regarding Judah and Jerusalem during the period from 792 to 686 BCE. In the first prophetic oracle, God is depicted as disappointed with his people: they have forsaken his word. Cultic observance alone is insufficient; what is required instead is the love of God. The second oracle continues this theme – the people have rebelled against the Lord. Yet Isaiah prophesies the eventual triumph of God's kingdom on earth:

It shall come to pass in the latter days
that the mountain of the house of the Lord
shall be established as the highest of the mountains,
and shall be raised above the hills;
and all the nations shall flow to it,
and many peoples shall come, and say:
'Come, let us go up to the mountain of the Lord,
to the house of the God of Jacob;
that he may teach us his ways
and that we may walk in his paths.'
For out of Zion shall go forth the law,
and the word of the Lord from Jerusalem.
He shall judge between the nations,
and shall decide for many peoples;
and they shall beat their swords into ploughshares,
and their spears into pruning hooks;
nation shall not lift up sword against nation,
neither shall they learn war any more. (2: 2–4)

This future vision is none the less overshadowed by present calamity. Beginning with chapter 2 prophetic criticism is levelled against idolatry, and the prophet foretells that such disobedience will eventually be eliminated with the destruction of Jerusalem. Chapter 5 proceeds with the song of the vineyard: Israel is compared to a vineyard which produces bad fruit. Because of their disobedience the nation will be sent into exile.

At this point the narrative provides background information about the prophet. In the year of King Uzziah's death in 740 BCE, Isaiah had a vision of the Lord in the temple commissioning him to be his servant:

> I saw the Lord sitting upon a throne, high and lifted up; and his train filled the temple. Above him stood the seraphim; each had six wings: with two he covered his face, and with two he covered his feet, and with two he flew. And one called to another and said:
>   'Holy, holy, holy is the Lord of hosts; the whole earth is full of his glory.' (6: 1–3)

Chapter 7 sets out the historical situation during the period of the Syro-Ephramite War in 735 BCE. Confronted by Assyrian aggression, Amram and the northern kingdom attempted to persuade Judah to join a coalition. When King Ahaz agreed, Jerusalem came under attack. Isaiah urged Ahaz to stand firm – as a sign he referred to a young woman giving birth to a son, possibly indicating that within nine months the threat would pass. After discussing the role of Assyria in God's providential plan, the prophet returned to the promise of salvation. A child will be born, he stated, who will be a Prince of Peace. This declaration of hope, however, is placed in the context of divine punishment. In Isaiah's view, God will use Assyria as an instrument whereby the Jewish nation will be devastated because of their sins. Only a faithful remnant will remain, and from this segment a redeemer will issue forth who will usher in a new period of Israelite history:

> There shall come forth a shoot from the stump of Jesse,
> and a branch shall grow out of his roots.
> And the Spirit of the Lord shall rest upon him ...
> He shall not judge by what his eyes see,
> or decide by what his ears hear;
> but with righteousness he shall judge the poor,
> and decide with equity for the meek of the earth; ...
> The wolf shall dwell with the lamb,
> and the leopard shall lie down with the kid,
> and the calf and the lion and the fatling together. (11: 1–2, 3–4, 6)

The Book of Isaiah continues with an account of God's judgement against the surrounding nations including Babylon, Assyria, Philistia, Moab, Syria, Ethiopia, Edom, Arabia, concluding with a prophecy concerning Jerusalem. Isaiah emphasized that the Lord would be totally victorious over all the earth, yet such divine judgement will provide deliverance for the people of God. In this context the prophet presents a song of praise to be sung on the day of Israel's deliverance:

> In that day this song will be sung in the land of Judah:
> 'We have a strong city;
> he sets up salvation
> as walls and bulwarks.
> Open the gates,
> that the righteous nation which keeps faith
> may enter in.
> Thou dost keep him in perfect peace,
> whose mind is stayed on thee,
> because he trusts in thee.
> Trust in the Lord for ever,
> for the Lord God is
> is an everlasting rock. (26: 1–4)

The next section of the book begins with a statement that God will punish unbelief. If the inhabitants of Jerusalem will not hearken to the word of the Lord, they will have to listen to the language of strangers – this is a reference to the invasion of the Assyrians and the threat of deportation. According to Isaiah, Israel must trust in the Lord rather than depend on their own strength or allies. This assurance is followed by the promise of a future king who will reign in peace and righteousness in Judah. A final prophecy emphasized that in the end of days all nature will rejoice with the entry of the redeemed people into Zion: 'And the ransomed of the Lord shall return, and come to Zion with singing; everlasting joy shall be upon their heads; they shall obtain joy and gladness, and sorrow and sighing shall flee away.' (35: 10).

Such prophecies about destruction and hope are overshadowed in chapters 36 to 39 by an account of the siege of Judah by Sennacherib. In 725 BCE King Shalmaneser V of Assyria invaded Samaria, and besieged the northern kingdom for three years. Once the kingdom of Israel had been conquered, Shalmaneser's successor Sennacherib advanced against Judah, but the assault against Jerusalem failed.

Second Isaiah

By the time of Second Isaiah, the prophecies of First Isaiah had been fulfilled. Judah was conquered and its inhabitants taken into Babylonian exile. In place of oracles of denunciation, Second Isaiah offered the promise of hope and restoration. The fortieth chapter begins with comforting words – the time of exile is over, and God declares that he is preparing for his people's return to Zion:

> Comfort, comfort my people,
> says your God.
> Speak tenderly to Jerusalem,
> and cry to her
> that her warfare is ended,
> that her iniquity is pardoned,
> that she has received from the Lord's hand
> double for all her sins.
> A voice cries:
> 'In the wilderness prepare the way of the Lord
> make straight in the desert a highway for our God.' (40: 1–3)

According to the prophet, the Lord will return in triumph to Jerusalem – he will act as a shepherd leading his flock: 'He will feed his flock like a shepherd, he will gather the lambs in his arms, he will carry them in his bosom, and gently lead those that are with young' (Isaiah 40: 11). All the world will see this act of deliverance and acknowledge that there is no redeemer except for the Lord of Israel. This theme is emphasized in chapter 44 where idolatry is severely criticized:

> All who make idols are nothing, and the things they delight in do not profit; their witnesses neither see nor know, that they may be put to shame. Who fashions a god or casts an image, that is profitable for nothing? (44: 9–10)

This condemnation of idolatry is followed by a prophecy of the fall of Babylon. Reflecting on the joy of Israel's deliverance from Babylonian domination, Second Isaiah rebuked the practices of Israel's captors: the gods of Babylon are incapable of preventing the collapse of the empire. God will send Cyrus, king of Persia against Babylon, and in this act of devastation the nation will be redeemed. In chapter 49 the prophet depicts the servant of the Lord through whom salvation will be brought to the ends of the earth. Chapter 49 illustrates that this servant will be mocked and despised and this theme is further developed in chapter 53:

He was despised and rejected by men;
a man of sorrows, and acquainted with grief;
and as one from whom men hide their faces
he was despised, and we esteemed him not.
Surely he has borne our griefs
and carried our sorrows;
yet we esteemed him stricken,
smitten by God, and afflicted.
But he was wounded for our transgressions,
he was bruised for our iniquities;
upon him was the chastisement that made us whole
and with his stripes we are healed. (53: 3–5)

Second Isaiah concludes with a vision of the future glory of Zion: God will be reunited with his people, and all will be fulfilled.

Third Isaiah

Echoing the prophecies about the restoration of Zion in Second Isaiah, Third Isaiah focuses on the role of the Jewish people in God's providential scheme. In chapter 58, the prophet draws a parallel between the regulations laid down for Israel after their escape from Egyptian bondage and the obligations placed upon the nation after its return from Babylonia. Through Israel's redemption all nations will be blessed, and the temple in Jerusalem will become a focus of worship for all peoples: 'My house shall be called a house of prayer for all peoples' (Isaiah 56: 7). In the next chapters God directs his criticism against those who have deserted him, yet despite this rebuke the Lord offered his promise of hope for those who are repentant. What is required is true worship, penitence and confession.

Chapter 60 continues with a description of the glory of Zion. Jerusalem, the prophet declares, will be honoured throughout the world because of God's greatness:

Arise, shine; for your light has come,
and the glory of the Lord has risen upon you.
For behold, darkness shall cover the earth,

and thick darkness the peoples;
but the Lord will arise upon you,
and his glory will be seen upon you.
And nations shall come to your light,
and kings to the brightness of your rising. (60: 1–3)

This theme is developed in the next chapter which speaks of a figure on whom the Spirit of God will rest; it is he who will liberate all captives, bring tidings to the afflicted, and rebuild Zion:

The Spirit of the Lord God is upon me,
because the Lord has anointed me
to bring good tidings to the afflicted;
he has sent me to bind up the brokenhearted,
to proclaim liberty to the captives,
and the opening of the prison to those who are bound; ...
They shall build up the ancient ruins,
they shall raise up the former devastations;
they shall repair the ruined cities,
the devastations of many generations. (61: 1, 4)

In such a time Jerusalem will be acknowledged as the place where the Lord's redeemed dwell. Beginning with chapter 63, the prophet recounts the great acts of the Lord – it is he who delivered his people from captivity and directs their history. Although God will judge those who have forsaken him, the promise of restoration is offered to all who are faithful. Here the prophet proclaims that a new heaven and a new earth will be created at the end of days:

'For behold, I create new heavens
and a new earth;
and the former things shall not be remembered
or come into mind.
But be glad and rejoice for ever
in that which I create;
for behold, I create Jerusalem a rejoicing,
and her people a joy ...
The wolf and the lamb shall feed together,
the lion shall eat straw like the ox;
and dust shall be the serpent's food.
They shall not hurt or destroy
in all my holy mountain.' (65: 17–18, 25)

11. Jeremiah

      b. Broken covenant (11: 1–13: 27)
         i.   Covenant (11: 1–14)
         ii. Destruction (11: 15–17)
         iii. Plot against Jeremiah (11: 18–12: 6)
         iv. God's complaint (12: 7–13)
         v. Judah's neighbours (12: 14–17)
         vi. Discourses (13: 1–14)
            1. Rotten loincloth (13: 1–11)
            2. Broken wineflasks (13: 12–14)
         vii. Threats (13: 15–27)
            1. Dark night (13: 15–17)
            2. Exile (13: 18–19)
            3. Sickness (13: 20–27)
      c. Disobedience and punishment (14: 1–17: 27)
         i.   Drought (14: 1–15: 9)
            1. Drought (14: 1–16)
            2. Lament (14: 17–15: 4)
            3. Tragedy (15: 5–9)
         ii. Renew of the call (15: 10–21)
         iii. Celibacy (16: 1–13)
         iv. Sayings (16: 14–17: 18)
         v. Sabbath observance (17: 19–27)
      d. Symbolic significance of the prophet's life (18: 1–20: 18)
         i.   The potter (18: 1–12)
         ii. Israel forgets God (18: 13–17)
         iii. Prayer for vengeance (18: 18–23)
         iv. Broken flask and Topheth (19: 1–20: 6)
         v. Despair (20: 7–18)
  4. Under Zedekiah (21: 1–24: 10)
      a. Consultation from Zedekiah (21: 1–10)
      b. Booklet on kings (21: 11–23: 8)
         i.   Address to the royal house (21: 11–22: 9)
         ii. Jehoahaz (22: 10–12)
         iii. Jehoiakim (22: 13–19)
         iv. Jehoiachin (22: 20–30)
         v. Future king (23: 1–8)
      c. Booklet on the prophets (23: 9–40)
      d. Baskets of figs (24: 1–10)
  5. Captivity of Judah and end of Babylon (25: 1–13)
  6. Judgement on the nations (25: 13–38)

3. Restoration of Israel (26: 1–35: 19)
   1. Persecution of Jeremiah (26: 1–24)
   2. Controversy with false prophets (27: 1–29: 32)
      a. Coalition of the west (27: 1–22)
      b. Against prophecy (28: 1–17)
      c. Letter to the exiles (29: 1–32)
   3. Restoration of Israel (30: 1–31: 40)
      a. Restoration of northern Israel (30: 1–31: 22)
         i. Introduction (30: 1–3)
         ii. Jacob's distress (30: 4–11)
         iii. Healing of Israel's wounds (30: 12–17)
         iv. Restoration (30: 18–24)
         v. Return (31: 1–6)
         vi. New exodus (31: 7–14)
         vii. Rachel's mourning (31: 15–20)
         viii. On route (31: 21–22)
      b. Additions (31: 23–40)
   4. Restoration of Judah (32: 1–33: 26)
      a. Pledge of restoration (32: 1–44)
      b. Restoration of Judah and Jerusalem (33: 1–26)
   5. Conditions for salvation (34: 1–35: 19)
      a. Fate of Zedekiah (34: 1–7)
      b. Dishonesty (34: 8–22)
      c. Rechabites (35: 1–19)

4. Martyrdom of Jeremiah (36: 1–45: 5)
   1. Scroll (36: 1–32)
   2. Zedekiah and the prophet (37: 1–38: 28)
   3. Fall of Jerusalem (38: 28–39: 18)
   4. Tragedy at Mizpah (40: 1–41: 18)
   5. Sojourn in Egypt (42: 1–44: 30)
      a. Search for guidance (42: 1–6)
      b. God's answer (42: 7–18)
      c. Refusal to remain home (42: 19–43: 7)
      d. Nebuchadnezzar (43: 8–13)
      e. Jeremiah's last words (44: 1–30)
   6. Baruch (45: 1–5)

5. Oracles against the nations (46: 1–51: 64)
   1. Egypt (46: 1–28)
   2. Philistia (47: 1–7)
   3. Moab (48: 1–47)

4. Ammon (49: 1–6)
5. Edom (49: 7–22)
6. Damascus (49: 23–27)
7. Arabia (49: 28–33)
8. Elam (49: 34–39)
9. Babylon (50: 1–51: 58)
10. Oracle in the Euphrates (51: 59–64)

6. Historical appendix (52: 1–34)

In 626 BCE Jeremiah was commissioned as a prophet during the reign of Josiah, king of Judah – his ministry continued during the reigns of Jehoahaz (609 BCE), Jehoiakim (609–598 BCE), Jehoiachin (598–597 BCE), and Zedekiah (597–586 BCE). During this period the kingdom of Judah underwent a series of major events beginning with Josiah's reform. After Josiah died in battle against the Egyptians who came to the aid of the Assyrians, the Assyrian army was defeated by the Babylonians. In 605 BCE the Egyptians were defeated by the Babylonians who then laid siege to Jerusalem during the reign of Jehoiakim; eventually they conquered the city in 598–597 BCE taking Jehoiachin into captivity. Zedekiah was then installed as king; when he rebelled against the Babylonians, Jerusalem was besieged. In this onslaught Jeremiah fled to Egypt.

The Book of Jeremiah opens with God's call to the prophet in 626 BCE during Josiah's reign. According to Scripture, Jeremiah was chosen by God to be his servant even before he was born: 'Before I formed you in the womb I knew you, and before you were born I consecrated you; I appointed you a prophet to the nations' (1: 5).

Subsequently Jeremiah experienced two visions. In the first he saw an almond tree (whose meaning in Hebrew is similar to the word 'watching') – the interpretation of this image is that God watches over his chosen people. In the second vision Jeremiah saw a boiling pot tilted away from the north – the interpretation is that the southern kingdom will experience a disaster coming from the north. In this passage Jeremiah was encouraged to remain faithful to God despite his loneliness in proclaiming God's message: 'But you, gird up your loins; arise, and say to them everything that I command you. Do not be dismayed by them, lest I dismay you before them' (1: 17).

Jeremiah's earliest prophecies dating from the time of Josiah begin in chapter 2. Judah, he declared, had forsaken God and in consequence he will be punished. The southern kingdom has become like Israel which was destroyed by Assyria. What is now required is repentance. Yet, if the inhabitants refuse, God will send forth an invader to subdue the country:

Flee for safety, O people of Benjamin,
from the midst of Jerusalem!
Blow the trumpet in Tekoa,
and raise a signal on Beth-haccherem;
for evil looms out of the north. (6: 1)

In the next section of the book, Jeremiah predicts further judgements against Judah. In his view, the religious life of the southern kingdom is worthless. At the gate of Solomon's temple, he declared that the inhabitants of Jerusalem are misguided in believing that cultic practice ensures their security. At the time of the conquest of Canaan, the existence of the tabernacle did not prevent Shiloh from being overthrown by the Philistines; so the temple will not protect the people unless they are faithful to God. In this context Jeremiah emphasized the prevalence of paganism in the religious life of the nation; even child sacrifice had been introduced. God will not stand for such disobedience: he will bring punishment to those who have turned away from him. Grieving over this state of affairs, Jeremiah wept for his people:

My grief is beyond healing,
my heart is sick within me ...
For the wound of the daughter of my people is my heart wounded,
I mourn, and dismay has taken hold on me. (8: 18, 21)

In a series of dire warnings, Jeremiah portrayed the devastation that would come to this wayward nation.

In chapter 9, Jeremiah turns his attention to idolatry – bitterly he castigates pagan practices as empty:

'A tree from the forest is cut down,
and worked with an axe by the hands of a craftsman.
Men deck it with silver and gold;
they fasten it with hammer and nails
so that it cannot move.
Their idols are like scarecrows in a cucumber field,
and they cannot speak;

they have to be carried,
for they cannot walk.
Be not afraid of them,
for they cannot do evil,
neither is it in them to do good.' (10: 3–5)

Chapter 11 continues with the theme of corruption and punishment: here the prophet emphasizes that the covenant places mutual obligations on both parties. Since Israel has violated God's commandments, doom is inevitable. Not surprisingly Jeremiah's prophecies evoked hostility – beginning with this chapter he recounts the anguish he endured because of his ministry. Yet the Lord reassured Jeremiah that he had no other option. Judah had sinned and would be destroyed: Jeremiah once again proclaimed that judgement will come from foreign invaders: 'Lift up your eyes and see those who come from the north' (13: 20).

In the following chapters Jeremiah describes a serious drought in the land; this, he believed, was a further condemnation of the nation. A day of disaster will eventually come – Judah will be devastated and its inhabitants taken into exile. However, accompanying this prophecy of doom is the promise of restoration. Just as God delivered the people in times past, so he will do so again despite their evil ways:

Therefore, behold, the days are coming, says the Lord, when it shall no longer be said, 'As the Lord lives who brought up the people of Israel out of the land of Egypt,' but 'As the Lord lives who brought up the people of Israel out of the north country and out of the countries where he had driven them.' For I will bring them back to their own land which I gave to their fathers. (16: 14–15)

After discussing the significance of Sabbath observance, Jeremiah visited a potter's house; there he observed the potter at work. Unhappy with his first attempt, the potter broke down the clay and refashioned it. So, Jeremiah argued, God will remould his chosen people: 'O house of Israel, can I not do with you as this potter has done? says the Lord. Behold, like the clay in the potter's hand, so are you in my hand, O house of Israel' (18: 6). Jeremiah then purchased a clay jar and smashed it in public – this action symbolized the way in which the Lord would deal with the Jewish nation. Judah and Jerusalem will be decimated because of their disobedience: 'Thus says the Lord of hosts: So will I break this people and this city, as one breaks a potter's vessel, so that it can never be mended' (19: 11). This action outraged one of the priests who planned for Jeremiah to be beaten; demoralized by this experience, Jeremiah complained to the Lord:

> O Lord, thou has deceived me,
> and I was deceived;
> thou art stronger than I,
> and thou has prevailed.
> I have become a laughingstock all the day;
> every one mocks me.
> For wherever I speak, I cry out,
> I shout, 'Violence and destruction!'
> For the word of the Lord has become for me
> a reproach and derision all day long. (20: 7–8)

Chapter 21 moves forward to events during the reign of Zedekiah who was installed as king by the Babylonians in 597 BCE. Nearly ten years later Zedekiah promoted rebellion against Babylon and sought reassurance from Jeremiah. The prophet, however, reaffirmed his conviction that the Lord would use the Babylonian army as an instrument of his wrath. In this context Jeremiah blamed both past and present rulers for their waywardness, yet he was convinced that a remnant would return from whom a new king would arise to redeem his people:

> Behold the days are coming, says the Lord, when I will raise up for David a righteous Branch, and he shall reign as king and deal wisely, and shall execute justice and righteousness in the land. In his days Judah will be saved, and Israel will dwell securely. (23: 5–6)

After denouncing false prophecy, Jeremiah had a vision of two baskets of figs – one contained good fruit but the other only rotten. The former he interpreted as the people of Jerusalem who had been taken into exile in Babylon; the latter was Zedekiah and his court who remained in Jerusalem. The exiles, he stated, will eventually return to Zion but the king and his court will be cut off forever. For seventy years Jerusalem will remain barren, but then the Lord will punish Babylon and set the Jewish exiles free. In a further vision Jeremiah saw the cup of God's wrath. When the nations drink from it, they will become drunk and then die by the sword. Again Jeremiah was threatened because of these utterances, and false prophets declared that Jerusalem was safe from danger. Aware of such false prophecies Jeremiah warned that the only hope was to return to God's ways.

The false prophets countered Jeremiah's message. Hananiah, for example, proclaimed that the Lord would soon overwhelm the Babylonians and restore the temple. Opposing these words, Jeremiah went about the city wearing a yoke around his neck as a symbol of the need to submit to Babylon. After Hananiah broke this yoke, the word of the Lord came to Jeremiah saying:

> Go tell Hananiah, 'Thus says the Lord: You have broken wooden bars, but I will make in their place bars of iron. For thus says the Lord of hosts, the God of Israel: I have put upon the neck of all these nations an iron yoke of servitude to Nebuchadnezzar king of Babylon, and they shall serve him.' (28: 13–14)

Concerned with those who had been taken into captivity, Jeremiah wrote a letter urging them to settle in Babylonia – such advice contradicted the optimistic pronouncements of such false prophets as Shemiah. Only later, Jeremiah predicted, would the Lord redeem his chosen people from bondage in a foreign land. To illustrate this belief, Jeremiah bought a plot of land in Anathoth as a symbol that the people would eventually return to their own country.

Chapters 36 to 38 contain Jeremiah's woes. His words evoke continually animosity, particularly from the royal court. In 605 BCE, the fourth year of Jehoiakim's reign, Jeremiah prophesied that Jerusalem would be held captive for seventy years. With the assistance of his scribe Baruch, Jeremiah recorded these words at the Lord's command. After reading out this scroll from a room near the temple, Baruch was requested to repeat them to a group of court officials who insisted that the king should hear them as well. Unmoved by Jeremiah's warnings, the king cut off a section of the scroll and cast it onto a burning brazier. Subsequently under Zedekiah, Jeremiah's message was similarly ignored. Prior to the Babylonian advance against Jerusalem in 588 BCE, Jeremiah once again pronounced doom and attempted to leave the city – as a consequence, he was accused of aligning himself with the Babylonians and cast into prison. Eventually, however, the king summoned him and asked whether he had received any further communication from the Lord. Unable to provide the reassurance the king desired, Jeremiah reiterated his prophecy of destruction.

Although Jeremiah continued to be held prisoner, he was allowed to receive visitors. When asked about the future of the nation, he once more urged his hearers to submit to the Babylonians with a dire warning:

> Thus says the Lord, He who stays in this city shall die by the sword, by famine, and by pestilence; but he who goes out to the Chaldeans shall live; he shall have his life as a prize of war, and live. (38: 2)

Alarmed by this pronouncement, the officials cast Jeremiah into a cistern within the courtyard of the guard. But when the king learned of such treatment, he arranged for Jeremiah to be released. Again, the prophet urged the king to submit to the Babylonians; he was then imprisoned until the city was devastated. During this siege, Zedekiah was killed and the city set on fire; those who surrendered were carried off into exile. Jeremiah, however, was compelled by King Nebuchadnezzer of Babylon to live in the house of Gedaliah, the governor of Judah who was stationed in Mizpah north of the city. When Gedaliah was assassinated, Jeremiah declared that those who fled for safety to Egypt would be punished. Angered by such prophecy, the senior officials accused Jeremiah of deceit and prepared to set out for Egypt taking Jeremiah and Baruch with them.

Jeremiah's final prophecy was concerned with the idolatrous practices of those who had escaped to Egypt. Because of their disobedience, he predicted that they would be punished. Unimpressed by Jeremiah's pronouncement, the Egyptian exiles argued that the fall of Jerusalem was caused by the failure to worship foreign gods during Josiah's reign: 'But since we left off burning incense to the queen of heaven and pouring out libations to her, we have lacked everything and have been consumed by the sword and by famine' (44: 18). Furious with all these words of blasphemy Jeremiah rebuked the exiles, prophesying total destruction of the Egyptian community:

> As for the incense that you burned in the cities of Judah and in the streets of Jerusalem, you and your fathers, your kings and your princes, and the people of the land, did not the Lord remember it? Did it not come into his mind? The Lord could no longer bear your evil doings and the abominations which you committed; therefore your land has become a desolation and a waste and a curse, without inhabitant ... all the men of Judah who are in the land of Egypt shall be consumed by the sword and by famine, until there is an end of them. (44: 21–22, 27)

The Book of Jeremiah concludes with a series of oracles against the nations including Judah itself.

12. Ezekiel

      ii.   Jehoiachin (19: 5–9)

      iii. Zedekiah (19: 10–14)

  6. Condemnation (20: 1–24: 27)

    a. Israel's infidelity (20: 1–44)

    b. Prophecies of the sword (20: 45–21: 32)

      i.   Sword against the south (20: 45–21: 7)

      ii. Sword polished for destruction (21: 8–17)

      iii. Sword against the king of Babylon (21: 18–27)

      iv. Sword against the Ammonites (21: 28–32)

    c. Sins of Jerusalem (22: 1–31)

    d. Harlotry of Oholah and Oholibah (23: 1–49)

    e. Signs of the end (24: 1–27)

      i.   Boiling pot (24: 1–14)

      ii. Death of Ezekiel's wife (24: 15–27)

2. Oracles against surrounding nations (25: 1–32: 32)

  1. Against small neighbours (25: 1–17)

    a. Ammon (25: 1–7)

    b. Moab (25: 8–11)

    c. Edom (25: 12–14)

    d. Philistines (25: 15–17)

  2. Against Tyre (26: 1–28: 19)

  3. Against Sidon (28: 20–26)

  4. Against Egypt (29: 1–32: 32)

3. Oracles of restoration (33: 1–39: 29)

  1. Second commission (33: 1–33)

    a. Role as watchman (33: 1–9)

    b. Message of righteousness (33: 10–20)

    c. New land (33: 21–33)

  2. Shepherd of Israel (34: 1–31)

  3. Prophecy against Mount Seir (35: 1–15)

  4. Judgement and restoration (36: 1–38)

    a. Judgement on Israel's oppressors (36: 1–7)

    b. Israel to be restored (36: 8–38)

  5. Restoration of Israel (37: 1–28)

    a. Vision of dry bones (37: 1–14)

    b. Two sticks rejoined (37: 15–28)

  6. Vision of Gog (38: 1–39: 29)

    a. Gog against Israel (38: 1–16)

    b. God's war against Gog (38: 17–23)

    c. Victory over Gog (39: 1–16)

According to Scripture the prophet Ezekiel began his ministry during the fifth year of Jehoiachin's exile, seven years before the conquest of Jerusalem. Dwelling in Babylon, Ezekiel prophesied about the state of affairs of Judah: during the first part of his ministry, the temple in Jerusalem was functioning and most of the book deals with this period. For Ezekiel the nation's sinfulness will bring about its destruction. Yet following the fall of Jerusalem in 586 BCE, Ezekiel offered words of comfort to his people. Although the nation had lost its homeland, it would one day return to the Promised Land.

The book begins in chapter 1 with Ezekiel's call. In this passage, Ezekiel sees a great cloud with brightness surrounding it; in its midst there was something resembling the flash of amber. From this appeared four living creatures; each resembled a man in form with four faces of a man, a lion, an ox and an eagle. In addition, each of these had four wings. There were also wheels full of eyes and wheels within wheels. Above the living creatures was a firmament on which rested the great throne which supported God's glory:

> As I looked, behold, a stormy wind came out of the north, and a great cloud, with brightness round about it, and fire flashing forth continually, and in the midst of the fire, as it were gleaming bronze. And from the midst of it came the likeness of four living creatures. And this was their appearance: they had the form of men, but each had four faces, and each of them had four wings ...
> Now as I looked at the living creatures, I saw a wheel upon the earth

beside the living creatures, one for each of the four of them ... And above the firmament over their heads there was the likeness of a throne, in appearance like sapphire; and seated above the likeness of a throne was a likeness as it were of a human form. (1: 4–6, 15, 26)

Subsequently in Jewish mystical reflection the first chapter of Ezekiel played a pivotal role: Ezekiel's vision of the divine chariot was described in detail and this scriptural source served as the basis for speculation about the nature of the deity.

In the following chapters the Lord calls Ezekiel, referring to him as a 'son of man'; he was commanded to instruct the people, and as a token of his ministry he was given a scroll on which were written words of lament and warning. When Ezekiel was told to eat this scroll, he found it tasted sweet. As a watchman of Israel, Ezekiel's task was to warn the people of God's judgement. In chapter 4, the siege against Jerusalem is symbolized by a series of actions. First, Ezekiel was commanded to draw a clay tablet depicting Jerusalem under siege. He was then told to lie on his left and right side – this symbolized the sin of the northern and southern kingdoms and the ensuing punishment. In the next symbolic act Ezekiel was compelled to eat grain and vegetables as well as use dung as fuel – these gestures signified the conditions that would prevail during the impending siege. A further symbol involved the cutting of Ezekiel's hair: a third was burnt; a third cut with a sword; and a third scattered to the wind. This action symbolized the fate of the Jewish nation – a third would die of plague or famine; a third would be massacred; and a third scattered among the nations.

In chapters 6 to 9 Ezekiel castigates places of pagan worship – they will be destroyed along with those who worship there. Not only are detestable practices taking place on mountain tops, they are also found inside the temple. In the temple court Ezekiel saw abominations on the wall: 'there, portrayed upon the wall round about, were all kinds of creeping things, and loathsome beasts, and all the idols of the house of Israel' (8: 10). Similarly in the inner court at the door of the temple between the east porch and the altar, Ezekiel saw twenty men with their backs to the temple of the Lord, 'and their faces toward the east, worshipping the sun toward the east' (8: 16). As a consequence of such impiety, God's glory departed from the temple:

And the cherubim mounted up. These were the living creatures that I saw by the river Chebar. And when the cherubim went, the wheels went beside them; and when the cherubim lifted up their wings to mount up from the earth, the wheels did not turn from beside them. When they stood still, these stood still, and when they mounted up, these mounted up with them; for the spirit of the living creatures was in them.

Then the glory of the Lord went forth from the threshold of the house and stood over the cherubim. And the cherubim lifted up their wings and mounted up from the earth in my sight as they went forth, with the wheels beside them; and they stood at the door of the east gate of the house of the Lord; and the glory of the God of Israel was over them. (10: 15–19)

Yet despite the departure of God's glory from his holy place, Ezekiel reassured the nation that it would not be abandoned: 'Thus says the Lord God: I will gather you from the peoples, and assemble you out of the countries where you have been scattered, and I will give you the land of Israel' (11: 17).

Notwithstanding such words of consolation, Ezekiel was commanded in chapters 12 to 14 to perform a symbolic act to stress the fate of Israel. He was told to pack his possessions and put them over his shoulder – this symbolized the long trek into exile. There will be no way to escape such punishment: when the false prophets foretell the reign of peace, they have no authority to speak on behalf of the Lord. Since the Jewish nation has disobeyed God's precepts, it will be cut off. To illustrate the hopelessness of Israel's plight, the nation is compared to a useless vine; at best it can only be used for firewood. Again, Judah's worthlessness is stressed by the image of an infant abandoned at birth. The Lord took compassion on this child, providing her with food and loving care. What was the Lord's reward for his concern? The child he nourished has become a prostitute. The implication is that Jerusalem is returning to its pagan origins in spite of God's loving kindness; because of its wayward-ness, Israel will be stripped naked so that all may see their shame.

This prophecy is followed by a parable about two eagles and a vine. Here the eagles symbolize Nebuchadnezzar and an Egyptian pharaoh. Ezekiel envisioned the Babylonians taking some of the inhabitants of Jerusalem to Babylonia where they will flourish, whereas those who remain in the land will become involved with Egypt and wither. This is followed by a declaration of individual responsibility:

The son shall not suffer for the iniquity of the father, nor the father suffer for the iniquity of the son; the righteousness of the righteous shall be upon himself, and the wickedness of the wicked shall be upon himself. (18: 20)

But those who truly repent will be forgiven – what the Lord requires is that the wicked turn from their evil ways and live: 'Have I any pleasure in the death of the wicked, says the Lord God, and not rather that he should turn from his way and live?' (18: 23). Thus the inhabitants of Jerusalem can still be saved if only they will return to the Lord with a contrite heart:

> Repent and turn away from all your transgressions, lest iniquity be your ruin. Cast away from you all the transgressions which you have committed against me, and get yourselves a new heart and a new spirit! (18: 30–31)

In chapter 20 the rebellious nature of Israel is again emphasized. Here the prophecy dates from 591 BCE: Ezekiel outlined the history of the nation's rebellious acts against the Lord from the sojourn in Egypt to its entry into the Holy Land. In the following chapter Babylonia is explicitly identified as the instrument of God's wrath; through this foreign invader the nation will be punished for its sinfulness: 'A sword, a sword is sharpened and also polished, sharpened for slaughter, polished to flash like lightning!' (21: 9–10).

In another passage Ezekiel proclaims that Israel will be consumed by God's wrath:

> And I will pour out my indignation upon you;
> I will blow upon you with the fire of my wrath;
> and I will deliver you into the hands of brutal men,
> skilful to destroy. You shall be fuel for the fire;
> your blood shall be in the midst of the land. (21: 31–32)

The next prophecy dates from 588 BCE. The Babylonians have besieged Jerusalem, and Ezekiel compares Judah to a cooking pot. The pot symbolizes Jerusalem – all the best pieces were left in the pot, but now the heat has increased and all will be consumed:

> Set on the pot; set it on,
> pour in water also;
> put in it the pieces of flesh,
> all the good pieces, the thigh and
> the shoulder;

fill it with choice bones.
Heap on the logs, kindle the fire, boil well the
flesh, and empty out the broth, and let the bones be
burned up. Then set it empty upon the coals, that
it may become hot, and its copper may burn, that
its filthiness may be melted in it, its rust consumed.
(24: 3–4, 10–11)

The Book of Ezekiel continues in chapters 25 to 32 with an account
of God's dealing with the nations surrounding Judah. Paralleling
Jeremiah's oracles against the nations, Ezekiel pronounced judgement on the enemies of the southern kingdom: Ammon (25: 1–7),
Moab (25: 8–11), Edom (25: 12–14), Philistia (25: 15–17), Tyre (26:
1–28: 19), Sidon (28: 20–26), and Egypt (29: 1–32: 32). The general
theme of these denunciations is that the nations surrounding Judah
will be compelled to recognize God's might. Significantly, Babylon
is not included among the peoples who will be destroyed; instead, it
is perceived as God's instrument through which these foreign
powers will be devastated.

The next section dates from after the fall of Jerusalem. Previously
Ezekiel prophesied doom and destruction, but after the fall of Judah
he offered words of comfort and hope. According to Ezekiel, God
takes no pleasure in the death of sinners; what he requires instead is
a contrite heart: chapter 34 continues with a prophecy of restoration.
Here the Lord declares that the shepherds of Israel have failed them;
yet Ezekiel reassuringly proclaims that God will be the shepherd of
his flock: he will gather the people from exile and return them to the
Promised Land:

For thus says the Lord God: Behold, I, I myself will search for my sheep,
and will seek them out. As a shepherd seeks out his flock when some of
his sheep have been scattered abroad, so will I seek out my sheep; and I
will rescue them from all places where they have been scattered on a
day of clouds and thick darkness. (34: 11–12)

This prophecy is followed by a further vision of restoration – the
Lord promised that the cities will be reinhabited and their ruins will
be rebuilt. Such national restoration, Ezekiel argued, will be
accompanied by personal dedication to the covenant. This
reassurance was reinforced by the prophet's vision of dry bones.
Although the nation had been destroyed, it will be renewed in a
future deliverance:

As I prophesied, there was a noise, and behold, a rattling; and the bones came together, bone to its bone. And as I looked, there were sinews on them, and flesh had come upon them, and skin had covered them ... Then he said to me, 'Son of man, these bones are the whole house of Israel. Behold, they say, "Our bones are dried up, and our hope is lost; we are clean cut off." Therefore prophesy, and say to them, Thus says the Lord God: Behold, I will open your graves, and raise you from your graves, O my people; and I will bring you home into the land of Israel ... And I will put my Spirit within you, and you shall live, and I will place you in your own land.' (37: 7–8, 11, 14)

This vision is followed by a prophecy concerning a future king who will rule over his people – under his dominion Jerusalem will benefit from the promises of the covenant. The book concludes with a final vision of a new temple in which God will once again dwell among his people.

13. Hosea

1. Marriage (1–3)
   1. Hosea's children (1: 2–2: 3)
   2. Marital unfaithfulness (2: 4–17)
   3. Reconciliation (2: 18–25)
   4. Hosea and his wife (3: 1–5)

2. Denunciation of contemporaries (4: 1–9: 9)
   1. God's case against Israel (4: 1–3)
   2. Criticism of the leaders of the nation (4: 4–5: 7)
   3. Political unrest (5: 8–14)
   4. False repentance (5: 15–7: 2)
   5. The corruption of the kings (7: 3–12)
   6. Lament (7: 13–16)
   7. Israel's sin (8: 1–14)
   8. Punishment for Israel (9: 1–6)
   9. Rejection of prophecy (9: 7–9)

3. The consequence of sinfulness (9: 10–13: 16)
   1. Israel's decline (9: 10–17)
   2. Destruction of Israel's idols (10: 1–8)
   3. Devastation of Israel's fortresses (10: 9–15)
   4. Israel will be captive of Assyria (11: 1–7)
   5. God's tenderness (11: 8–9)
   6. Israel's restoration (11: 10–11)
   7. Punishment for Ephraim (11: 12–12: 1)
   8. Judgement on Jacob (12: 2–6)
   9. Ephraim's sins (12: 7–15)
   10. Ephraim's doom (13: 1–16)

4. Repentance and salvation (14: 1–9)

Born in the northern kingdom, Hosea was an eighth-century prophet during the reign of Jeroboam. Overlapping with the ministry of

Amos, Isaiah and Micah, he protested against religious apostasy. In his view, the leaders of the nation had put their trust in foreign gods as well as in the powers of Assyria and Egypt. This, he believed, was gross indecency which would be punished by divine retribution. In proclaiming this message, the prophet drew on his own personal grief. Previously he was commanded to marry a woman who was unfaithful, yet despite Hosea's anguish he remained loyal to her. In Hosea's view, his marriage symbolized God's relationship to Israel: although the nation had abandoned the Lord, God's love for his chosen people would continue.

The Book of Hosea commences with an account of the prophet's wife and children. Hosea married Gomer, a woman already guilty of adultery: 'When the Lord first spoke through Hosea, the Lord said to Hosea, "Go, take to yourself a wife of harlotry and have children of harlotry, for the land commits great harlotry by forsaking the Lord."' (1: 2). After bearing a son, Gomer subsequently had two more children. Each was given a name symbolic of Israel's waywardness: Lo-ruhamah ('Not pitied') symbolized that no mercy would be extended to the northern kingdom: and Lo Ami ('Not my people'), a symbol of God's rejection of the apostate nation:

> She conceived again and bore a daughter. And the Lord said to him, 'Call her name Not pitied, for I will no more have pity on the house of Israel, to forgive them at all. But I will have pity on the house of Judah, and I will deliver them by the Lord their God; I will not deliver them by bow, nor by sword, nor by war, nor by horses, nor by horsemen.' (1: 6–8)

Despite such condemnation, however, the prophet promised future redemption, a theme paralleled in other prophetic books:

> Yet the number of the people of Israel shall be like the sand of the sea, which can be neither measured nor numbered; and in the place where it was said to them, 'You are not my people,' it shall be said to them, 'Sons of the living God.' And the people of Judah and the people of Israel shall be gathered together, and they shall appoint for themselves one head; and they shall go up from the land, for great shall be the day of Jezreel. (1: 10–11)

In the second chapter of the book the northern kingdom's punishment is explained. In a song about Gomer's adultery (which is a symbol of Israel), Hosea accused his wife of playing the harlot; as a result she is to be pitied:

Plead with your mother, plead –
for she is not my wife, and I am not her husband –
that she put away her harlotry from her face, and her adultery from
between her breasts; . . .
Upon her children also I will have no pity,
because they are children of harlotry.
For their mother has played the harlot;
she that conceived them has acted shamefully.
For she said, 'I will go after my lovers,
who give me my bread and my water,
my wool and my flax, my oil and my drink.' (2: 2, 4–5)

None the less just as Gomer will be restored to her husband, so God
intends to restore Israel:

And in that day, says the Lord,
I will answer the heavens
and they shall answer the earth;
and the earth shall answer the grain, the wine, and oil,
and they shall answer Jezreel;
and I will sow him for myself in the land.
and I will have pity on Not pitied,
and I will say to Not my people, 'You are my people';
and he shall say, 'Thou art my God.' (2: 21–23)

In chapter 3 Hosea's restoration with his wife is depicted as a
symbol of reconciliation with the northern kingdom. Although God
is incensed by the nation's unfaithfulness, he will restore the people
to their former glory:

And the Lord said to me, 'Go again, love a woman who is beloved of a
paramour and is an adulteress; even as the Lord loves the people of
Israel, though they turn to other gods and love cakes and raisins.' So I
bought her for fifteen shekels of silver and a homer and a lethech of
barley. And I said to her, 'You must dwell as mine for many days; you
shall not play the harlot, or belong to another man; so will I also be to
you.' For the children of Israel shall dwell many days without king or
prince, without sacrifice or pillar, without ephod or teraphim. Afterward
the children of Israel shall return and seek the Lord their God, and
David their king; and they shall come in fear to the Lord and to his
goodness in the latter days. (3: 1–5)

Throughout the Book of Hosea, the prophet emphasizes the
symbolic nature of his marriage to Gomer: her adultery signifies

Israel's relationship with the Lord. Just as Gomer abandoned her husband, the northern kingdom has been faithless. As Hosea explained, the people have deserted God for idols and Canaanite altars:

> For a spirit of harlotry has led them astray,
> and they have left their God to play the harlot.
> They sacrifice on the tops of mountains,
> and make offerings upon the hills,
> under oak, poplar, and terebinth ... (4: 12–13)

To God's dismay the leaders of the nation did not attempt to curtail such deviation from covenantal worship – instead they turned to Assyria for help. Such behaviour, Hosea asserted, will not be forgiven. Although Hosea's words were directed principally to the northern kingdom, he included Judah in his denunciation:

> When Ephraim saw his sickness,
> and Judah his wound,
> then Ephraim went to Assyria,
> and sent to the great king.
> But he is not able to cure you
> or heal your wound.
> For I will be like a lion to Ephraim,
> and like a young lion to the house of Judah
> I, even I, will rend and go away,
> I will carry off, and none shall rescue. (5: 13–14)

Yet even though God will bring about the punishment of his faithless servants, Hosea insisted that he will not abandon them. If the people acknowledge their sin and repent, they can be forgiven. Here Hosea compares God's mercy to the arrival of rains which replenish the earth:

> Let us know, let us press on to know the Lord;
> his going forth is sure as the dawn;
> he will come to us as showers,
> as the spring rains that water the earth. (6: 3)

The Israelites, however, stubbornly refused to mend their ways – as a result, Hosea predicted that God's judgement will be meted out on the unfaithful. Utilizing imagery drawn from nature, he portrayed their doom:

Ephraim is like a dove,
silly and without sense,
calling to Egypt, going to Assyria.
As they go, I will spread over them my net;
I will bring them down like birds of the air;
I will chastise them for their wicked deeds.
Woe to them, for they have strayed from me!
Destruction to them, for they have rebelled against me! (7: 11–13)

Israel is thus destined to reap a whirlwind – a day of reckoning will take place:

The days of punishment have come,
the days of recompense have come;
Israel shall know it ...
They have deeply corrupted themselves
as in the days of Gibeah:
he will remember their iniquity,
he will punish their sins. (9: 7, 9)

In chapter 9 Hosea reminds Israel of their youth. When the people came out of Egypt, they were innocent. But after entering the Promised Land, they lapsed into pagan worship. And as the nation grew prosperous, it came to believe that its prosperity was due to the influence of Canaanite deities:

Israel is a luxuriant vine
that yields its fruit.
The more his fruit increased
the more altars he built;
as his country improved
he improved his pillars. (10: 1)

Such abomination can no longer be endured. Because the people have done iniquitously, they will be devastated through war and destruction:

You have ploughed iniquity,
you have reaped injustice,
you have eaten the fruit of lies.
Because you have trusted in your chariots
and in the multitude of your warriors,
therefore the tumult of war shall arise among your people,

and all your fortresses shall be destroyed,
as Shalman destroyed Beth-arbel on the day of battle;
mothers were dashed in pieces with their children.
Thus it shall be done to you, O house of Israel,
because of your great wickedness.
In the storm the king of Israel
shall be utterly cut off. (10: 13–15)

Returning to the theme of restoration, Hosea recalled the earlier relationship between Israel and God. When the Israelites escaped from Egyptian bondage, they held fast to their belief that the Lord would guide them to their ultimate destination. Yet, as time passed the nation grew away from the Lord. Justice demands that such waywardness be punished, yet the Lord in his compassion will not abandon his chosen people. In a future age Israel will be restored:

They shall go after the Lord,
he will roar like a lion;
yea, he will roar,
and his sons shall come trembling from the west;
they shall come trembling like birds from Egypt,
and like doves from the land of Assyria;
and I will return them to their homes, says the Lord. (11: 10–11)

In a final section of the book, Hosea reiterates Israel's sinfulness: Israel has become wealthy by illicit means; the nation has paid tribute to foreign powers; the people have turned away from worshipping God. This catalogue of wickedness, however, is not the last word. In his mercy God will heal the nation's wounds and draw it back to himself:

I will heal their faithlessness;
I will love them freely,
for my anger has turned from them.
I will be as the dew to Israel;
he shall blossom as the lily,
he shall strike root as the poplar;
his shoots shall spread out;
his beauty shall be like the olive,
and his fragrance like Lebanon.
They shall return and dwell beneath my shadow,
they shall flourish as the garden; they shall blossom as the vine,
their fragrance shall be like the wine of Lebanon. (14: 4–7)

14. Joel

The Book of Joel is attributed to Joel, son of Pethuel: 'The word of the Lord that came to Joel, the son of Pethuel' (1: 1). However, it is unclear who such a person was since Scripture contains a number of figures named Joel – arguably the prophet should not be identified with any of these individuals. Presumably Joel lived in the environs of Jerusalem which provides the background to this book; due to his familiarity with temple worship, some scholars have identified him as a cultic prophet. Yet since there is no concrete evidence when the book was written, commentators have advanced various views, ranging from the ninth century BCE during the time of Joash to the six, fifth, fourth, third and second centuries BCE.

The book itself begins with an account of the invasion of locusts. In chapter 1 Joel describes the devastation caused by this plague – this he interpreted as a sign of God's judgement on his people:

What the cutting locust left,
the swarming locust has eaten.
What the swarming locust left,
the hopping locust has eaten,
and what the hopping locust left,

the destroying locust has eaten.
Awake, you drunkards, and weep;
and wail, all you drinkers of wine,
because of the sweet wine,
for it is cut off from your mouth.
For a nation has come up against my land,
powerful and without number;
its teeth are lions' teeth,
and it has the fangs of a lioness.
It has laid waste my vines,
and splintered my fig trees;
it has stripped off their bark and thrown it down;
their branches are made white. (1: 4–7)

According to Joel a day of darkness will descend upon the land; this is symbolized by the locusts, a manifestation of divine destructiveness:

Blow the trumpet in Zion;
sound the alarm on my holy mountain!
Let all the inhabitants of the land tremble,
for the day of the Lord is coming, it is near,
a day of darkness and gloom,
a day of clouds and thick darkness!
Like blackness there is spread upon the mountains
a great and powerful people;
their like has never been from of old,
nor will be again after them
through the years of all generations.

Fire devours before them
and behind them a flame burns.
The land is like the garden of Eden before them,
but after them a desolate wilderness,
and nothing escapes them ...

The earth quakes before them, the heavens tremble.
The sun and moon are darkened,
and the stars withdraw their shining. (2: 1–3, 10)

In chapter 2 Joel outlines the disaster that is destined to befall the nation if the people do not repent. Such repentance must be genuine; the Lord is not satisfied with outward signs. Instead he searches the heart — what is demanded is true contrition:

'Yet even now,' says the Lord, 'return to me with all your heart, with fasting, with weeping, and with mourning; and rend your hearts and not your garments.' Return to the Lord, your God, for he is gracious and merciful, slow to anger, and abounding in steadfast love, and repent of evil. (2: 12–13)

In the prophet's view, it is not too late. Here Joel depicts the promised deliverance following such remorse. No longer will Israel be a reproach to the nations; rather, the Lord will cause the land to prosper, and the destruction brought about by the locusts will be forgotten:

Fear not, O land;
be glad and rejoice,
for the Lord has done great things!
Fear not, you beasts of the field,
for the pastures of the wilderness are green;
the trees bears its fruit,
the fig tree and vine give their full yield.

Be glad, O sons of Zion,
and rejoice in the Lord, your God:
for he has given the early rain for your vindication,
he has poured down for you abundant rain,
the early and the latter rain, as before.

The threshing floors shall be full of grain,
the vats shall overflow with wine and oil.
I will restore to you the years
which the swarming locust has eaten,
the hopper, the destroyer, and the cutter,
my great army, which I sent among you. (2: 21–25)

This depiction of Israel's recovery is followed by an even greater hope: God's spirit will be poured out on all people: 'And it shall come to pass afterward, that I will pour out my spirit on all flesh; your sons and your daughters shall prophesy, and your old men shall dream dreams, and your young men shall see visions.' (2: 28). Chapter 3 continues with a portrayal of the restoration of Judah and Jerusalem:

For behold, in those days and at that time, when I restore the fortunes of Judah and Jerusalem, I will gather all the nations and bring them down to the valley of Jehoshaphat, and I will enter into judgement with them there, on account of my people and my heritage Israel, because they have scattered them among the nations, and have divided up my land. (3: 1–2)

Here Joel lists the sins of Israel's enemies, yet with the restoration of the nation its foes will be undone. The Lord will bring about their destruction, but Israel will be saved:

Multitudes, multitudes,
in the valley of decision!
For the day of the Lord is near
in the valley of decision.
The sun and moon are darkened,
and the stars withdraw their shining.

And the Lord roars from Zion,
and utters his voice from Jerusalem,
and the heavens and the earth shake.
But the Lord is a refuge to his people,
a stronghold to the people of Israel. (3: 14–16)

In the future, Joel proclaimed, Jerusalem would be restored and become the Lord's.

So you shall know that I am the Lord your God,
who dwell in Zion, my holy mountain.
And Jerusalem shall be holy
and strangers shall never again pass through it.

And in that day
the mountains shall drip sweet wine,
and the hills shall flow with milk,
and all the stream beds of Judah
shall flow with water;
and a fountain shall come forth from the house of the Lord
and water the valley of Shittim. (3: 17–18)

15. Amos

1. Judgement on the surrounding nations (1: 1–2: 3)
    1. Introduction (1: 1–2)
    2. Damascus (1: 3–5)
    3. Gaza (1: 6–8)
    4. Tyre (1: 9–10)
    5. Edom (1: 11–12)
    6. Ammon (1: 13–15)
    7. Moab (2: 1–3)

2. Prophecies against God's chosen people (2: 4–16)
    1. Judah (2: 4–5)
    2. Israel (2: 6–16)

3. Judgement against Israel (3: 1–8)
    1. Israel's relation to God (3: 1–6: 14)
    2. Sins of Samaria (3: 9–4: 3)
    3. Israel's failure to return to God (4: 4–13)
    4. God's lamentation over Israel (5: 1–3)
    5. Call to repentance (5: 4–17)
    6. Israel's woes (5: 18–6: 14)
        1. Exile beyond Damascus (5: 18–25)
        2. Prediction of desolation, oppression and want (6: 1–14)

4. Five visions of judgement and blessings (7: 1–8: 14)
    1. Plague of locusts (7: 1–3)
    2. Fire devouring the deep (7: 4–6)
    3. Plumb line (7: 7–17)
    4. Basket of summer fruit (8: 1–14)
    5. Israel's ruin (8: 1–3)
    6. Lust for money (8: 1–10)
    7. Famine of the Word of God (8: 11–14)

5. Destruction of the sanctuary (9: 1–10)

6. Promise of blessing (9: 11–15)
    1. Restoration of kingdom of David (9: 11–12)
    2. Productivity of the earth (9: 13)
    3. Blessings of the kingdom (9: 14–15)

Amos was a prophet during the eighth century BCE in the northern kingdom. According to Scripture, he was a herdsman in Tekoa who prophesied during the reign of Jeroboam, king of Israel, and Uzziah, king of Judah. His prophecy was essentially a judgement on Israel and the surrounding nations for their iniquity. The book begins with a series of oracles against other peoples: Damascus (1: 3–5), Gaza (1: 6–8), Tyre (1: 9–10), Edom (1: 11–12), Ammon (1: 13–15), Moab (2: 1–3). Amos' audience would have approved of such denunciations of foreign powers who were the historic enemies of Israel, yet his proclamation of judgement and doom on the Jewish people no doubt caused dismay and consternation.

Amos' first oracle against God's chosen people was pronounced over the inhabitants of Judah – here the prophet condemns them for their transgressions:

Thus says the Lord:
'For three transgressions of Judah,
and for four, I will not revoke the punishment;
because they have rejected the law of the Lord,
and have not kept his statutes,
but their lies have led them astray,
after which their fathers walked.
So I will send a fire upon Judah,
and it shall devour the strongholds of Jerusalem.' (2: 4–5)

Turning next to the northern kingdom, Amos castigated Israel for neglecting God's law. Outlining a series of sins, the prophet illustrated that the Jewish people had become as corrupt as their neighbours. As a consequence of such disobedience, the nation would be destroyed. Israel had sinned, Amos declared,

because they sell the righteous for silver,
and the needy for a pair of shoes –
they that trample the head of the poor in the dust of the earth,
and turn aside the way of the afflicted;
a man and his father go in to the same maiden,
so that my holy name is profaned;

they lay themselves down beside every altar
upon garments taken in pledge;
and in the house of their God they drink
the wine of those who have been fined. (2: 6b–8)

As a consequence of such iniquity, the nation will be punished. Not even warriors or weapons will be able to save the people from impending catastrophe:

'Behold, I will press you down in your place,
as a cart full of sheaves presses down.
Flight shall perish from the swift,
and the strong shall not retain his strength,
nor shall the mighty save his life;
he who handles the bow shall not stand,
and he who is swift of foot shall not save himself,
nor shall he who rides the horse save his life;
and he who is stout of heart among the mighty
shall flee away naked in that day,' says the Lord. (2: 13–16)

In chapter 3 Amos continues his dispute with the nation. First, he emphasized God's concern for his people: Israel was chosen from among all humankind to be the Lord's favourite, yet such special concern entails obligations. The Lord summoned all foreign powers to hear his condemnation. In a catalogue of Samaria's sins, the prophet singled out Israel's reversion to pagan practices as the most grave:

'Hear, and testify against the house of Jacob,'
says the Lord God, the God of hosts,
'that on the day I punish Israel for his transgressions,
I will punish the altars of Bethel,
and the horns of the altar shall be cut off
and fall to the ground.' (3: 13–14)

In the next chapter Amos scornfully compares Israelite women to the fat cows of Bashan, a rich grain-producing land; they indulge themselves while the poor continue to be oppressed. Such sinners will not be rescued from God's harsh judgement:

Hear this word, you cows of Bashan,
who are in the mountain of Samaria,
who oppress the poor, who crush the needy,

who say to their husbands, 'Bring, that we may drink!'
The Lord God has sworn by his holiness
that, behold, the days are coming upon you,
when they shall take you away with hooks,
even the last of you with fishhooks. (4: 1–2)

Even when the Lord sent famine and drought upon the land, the
people failed to return to the Lord. For such disobedience, God will
unleash his fury:

And I also withheld the rain from you
when there were yet three months to the harvest; ...
yet you did not return to me ...
I smote you with blight and mildew;
I laid waste your gardens and your vineyards;
your fig trees and your olive trees the locust devoured;
yet you did not return to me ...
I sent among you a pestilence after the manner of Egypt;
I slew your young men with the sword;
I carried away your horses; and I made the stench of your camp go up
into your nostrils;
yet you did not return to me ...

I overthrew some of you,
as when God overthrew Sodom and Gomorrah,
and you were as a brand plucked out of the burning;
yet you did not return to me ...

Therefore thus I will do to you, O Israel;
because I will do this to you,
prepare to meet your God, O Israel! (4: 7–12)

Despite the nation's stubbornness, the Lord urged his people to
return to him. In chapter 5 the phrase 'seek the Lord and live' is
repeatedly emphasized:

Seek me and live;
but do not seek Bethel,
and do not enter into Gilgal
or cross over to Beer-sheba; ...
Seek the Lord and live,
lest he break out like fire in the house of Joseph,
and it devour, with none to quench it for Bethel ...
Seek good, and not evil,
that you may live;

and so the Lord, the God of hosts, will be with you,
as you have said.
Hate evil, and love good,
and establish justice in the gate. (5: 4b–6, 14–15)

Beginning with 5: 18, Amos turns to the theme of the 'Day of the Lord'. Previously the nation expected this to be a time of fulfilment, but Amos insisted that the 'Day of the Lord' would bring darkness rather than light:

Woe to you who desire the day of the Lord!
Why would you have the day of the Lord?
It is darkness, and not light;
as if a man fled from a lion,
and a bear met him;
or went into the house and leaned with his hand against the wall,
and a serpent bit him.
Is not the day of the Lord darkness, and not light,
and gloom with no brightness in it? (5: 18–20)

Israel was deceived into believing that by offering sacrifices to God, the population could be saved. Yet what is required is righteousness and social justice. Thus the Lord declared:

I hate, I despise your feasts,
and I take no delight in your solemn assemblies.
Even though you offer me your burnt offerings and cereal offerings,
I will not accept them,
and the peace offerings of your fatted beasts
I will not look upon.
Take away from me the noise of your songs;
to the melody of your harps I will not listen.
But let justice roll down like waters,
and righteousness like an everflowing stream. (5: 21–24)

In a series of woes, Amos predicted desolation for those who were at ease in Zion and those who felt secure in the mountains of Samaria: they indulge themselves with food, drink and wine, but they shall be led away into exile:

Woe to those who lie upon beds of ivory,
and stretch themselves upon their couches,
and eat lambs from the flock,

and calves from the midst of the stall;
who sing idle songs to the sound of the harp,
and like David invent for themselves instruments of music;
who drink wine in bowls,
and anoint themselves with the finest oils,
but are not grieved over the ruin of Joseph!
Therefore they shall now be the first of those to go into exile. (6: 4–7a)

The next section of Amos' prophecy consists of a series of visions in which the Lord revealed the fate of Israel. In the first Amos was shown a swarm of locusts that the Lord had prepared as a judgement. However, in response to Amos' prayer for compassion, the Lord withheld this devastation:

> Thus the Lord God showed me: behold, he was forming locusts in the beginning of the shooting up of the latter growth; and lo, it was the latter growth after the king's mowings. When they had finished eating the grass of the land, I said, 'O Lord God, forgive, I beseech thee! How can Jacob stand? He is so small!' The Lord repented concerning this; 'It shall not be,' said the Lord. (7: 1–3)

This revelation is followed by a vision of a plumb line, indicating the degree to which Israel had forsaken the Lord – such an architectural image illustrates the extent to which the nation was out of line with God's purposes. When Amaziah the priest of Bethel heard Amos' message, he declared to Jeroboam, the king of Israel: 'Amos has conspired against you in the midst of the house of Israel ... For thus has Amos said, "Jeroboam shall die by the sword, and Israel must go into exile away from his land" ' (7: 10–11). Amaziah then instructed Amos to depart to Judah and never prophesy again at Bethel. In reply Amos explained that he was not a cultic prophet but a herdsman and a dresser of sycamore trees; the Lord had told him to prophesy to Israel, and even though Amaziah wished him to desist this was not God's intention.

Amos' prophecy continued with a vision of a basket of ripe fruit – this produce denotes a time when God's judgement will have ripened:

> Thus the Lord God showed me; behold, a basket of summer fruit. And he said, 'Amos, what do you see?' And I said, 'A basket of summer fruit.' Then the Lord said to me, 'The end has come upon my people Israel; I will never again pass by them. The songs of the temple shall become wailings in that day,' says the Lord God. (8: 1–3)

The nature of such divine punishment is explained in a further vision in which the prophet saw the Lord judging the people from the altar of the temple. This was to have been a place of sanctuary, but instead it is represented as the starting point of God's verdict against his wayward people:

> I saw the Lord standing beside the altar, and he said:
> 'Smite the capitals until the thresholds shake,
> and shatter them on the heads of all the people;
> and what are left of them I will slay with the sword;
> not one of them shall flee away,
> not one of them shall escape.' (9: 1)

Such determination to chasten the population does not mean that the nation would be forsaken. Rather, Amos envisaged the coming of a future restoration when the ruined cities would be rebuilt and the land bring forth produce. Israel would then be restored and their enemies subdued:

> In that day I will raise up
> the booth of David that is fallen
> and repair its breaches,
> and raise up its ruins,
> and rebuild it as in the days of old; ...
> 'Behold the days are coming,' says the Lord,
> 'when the ploughman shall overtake the reaper
> and the treader of grapes him who sows the seed;
> the mountains shall drip sweet wine,
> and all the hills shall flow with it.
> I will restore the fortunes of my people Israel,
> and they shall rebuild the ruined cities and inhabit them; ...
> I will plant them upon their land,
> and they shall never again be plucked up
> out of the land which I have given them.' (9: 11, 13–15)

16. Obadiah

Little is known about the prophet Obadiah; according to some commentators he was a cultic prophet attached to the temple, yet there is insufficient evidence to reach a firm conclusion. Most scholars, however, believe that Obadiah prophesied in the sixth century BCE, either early during the Judean exile or at a later time – the evidence for this dating is the prophet's denunciations against Edom for its raids on Judah at the time of the fall of Jerusalem. On the other hand, several scholars regard the prophecy of Edom's destruction as a reflection on previous events, maintaining that they must have been composed subsequent to the destruction of Edom by the Nabateans in the late fifth century BCE.

In any event, the book itself begins with a description of the judgement against the Edomites. After the destruction of Judah, Edom took possession of territories which previously belonged to the southern kingdom. Here in the first chapter Obadiah predicts Edom's fall. In his view, this will be a just punishment for the nation's pride:

Thus says the Lord God concerning Edom:
We have heard tidings from the Lord,
and a messenger has been sent among the nations;
'Rise up! Let us rise against her for battle!'
Behold, I will make you small among the nations,

you shall be utterly despised.
The pride of your heart has deceived you,
you who live in the clefts of the rock,
whose dwelling is high,
who say in your heart,
'Who will bring me down to the ground?'
Though you soar aloft like the eagle,
though your nest is set among the stars,
thence I will bring you down, (1: 1–4)

Such destruction will be brought about by Edom's former allies: 'All your allies have deceived you, they have driven you to the border; your confederates have prevailed against you; your trusted friends have set a trap under you' (1: 7). Now Edom which previously benefited from the conquest of Zion will itself be humbled:

For the violence done to your brother Jacob,
shame shall cover you,
and you shall be cut off for ever.
On the day that you stood aloof,
on the day that strangers carried off his wealth,
and foreigners entered his gates
and cast lots for Jerusalem,
you were like one of them.
But you should not have gloated over the day of your brother
in the day of his misfortune;
you should not have rejoiced over the people of Judah
in the day of their ruin;
you should not have boasted
in the day of distress.
You should not have entered the gate of my people
in the day of his calamity;
you should not have gloated over his disaster
in the day of his calamity;
you should not have looted his goods
in the day of his calamity. (1: 10–13)

17. Jonah

1. The suffering prophet (1: 1–17)

2. The repentant and delivered prophet (2: 1–10)

3. The reluctantly obedient prophet (3: 1–10)

4. A merciful God (4: 1–11)

The central figure of the Book of Jonah is Jonah, the son of Amittai; according to 2 Kings 14: 25, he lived in Gath-hepher, north of Nazareth during the reign of Jeroboam II in the eighth century BCE. Traditionally, the book was interpreted as a true historical account, however, scholars generally believe it was composed by an unknown author who wished to emphasize God's universal concern for humanity. Nineveh which plays a major role in the story was the capital of Assyria which conquered Israel in 722 BCE.

The book begins with God's call to Jonah to go to Nineveh to preach to its inhabitants: 'Now the word of the Lord came to Jonah the son of Amittai, saying, "Arise, go to Nineveh, that great city, and cry against it; for their wickedness has come up before me"' (1: 1–2). Jonah, however, refused to comply. Instead of following God's command, he went to Joppa and boarded a ship going to Tarshish (probably Tartessus in southwestern Spain). During the voyage a great storm took place which caused panic on board. The sailors prayed to their gods, and cast goods overboard to lighten the ship's load. During this tumult Jonah had gone to the inner part of the ship and had fallen asleep. Awakened by the captain, he was told to pray to his God as well. Eventually the crew cast lots to determine on whose account the storm was raging. When the lot fell upon Jonah, they inquired: 'Tell us, on whose account this evil has come upon us? What is your occupation? And whence do you come? What is your country? And of what people are you?' (1: 8).

In response Jonah explained that he was an Israelite who

worshipped the God who created heaven and earth. Hearing this, the men became afraid and asked him what he had done to offend the Lord since Jonah told them that he had fled from God's presence. As the sea grew increasingly tempestuous, Jonah told the sailors to cast him overboard. The men rowed harder, but the storm did not abate. In desperation they cried out: 'We beseech thee, O Lord, let us not perish for this man's life, and lay not on us innocent blood; for you, O Lord, has done as it pleased thee' (1: 14).

They then cast Jonah into the sea, but the Lord appointed a great fish to swallow him up; the prophet was in the belly of the fish three days and nights. From the belly of the fish Jonah prayed to God, thanking him for his deliverance and repenting of his actions. At the end of this prayer the fish vomited Jonah onto dry land:

I called to the Lord, out of my distress,
and he answered me;
out of the belly of Sheol I cried,
and thou didst hear my voice.
For thou didst cast me into the deep,
into the heart of the seas,
and the flood was round about me;
all thy waves and thy billows
passed over me.
Then I said, 'I am cast out
from thy presence;
how shall I again look
upon thy holy temple?'
The waters closed in over me,
the deep was round about me;
weeds were wrapped about my head
at the roots of the mountains.
I went down to the land
whose bars closed upon me for ever;
yet thou didst bring up my life from the Pit,
O Lord my God.
When my soul fainted within me,
I remembered the Lord;
and my prayer came to thee,
into thy holy temple.
Those who pay regard to vain idols
forsake their true loyalty.
But I with the voice of thanksgiving
will sacrifice to thee;

what I have vowed I will pay.
Deliverance belongs to the Lord!'
And the Lord spoke to the fish, and it vomited out Jonah upon
the dry land. (2: 2–10)

Following this prayer, the word of the Lord came to Jonah that he
go to Nineveh to proclaim God's message. In response Jonah arose
and travelled to Nineveh. According to Scripture, the city was
exceedingly large, and as Jonah travelled across its breadth he cried:
'Yet forty days, and Nineveh shall be overthrown!' (3: 4). Hearing
this prophecy of doom, the inhabitants proclaimed a fast and put on
sackcloth; when these tidings reached the king, he too removed his
garments, put on sackcloth, and sat on ashes. He then made a
proclamation and published it throughout Nineveh:

> By the decree of the king and his nobles: Let neither man nor beast, herd
> nor flock, taste anything; let them not feed, or drink water, but let man
> and beast be covered with sackcloth, and let them cry mightily to God;
> yet, let every one turn from his evil way and from the violence which is
> in his hands. Who knows, God may yet repent and turn from his fierce
> anger, so that we perish not? (3: 7–8)

When God observed that the nation repented of its evil ways, he
refrained from bringing about the destruction he had planned.

Jonah, however, was furious with this outcome, and he cried out
to God. Although the Bible is not entirely clear why he felt such
anger, it is probable that in his view, the people of Nineveh should
not have been spared, given their hostility to Israel. Why should the
Lord be compassionate towards Israel's enemies? Here Jonah
explains that he did not go to Nineveh because he feared that his
message might bring about the repentance of the nation and thereby
ensure their deliverance from God's judgement:

> I pray thee, Lord, is not this what I said when I was yet in my country?
> That is why I made haste to flee to Tarshish; for I knew that thou art a
> gracious God and merciful, slow to anger, and abounding in steadfast
> love, and repentest of evil. (4: 2)

The Book of Jonah concludes with a depiction of God's compassion.
Because of the scorching sun, God had appointed a plant to shade
Jonah to save him from discomfort. The prophet was pleased by this,
but when dawn came up the next day, God devised that a worm

would attack the plant so that it would wither. Then God appointed a sultry east wind to beat on Jonah's head so that he felt faint. Overcome by such exposure Jonah said: 'It is better for me to die than to live' (4: 8). God then reasoned with Jonah to show him the error of his ways:

> But God said to Jonah, 'Do you do well to be angry for the plant?' And he said, 'I do well to be angry, angry enough to die.' And the Lord said, 'You pity the plant for which you did not labour, nor did you make it grow, which came into being in a night, and perished in a night. And should not I pity Nineveh, that great city, in which there are more than a hundred and twenty thousand persons ...? (4: 9–11)

Here the author of the book stressed the universality of God's concern and compassion.

18. Micah

1. Judgement on Israel and Judah (1: 1–2: 11)
   1. Introduction (1: 1)
   2. God's anger with Samaria and Judah (1: 2–7)
   3. Lamentation (1: 8–16)
      a. Situation in Jerusalem (1: 8–9)
      b. Fate of the southern cities (1: 10–16)
   4. Sins (2: 1–11)
      a. Oracle against oppressors (2: 1–5)
      b. Rejection of prophecy (2: 6–11)

2. Remnant will return (2: 12–13)

3. Condemnation of leaders (3: 1–12)
   1. Corrupt leaders (3: 1–4)
   2. Proclamation against prophets (3: 5–7)
   3. Micah's ministry (3: 8)
   4. Denunciation of leaders, prophets and priests (3: 9–12)

4. Renewed Israel (4: 1–5: 14)
   1. Nations to mount of the Lord's house (4: 1–5)
   2. Lord as king (4: 6–8)
   3. Destruction and exile (4: 9–14)
   4. Messiah (5: 1–3)
   5. Peace and deliverance (5: 4–5)
   6. Remnant of Jacob (5: 6–8)
   7. Destruction of sin (5: 9–14)

5. Condemnation of Israel (6: 1–7: 7)
   1. God's lawsuit (6: 1–8)
      a. Address (6: 1–2)
      b. Lamentation (6: 3–5)
      c. True worship (6: 6–7)
      d. Anger (6: 8)

2. Punishment of Jerusalem (6: 9–16)
3. Lamentation (7: 1–7)
   a. Injustice and punishment (7: 1–6)
   b. The prophet (7: 7)
6. Faith (7: 8–20)
   1. Sin and address to the enemy (7: 8–10)
   2. New Jerusalem (7: 11–13)
   3. Prayer (7: 14–17)
   4. Hymn (7: 18–20)

As the last of the prophets of the eighth century BCE, (Amos, Hosea, Isaiah) Micah originated from the foothills of Judah and prophesied in the southern kingdom during the period 750–686 BCE. His prediction of the fall of Samaria – the capital of Israel – indicates that part of his ministry in all likelihood took place before 722 BCE when the Assyrians conquered the northern kingdom. Like Isaiah, Micah combined prophecies of doom with assurances of the nation's restoration.

The Book of Micah opens by indicating the reigns during which Micah was active. Here the prophet condemns both Samaria and Judah for their wickedness. God, he declared, will bring about judgement of the people:

For behold, the Lord is coming forth out of his place,
and will come down and tread upon the high places of the earth.
And the mountains will melt under him
and the valleys will be cleft,
like wax before the fire,
like waters poured down a steep place. (1: 3–4)

In vivid terms, Micah predicted that Samaria will be ruined and the places of idolatry will be broken down:

All her images shall be beaten to pieces,
and her hires shall be burned with fire,
and all her idols I will lay waste. (1: 7)

Chapter 2 continues with a description of the reasons for God's anger. According to Micah, both Israel and Judah are guilty of a variety of transgressions including the exploitation of the weak, the dispossession of the poor, and the enslavement of children: 'They covet fields, and seize them; and houses, and take them away; they oppress a man and his house, a man and his inheritance' (2: 2). As a consequence, God is determined to punish the guilty. Critical of the false prophets, Micah explained that they have mistakenly believed that Israel was not in danger: 'Do not preach' – thus they preach – 'one should not preach of such things; disgrace will not overtake us' (2: 6). Yet, the Lord is impatient and will send his wrath upon the people. Despite this dire prediction, the prophet was anxious to reassure the nation that it would not be utterly cut off. God had a purpose for them in the future:

> I will surely gather all of you, O Jacob,
> I will gather the remnant of Israel;
> I will set them together
> like sheep in a fold,
> like a flock in its pasture,
> a noisy multitude of men.
> He who opens the breach will go up before them;
> they will break through and pass the gate,
> going out by it.
> Their king will pass on before them,
> the Lord at their head. (2: 12–13)

Repeatedly Micah reiterated this theme of God's judgement. In chapter 3 he utilizes dramatic imagery to portray the sinfulness of the rulers of the house of Israel – they are the ones who hate good and love evil:

> who tear the skin from off my people,
> and their flesh from off their bones;
> who eat the flesh of my people,
> who flay their skin from off them,
> and break their bones in pieces,
> and chop them up like meat in a kettle,
> like flesh in a cauldron. (3: 2–3)

The prophets too have led the people astray: they cry 'peace' when they are well fed, but proclaim war against those who deprive them of sustenance. Because of such wickedness, darkness shall fall upon the nation: 'It shall be night to you, without vision, and darkness to you, without divination. The sun shall go down upon the prophets, and the day shall be black over them; the seers shall be disgraced, and the diviners put to shame' (3: 6c–7). There is no hope for such waywardness – Israel is doomed to destruction: 'Zion shall be plowed as a field; Jerusalem shall become a heap of ruins' (3: 12).

Despite these pronouncements Micah was confident that restoration would take place; in the next chapter, he looks forward to an age of prosperity and fulfilment. Like Isaiah, he predicted a time of messianic redemption. All nations, he declared, shall go to the mountain of the Lord and dwell together in peace – in those days swords will be turned into ploughshares and each man will sit under his vine and fig tree:

It shall come to pass in the latter days
that the mountain of the house of the Lord
shall be established as the highest of the mountains,
and shall be raised up above the hills;
and peoples shall flow to it,
and many nations shall come, and say:
'Come, let us go up to the mountain of the Lord,
to the house of the God of Jacob;
that he may teach us his ways
and we may walk in his paths.'
For out of Zion shall go forth the law,
and the word of the Lord from Jerusalem.
He shall judge between many peoples,
and shall decide for strong nations afar off;
and they shall beat their swords into ploughshares,
and their spears into pruning hooks;
nation shall not lift up sword against nation,
neither shall they learn war any more;
but they shall sit every man under his vine and under his fig tree,
and none shall make them afraid ... (4: 1–4)

Following this description of a future age, Micah went on to depict the coming ruler of Israel and Judah who will come from Bethlehem in the region of Ephrathah: 'But you, O Bethlehem Ephrathah, who are little to be among the clans of Judah, from you shall come forth for me one who is to be ruler in Israel' (5: 2). Such a deliverer is needed since the Assyrians are soon to invade and conquer the land; as a result, those who survive will be scattered among the nations. The purpose of such devastation is to eliminate all forms of pagan worship from the land:

And in that day ...
and I will cut off sorceries from your hand,
and you shall have no more soothsayers;
and I will cut off your images
and your pillars from among you,
and you shall bow down no more
to the work of your hands. (5: 10a, 12–13)

What the Lord requires is not sacrifice, but faithful obedience to his
word; his servants are to do justly, love mercy and walk humbly
with their God:

'With what shall I come before the Lord,
and bow myself before God on high?
Shall I come before him with burnt offerings,
with calves a year old?
Will the Lord be pleased with thousands of rams,
with ten thousands of rivers of oil?
Shall I give my first-born for my transgression,
the fruit of my body for the sin of my soul?'
He has showed you, O man, what is good;
and what does the Lord require of you
but to do justice, and to love kindness,
and to walk humbly with your God? (6: 6–8)

Even though the nation has gone astray and will be punished for its
iniquity, the prophet trusted in the Lord's deliverance. God will
shepherd his people and show compassion to them. Then the
nations will see and fear the Lord. God's anger will not endure
forever – he will tread the nation's iniquity underfoot and show love
to his chosen people:

He does not retain his anger for ever
because he delights in steadfast love.
He will again have compassion upon us,
he will tread our iniquities under foot.
Thou wilt cast all our sins
into the depths of the sea.
Thou wilt show faithfulness to Jacob
and steadfast love to Abraham,
as thou hast sworn to our fathers
from the days of old. (7: 18–20)

19. Nahum

1. The Lord's majesty (1: 1–15)
2. Siege and fall of Nineveh (2: 1–13)
3. Reasons for the destruction of Nineveh (3: 1–19)
   1. The iniquity of Nineveh (3: 1–7)
   2. God's judgement (3: 8–19)

According to tradition, the writer of this book was Nahum the Elkoshite who was in all likelihood from Judah. He appears to have been a contemporary of Zephaniah, Habakkuk and Jeremiah prophesying during the second half of the seventh century BCE. Since the book treats the fall of Thebes (633 BCE) as a past event and presents the destruction of Nineveh (612 BCE) as a future occurrence, it is probable that it was composed during this period. The Book of Jonah contains a prediction of Nineveh's devastation; here the time has passed for such deliverance. Although the background of this book is the impending fall of Judah, a large part of Nahum's prophecy deals with the Assyrian capital which had grown increasingly menacing after the fall of the northern kingdom.

The book opens with a description of God's anger against the inhabitants of Nineveh – the prophet rejoices in the overthrow of the Assyrian empire. Employing the same image used by Isaiah to express the joy that would accompany the restoration of Judah from Babylonian captivity, Nahum looks forward to the devastation of Nineveh. God's verdict against the city will bring about relief for the Israelite nation:

The Lord is a jealous God and avenging,
the Lord is avenging and wrathful;
the Lord takes vengeance on his adversaries
and keeps wrath for his enemies ...
Thus says the Lord,

'Though they be strong and many,
they will be cut off and pass away.
Though I have afflicted you,
I will afflict you no more.
And now I will break his yoke from off you
and will burst your bonds asunder.' ...
Keep your feasts, O Judah,
fulfil your vows,
for never again shall the wicked come against you,
he is utterly cut off. (1: 2, 12–13, 15b)

In the second chapter Nahum predicts the fall of Nineveh and the nation's future glory. In graphic detail he described the desolation that would come about in the impending siege:

The shield of his mighty men is red,
his soldiers are clothed in scarlet.
The chariots flash like flame
when mustered in array;
the chargers prance.
The chariots rage in the streets,
they rush to and fro through the squares;
they gleam like torches,
they dart like lightening. (2: 3–4)

Because of its iniquity the Lord is determined to bring destruction on the Assyrian empire: 'Behold, I am against you, says the Lord of hosts, and I will burn your chariots in smoke, and the sword shall devour your young lions; I will cut off your prey from the earth, and the voice of your messengers shall no more be heard' (2: 13).

In the next section the prophet compares the conquest of Nineveh to the fall of Thebes, the capital of Upper Egypt: 'Are you better than Thebes that sat by the Nile, with water around her, her rampart a sea, and water her wall?' (3: 8).

So too, Nineveh will fall amid the rejoicing of Judah and other nations:

Your shepherds are asleep,
O king of Assyria;
your nobles slumber.
Your people are scattered on the mountains
with none to gather them.
There is no assuaging your hurt,

your wound is grievous.
All who hear the news of you
clap their hands over you. (3: 18–19a)

20. Habakkuk

1. Dialogue between God and Habakkuk (1: 2–2: 5)
   1. First Dialogue (1: 2–11)
      a. Prophet's complaint (1: 2–4)
      b. God's response (1: 5–11)
   2. Second Dialogue (1: 12–2: 5)
      a. Prophet's complaint (1: 12–17)
      b. God's response (2: 1–5)

2. Five Woes (2: 6–20)
   1. Introduction (2: 6)
   2. Woe against greed (2: 6–8)
   3. Woe against presumption (2: 9–11)
   4. Woe against pride and violence (2: 12–14)
   5. Woe against assault on human dignity (2: 15–17)
   6. Woe against idolatry (2: 18–20)

3. Prayer of Habakkuk (3: 1–15)
   1. Prayer (3: 1)
   2. Fear and salvation (3: 2)
   3. The appearance of the Lord (3: 3–15)
      a. God's disclosure (3: 3–7)
      b. Battle with chaos (3: 8–15)
         i. Preparation for conflict (3: 8–9)
         ii. Reaction of nature (3: 10–11)
         iii. Battle charge (3: 11–13)
         iv. Victory (3: 13–15)

4. Fear and salvation (3: 16–19)
      a. Fear (3: 16–17)
      b. Salvation (3: 18–19)

It is probable that Habakkuk prophesied in the southern kingdom before the battle of Carchemish in 605 BCE; in this conflict the Egyptians were defeated by the Babylonian army. Subsequently Judah came under attack by the Babylonians leading to the onslaught against Jerusalem in 597 BCE and the final conquest of Judah in 586 BCE. Like his contemporary Jeremiah, Habakkuk predicted that the nation would be doomed unless it turns from its evil ways.

The book begins with the prophet's complaint to the Lord: why does evil go unpunished? In desperation, Habakkuk cried out to God:

O Lord, how long shall I cry for help,
and thou wilt not hear?
Or cry to thee 'Violence!'
and thou wilt not save?
Why dost thou make me see wrongs
and look upon trouble?
Destruction and violence are before me;
strife and contention arise.
So the law is slacked
and justice never goes forth.
For the wicked surround the righteous,
so justice goes forth perverted. (1: 2–4)

In response to these questions the Lord declared that he would use the Babylonians as instruments of his wrath. Even though they are not righteous themselves, they will exact punishment on God's behalf: 'For lo, I am rousing the Chaldeans, that bitter and hasty nation, who march through the breadth of the earth, to seize habitations not their own' (1: 6).

Following this dialogue, the prophet again engaged the Lord in debate. Why, he asked, does God use those who are wicked to punish those who are less sinful? Judah is guilty of iniquity, yet the Babylonians are worse. Replying to this entreaty, the Lord explained that the Chaldeans too will be devastated. In a series of woes, Habakkuk castigated the Babylonians for their corrupt ways. The nation, he asserted is greedy: 'His greed is as wide as Sheol; like death he has never enough. He gathers for himself all nations, and collects as his own all peoples' (2: 5b).

In addition, the Babylonians are covetous:

> Woe to him who gets evil gain for his house,
> to set his nest on high,
> to be safe from the reach of harm!
> You have devised shame to your house
> by cutting off many peoples;
> you have forfeited your life. (2: 9–10)

The Chaldeans are cruel as well: 'Woe to him who builds a town with blood, and founds a city on iniquity! ... Woe to him who makes his neighbours drink of the cup of his wrath, and makes them drunk, to gaze on their shame! (2: 12, 15).

Babylonia is also idolatrous. Bitterly Habakkuk condemned the pagan practices of its inhabitants:

> What profit is an idol
> when its maker has shaped it,
> a metal image, a teacher of lies?
> For the workman trusts in his own creation
> when he makes dumb idols!
> Woe to him who says to a wooden thing, Awake;
> to a dumb stone, Arise! (2: 18–19)

In place of such deceit and impiety the wise man must learn to put his trust in God. The ways of the Lord are righteous, Habakkuk declared, and knowledge of God's glory is manifest throughout the world: 'For the earth will be filled with the knowledge of the glory of the Lord, as the waters cover the sea' (2: 14).

Habakkuk's prophecy ends with a prayer in the form of a song. Here the prophet recounts God's majesty and creative acts:

> His glory covered the heavens,
> and the earth was full of his praise.
> His brightness was like the light,
> rays flashed from his hand;
> and there he veiled his power.
> Before him went pestilence,
> and plague followed close behind.
> He stood and measured the earth;
> he looked and shook the nations;
> then the eternal mountains were scattered,
> the everlasting hills sank low. (3: 3b–6)

Full of anger the Lord condemned the wicked – with vengeance he crushed the foes of Israel:

Thou didst bestride the earth in fury,
thou didst trample the nations in anger ...
Thou didst pierce with thy shafts the head of his warriors ...
Thou didst trample the sea with thy horses,
the surging of mighty waters. (3: 12, 14–15)

In conclusion Habakkuk proclaimed his faith in the Lord: with trembling he waits for the day of trouble to befall those who invade Judah, trusting God's saving power: 'I will rejoice in the Lord, I will joy in the God of my salvation. God, the Lord is my strength' (3: 18–19).

21. Zephaniah

The prophet Zephaniah was the son of Cushi, the son of Gedaliah, the son of Amaziah, the son of Hiskah (which is the same in Hebrew as Hezekiah). If this person was King Hezekiah, Zephaniah was of royal descent. In any event, Zephaniah lived in Jerusalem during the reign of Josiah in about 625 BCE. For fifty years before the prophet's appearance, Assyria had been a dominant power: from 686–641 BCE Manasseh, king of Judah, had paid tribute to Assyria; he was followed by his son Amnon who reigned for a short period and was succeeded by Josiah under whom religious reforms were instituted and the book of the law discovered. The death of King Asurbanipal of Assyria in 626 BCE marked the end of Assyrian ascendancy and the emergence of the Babylonian empire. As one of the last prophets before the Babylonian conquest of Judah, Zephaniah announced the impending destruction of the southern kingdom.

Chapter 1 of the Book of Zephaniah begins with an introduction

about the prophet: this is followed by Zephaniah's prophecy about
the sinfulness of the nation. Here he warns of impending destruction
due to the iniquity of the inhabitants of Judah. In particular the
prophet was concerned with pagan practices which the Lord firmly
condemns:

I will stretch out my hand against Judah,
and against all the inhabitants of Jerusalem;
and I will cut off from this place the remnant of Baal
and the name of the idolatrous priests;
those who bow down on the roofs
to the host of the heavens;
those who bow down and swear to the Lord
and yet swear by Milcom;
those who have turned back from following the Lord,
who do not seek the Lord or inquire of him. (1: 4–6)

The great day of the Lord is at hand, Zephaniah announced. This
will not be a time of fulfilment, but of calamity. It will be:

a day of distress and anguish,
a day of ruin and devastation,
a day of darkness and gloom,
a day of clouds and thick darkness,
a day of trumpet blast and battle cry
against the fortified cities
and against the lofty battlements. (1: 15–16)

Nothing will be able to prevent the outpouring of God's fury:
'Neither their silver nor their gold shall be able to deliver them on
the day of the wrath of the Lord. In the fire of his jealous wrath, all
the earth shall be consumed' ... (1: 18). Judah can only be saved if
the people turn back to God. 'Seek the Lord, all you humble of the
land, who do his commands,' the prophet cried out, 'Seek
righteousness, seek humility; perhaps you may be hidden on the
day of the wrath of the Lord' (2: 3).

This prophecy is followed by a series of oracles against the
surrounding nations; in each case Zephaniah prophesied doom and
destruction. Turning his attention first to Gaza and the Philistines
he proclaimed that Gaza would be deserted, Ashkelon become
desolate, Ashood's inhabitants driven out, and Ekron uprooted.
The word of the Lord will also be against those who resided on the

seacoast: 'And you, O seacoast, shall be pastures, meadows for shepherds and folds for flocks. The seacoast shall become the possession of the remnant of the house of Judah, on which they shall pasture' (2: 6–7).

Moab and Amnon, too, will be destroyed. These nations have taunted Israel and will thus be crushed: 'Moab shall become like Sodom, and the Ammonites like Gomorrah, a land possessed by nettles and salt pits, and a waste for ever' (2: 9).

Ethiopia and Assyria shall similarly be slain by the sword. The Lord will stretch out his hand against the North and annihilate Assyria; Nineveh shall become desolate, a dry waste like the desert. Certain of its downfall, the prophet ridiculed its future plight:

This is the exultant city
that dwelt secure,
that said to herself,
'I am and there is none else.'
What a desolation she has become,
a lair for wild beasts!
Every one who passes by her
hisses and shakes his fist. (2: 15)

These prophecies serve as the background for Zephaniah's dire warnings to Judah. If the nation does not forsake its evil ways, it too shall endure the same fate. The Lord is angry with his chosen people who refuse to obey his commands. The officials are impervious to God's degree; the judges rapacious; the prophets corrupt; the priests impious. Only the Lord is righteous:

Woe to her that is rebellious and defiled,
the oppressing city!
She listens to no voice,
She accepts no correction.
She does not trust in the Lord,
She does not draw near to her God.
Her officials within her
are roaring lions;
her judges are evening wolves
that leave her nothing till the morning.
Her prophets are wanton,
faithless men;
her priests profane what is sacred,
they do violence to the law.

The Lord within her is righteous,
he does no wrong. (3: 1–5)

Because of such defiance, the Lord is determined to punish the guilty. Yet the Jewish people will not be cut off forever. In the final section of the book, Zephaniah calls upon the Israelites to wait for God's vindication. He will gather the nations and pour out the heat of his anger – in this destruction all the earth shall be consumed. But at that time he will change the speech of the peoples so that they will call on the name of the Lord and serve him with one accord. From beyond the rivers of Ethiopia, suppliants shall bring offerings. On this day Israel will not be put to shame because of their rebellion. Rather, the Lord will remove from their midst the proud and haughty; in their place there will be a humble and lowly people who shall seek refuge in the name of the Lord: 'those who are left in Israel; they shall do no wrong and utter no lies, nor shall there be found in their mouth a deceitful tongue' (3: 13).

Knowing that their chastening is over, the people can rejoice. Assured of God's steadfast love, the nation can look forward to restoration and renewal. 'Sing aloud, O daughter of Zion; shout, O Israel!' the prophet exclaimed. 'Rejoice and exult with all your heart, O daughter of Jerusalem!' (3: 14). The Lord has taken away his judgement and cast out the nation's enemies; he is now in the midst of the land and there is no cause to fear. Confident of the future, Zephaniah proclaimed in God's name:

'Behold, at the time I will deal
with all your oppressors.
And I will save the lame
and gather the outcast,
and I will change their shame into praise
and renown in all the earth.
At that time I will bring you home,
at the time when I gather you together;
yea, I will make you renowned and praised
among all the peoples of the earth,
when I restore your fortunes
before your eyes,' says the Lord. (3: 19–20)

147

22. Haggai

Little is known about the prophet Haggai. Possibly he lived during the time of the exile; some scholars, however, believe he was born during the period of captivity. In any event, he returned to Judah after the exile and together with Zerubbabel engaged in the rebuilding of the temple. The four discourses that comprise his prophecy were in all likelihood composed during a four-month period in 520 BCE – the rebuilding of the temple was the primary theme of his ministry.

The book begins with God's call to rebuild the house of the Lord; this can be dated to 520 BCE on the basis of the first verse: 'In the second year of Darius the king, in the sixth month, on the first day of the month, the word of the Lord came by Haggai the prophet to Zerubbabel the son of She-alti-el, governor of Judah, and to Joshua the son of Jehozadak, the high priest' (1: 1). The first discourse consists of God's command to rebuild the temple; the time has come, the prophet announced, for the Jewish people to turn from their personal preoccupations to communal effort:

> Is it a time for you yourselves to dwell in your panelled houses, while this house lies in ruins? ... Go up to the hills and bring wood and build the house, that I may take pleasure in it and that I may appear in my glory, says the Lord. (1: 4, 8)

In response to this plea Zerubabbel, Joshua and a remnant of the people worked on the house of the Lord of hosts, beginning on the twenty-fourth day of the sixth month.

Chapter 2 continues with a description of the glory of the rebuilt temple. Here the prophet asserts that God is with his people. No longer is he determined that they be punished for their iniquities as he was when he used the Assyrians and Babylonians as the instruments of his wrath. Instead, the people can be assured of God's abiding presence and that the new temple will surpass the old temple in glory. Speaking to Zerubbabel and Joshua as well as to the remnant of the people in the land, Haggai asked: 'Who is left among you that saw this house in its former glory? How do you see it now? Is it not in your sight as nothing?' (2: 3). Urging these two leaders to take courage, the prophet proclaimed in the name of the Lord:

work, for I am with you, says the Lord of hosts, according to the promise that I made you when you came out of Egypt. My Spirit abides among you; fear not. ... The latter splendour of this house shall be greater than the former, says the Lord of hosts; and in this place I will give prosperity, says the Lord of hosts. (2: 4–5, 9)

Despite this promise of hope, the prophet was disturbed by those among the returning exiles who had become defiled. In Haggai's view, such a state of affairs posed a danger to the people in that their influence could lead to a disregard of the covenant. What is required, therefore, is the reconstruction of the temple whereby the nation can demonstrate its commitment to the Lord. In response, God will bless his people with prosperity:

Before a stone was placed upon a stone in the temple of the Lord, how did you fare? ... I smote you and all the products of your toil with blight and mildew and hail; yet you did not return to me, says the Lord. Consider from this day onward, from the twenty-fourth day of the ninth month. Since the day that the foundation of the Lord's temple was laid, consider: Is the seed yet in the barn? Do the vine, the fig tree, the pomegranate and the olive tree still yield nothing? From this day on I will bless you. (2: 15b, 16–19)

The final section of chapter 2 depicts God's victory over Israel's enemies and his commitment to Zerubbabel. Here the prophet proclaims that the Lord has chosen Zerubbabel as his servant – he is to be God's signet ring:

The word of the Lord came a second time to Haggai on the twenty-fourth day of the month, 'Speak to Zerubbabel, governor of Judah, saying, I am about to shake the heavens and the earth, and to overthrow the throne of kingdoms; I am about to destroy the strength of the kingdoms of the nations, and overthrow the chariots and their riders; and the horses and their riders shall go down, every one by the sword of his fellow. On that day, says the Lord of hosts, I will take you, O Zerubbabel my servant, the son of She-alti-el, says the Lord, and make you like a signet ring; for I have chosen you, says the Lord of hosts.' (2: 20–23)

23. Zechariah

1. Prophecy during the rebuilding of the temple (1: 1–8: 23)
   1. Prologue (1: 1–6)
   2. Eight night visions and oracles (1: 7–6: 15)
      a. Coloured horses and horsemen (1: 7–17)
      b. Four horns and the carvers (2: 1–4)
      c. Surveyor (2: 5–17)
      d. Joshua the high priest (3: 1–10)
      e. Lampstand and olive trees (4: 1–14)
      f. Flying scroll (5: 1–4)
      g. Women in the barrel (5: 5–11)
      h. Four chariots, crowns and leaders (6: 1–15)
   3. Oracles (7: 1–8: 23)
      a. Evaluation of past events (7: 1–14)
      b. Promises (8: 1–23)

2. Prophecy after the building of the temple (9: 1–14: 21)
   1. First collection (9: 1–11: 17)
      a. God the warrior (9: 1–8)
      b. King of peace (9: 9–10)
      c. Victory (9: 11–17)
      d. Against those who mislead the people (10: 1–3)
      e. God's victorious followers (10: 3–12)
      f. Devastation in Lebanon and Bashan (11: 1–3)
      g. Bad shepherds and flocks (11: 4–17)
   2. Second collection
      a. Jerusalem victorious (12: 1–9)
      b. Mourning and cleansing (12: 10–13: 1)
      c. Removal of idols and prophets (13: 2–6)
      d. The shepherd and his flock (13: 7–9)
      e. Deliverance of Israel (14: 1–21)
         i. Jerusalem delivered (14: 1–8)
         ii. Judah's king supreme over the earth (14: 9–15)

iii. Nations subjugated and Israel holy (14: 16–21)

According to the Book of Nehemiah, Zechariah's grandfather, Iddo, returned from the exile with Zerubbabel and Joshua. Given this chronology, it is likely the prophet was a contemporary of Haggai, possibly attached to the priesthood. Since the two sections of the book of Zechariah are strikingly dissimilar, a number of scholars argue that the book is the work of two authors; those who defend the unity of the book account for these differences by concluding that the latter part of Zechariah's prophecy was composed some decades after the first part. In any event, the central theme of the book is the rebuilding of the temple – throughout the prophet encouraged the people to continue the work which had been interrupted for some time. Unlike his contemporary Haggai, Zechariah employed symbolic language to convey his message.

The Book of Zechariah begins by identifying the prophet as the grandson of Iddo who is named in Nehemiah's list of those who returned to Jerusalem from Babylonia (Nehemiah 12: 4). The opening words of the prophecy proclaim the necessity of returning to the Lord; the people are not to be like their ancestors who transgressed God's word:

> Return to me, says the Lord of hosts, and I will return to you, says the Lord of hosts. Be not like your fathers, to whom the former prophets cried out, 'Thus says the Lord of hosts, Return from your evil ways and from your evil deeds.' But they did not hear or heed me. (1: 3–4)

Even though a remnant of the nation has returned to Zion, the people have not yet embraced God's covenant.

This prologue is followed by a series of night visions which took place about three months after the call of the prophet. In the first vision a horseman appeared among myrtle trees: 'I saw in the night, and behold, a man riding upon a red horse! He was standing among the myrtle trees in the glen; and behind him were red, sorrel, and white horses' (1: 8–9).

Although the Lord had punished Judah by sending its inhabitants into exile for seventy years, the nation has been sufficiently chastised. Now God's mercies will be made known to his chosen people – the land will prosper and the home of the Lord will be established in Jerusalem. In response to an angel standing among the myrtle trees who asked how long God would withhold his compassion, the

Lord spoke words of comfort. Zechariah was then commanded by the angel to proclaim a message of hope to the nation:

> So the angel who talked with me said to me, 'Cry out, Thus says the Lord of hosts: I am exceedingly jealous for Jerusalem and for Zion. And I am very angry with the nations that are at ease; for while I was angry but a little they furthered the disaster. Therefore, thus says the Lord, I have returned to Jerusalem with compassion; my house shall be built in it, says the Lord of hosts, and the measuring line shall be stretched out over Jerusalem. Cry again, Thus says the Lord of hosts: My cities shall again overflow with prosperity, and the Lord will again comfort Zion and again choose Jerusalem.' (1: 14–17)

A second vision of four horns and four smiths illustrates that the powers responsible for the nation's downfall will themselves be overthrown:

> And I lifted my eyes and saw, and behold, four horns! And I said to the angel who talked with me, 'What are these?' And he answered me, 'These are the horns which have scattered Judah, Israel, and Jerusalem.' Then the Lord showed me four smiths. And I said, 'What are these coming to do?' He answered, 'These are the horns which scattered Judah, so that no man raised his head; and these have come to terrify them, to cast down the horns of the nations who lifted up their horns against the land of Judah to scatter it.' (1: 18–21)

In Zechariah's third vision a man with a measuring line came to gauge the width and breadth of Jerusalem – a symbol of Jerusalem's restoration. Here the prophet declares that the Lord has chosen Jerusalem as his dwelling place:

> Sing and rejoice, O daughter of Zion; for lo, I come and I will dwell in the midst of you, says the Lord. And many nations shall join themselves to the Lord in that day, and shall be my people; and I will dwell in the midst of you, and you shall know that the Lord of hosts has sent me to you. And the Lord will inherit Judah as his portion in the holy land, and will again choose Jerusalem. (2: 10–12)

The fourth vision recounted in chapter 3 foretells the cleansing of sin from Israel and its restoration as a priestly nation. Joshua the high priest who together with Zerubbabel brought the people back from Babylon is depicted wearing dirty clothes; these are removed and replaced with garments of righteousness:

> Now Joshua was standing before the angel, clothed with filthy garments. And the angel said to those who were standing before him, 'Remove the filthy garments from him.' And to him he said, 'Behold I have taken your iniquity away from you, and I will clothe you with rich apparel.' (3: 3–4)

Zechariah's fifth vision was of a solid gold lampstand with seven lamps; nearby were two olive trees which provided a constant source of oil for the lampstand. These trees symbolize Zerubbabel and Joshua who are God's anointed servants:

> Then I said to him, 'What are these two olive trees on the right and the left of the lampstand?' ... He said to me, 'Do you not know what these are?' I said, 'No my lord.' Then he said, 'These are the two anointed who stand by the Lord of the whole earth.' (4: 11, 13)

Zechariah's prophecy concludes with a series of further visions – in the first a flying scroll symbolizes the universality of the law and the punishment for those who ignore it. The next vision depicts an ephah in which a woman symbolizing wickedness was sitting; according to the prophet, the ephah will be transported to Babylon. The final vision of four chariots of divine judgement symbolizes God's victory over all the earth. In a sequel to these visions, Zechariah saw Joshua the high priest crowned in glory; he is the one who will complete the restoration of the temple:

> It is he who shall build the temple of the Lord, and shall bear royal honour, and shall sit and rule upon his throne. And there shall be a priest by his throne, and peaceful understanding shall be between them both ... And those who are far off shall come and help to build the temple of the Lord; and you shall know that the Lord of hosts has sent me to you ... (6: 13, 15)

The second part of the Book of Zechariah opens with events that took place some time after the eight night visions. The word of the Lord came to Zechariah again, condemning Jerusalem for its lack of justice, mercy and compassion. What the Lord requires is obedience to his commandments:

> 'Thus says the Lord of hosts, Render true judgments, show kindness and mercy each to his brother, do not oppress the widow, the fatherless, the sojourner, or the poor: and let none of you devise evil against his brother in your heart.' But they refused to hearken, and turned a

154

stubborn shoulder, and stopped their ears that they might not hear. They made their hearts like adamant lest they should hear the law and the words which the Lord of hosts had sent by his Spirit through the former prophets ... (7: 9–12)

Yet despite its iniquity, Jerusalem is precious to the Lord; his love of Zion is so great that he cannot bear to lose it. In the past Zion was an object of cursing, but now it will be full of joy and prosperity:

Thus says the Lord of hosts: Old men and old women shall again sit in the streets of Jerusalem, each with staff in hand for every age. And the streets of the city shall be full of boys and girls playing in its streets. (8: 4–5)

Chapter 9 begins with an oracle about a coming king who will rule over the people. In a vision of hope, the prophet described this messianic figure who will be a descendant of David; he shall enter the city in triumph riding upon an ass: 'Rejoice greatly, O daughter of Zion! Shout aloud, O daughter of Jerusalem! Lo, your king comes to you; triumphant and victorious is he, humble and riding on an ass, on a colt the foal of an ass' (9: 9).

According to Zechariah, God will redeem his people – he will strengthen them and bring them back to Zion. Then the inhabitants of Jerusalem shall be as though they had never been rejected:

I will signal for them and gather them in,
for I have redeemed them,
and they shall be as many as of old.
Though I scattered them among the nations,
yet in far countries they shall remember me,
and with their children they shall live and return. (10: 8–9)

A transition is made in chapter 12 from this depiction of a messianic king. Here the prophet presents a vision of the destruction of Jerusalem's enemies. Those who attack the city are not the Babylonians, but armies from throughout the world. Yet Judah will triumph over its foes:

All the nations of the earth will come together against it ... On that day I will make the clans of Judah like a blazing pot in the midst of wood, like a flaming torch among sheaves ... On that day the Lord will put a shield about the inhabitants of Jerusalem ... I will seek to destroy all the nations that come against Jerusalem. (12: 3, 6, 8–9)

In the next section two images are presented. In the first the inhabitants of Jerusalem are depicted as looking with compassion on one who has been pierced: 'I will pour out on the house of David and the inhabitants of Jerusalem a spirit of compassion and supplication, so that, when they look on him whom they have pierced, they shall mourn for him' (12:10). The second related theme is a prophecy of a fountain which will cleanse the descendants of David: 'On that day there shall be a fountain opened for the house of David and the inhabitants of Jerusalem to cleanse them from sin and uncleanliness' (13:1). Although it is unclear who is being referred to, these prophecies appear to point to a process of redemption for the people of Israel.

In the final chapter Zechariah returns to the topic of the Day of the Lord. At this time Jerusalem and its population will again be attacked, yet the Lord will triumph over those who beseige his holy city:

> Behold, a day of the Lord is coming, when the spoil taken from you will be divided in the midst of you. For I will gather all the nations against Jerusalem to battle, and the city shall be taken and the houses plundered and the women ravished ... Then the Lord will go forth and fight against those nations as when he fights on a day of battle ... And the Lord will become king over all the earth; on that day the Lord will be one and his name one. (14: 1, 2, 3, 9)

24. Malachi

Like Haggai and Zechariah, Malachi was in all likelihood a post-exilic prophet who was active after the return of the exiles from Babylonia to Jerusalem. According to tradition, he was the last of the prophets of Israel. His prophecy begins with an assertion of God's love for his chosen people; this is contrasted with the Lord's rejection of Esau and his descendants the Edomites:

> 'I have loved you,' says the Lord. But you say, 'How hast thou loved us?'
> 'Is not Esau Jacob's brother?' says the Lord. 'Yet I have loved Jacob, but I have hated Esau; I have laid waste his hill country and left his heritage to jackals of the desert.' (1: 2–3)

However, despite such a close relationship, Israel has been contemptuous of its cultic obligations. With anger and disgust, the Lord condemned the priests for neglecting his statutes:

> And if I am a master, where is my fear? says the Lord of hosts to you, O priests, who despise my name. You say, 'How have we despised thy name?' By offering polluted food upon my altar. And you say, 'How have we polluted it?' By thinking that the Lord's table may be despised. When you offer blind animals in sacrifice, is that no evil? And when you offer those that are lame or sick, is that no evil? ... (1: 6–8)

By way of contrast, the Lord stressed that he is acknowledged among the nations of the earth – but in Israel his statutes are despised:

> For from the rising of the sun to its setting my name is great among the nations, and in every place incense is offered to my name, and a pure offering; for my name is great among the nations, says the Lord of hosts. But you profane it when you say that the Lord's table is polluted, and the food for it may be despised. (1: 11–12)

Chapter 2 continues this diatribe. Warning the priests of the consequence of their neglect, the Lord resolved to punish those who are unfaithful to him – they will be hated and their offspring will be cursed. Here the prophet specifically mentions the sin of intermarriage: Judah has profaned the sanctuary of the Lord and has married the daughters of a foreign god: 'May the Lord cut off from the tents of Jacob, for the man who does this,' the prophet declared (2: 12). Further, God is displeased with those who have divorced their wives. Aware of such divine displeasure, the people cried out to God in despair yet the Lord will not heed such wailing because of this profanity against his name:

> You cover the Lord's altar with tears, with weeping and groaning because he no longer regards the offering or accepts it with favour at your hand. You ask, 'Why does he not?' Because the Lord was witness to the covenant between you and the wife of your youth, to whom you have been faithless, though she is your companion and your wife by covenant. Has not the one God made and sustained for us the spirit of life? And what does he desire? Godly offspring. So take heed to yourselves, and let none be faithless to the wife of his youth. 'For I hate divorce, says the Lord the God of Israel ...' (2: 13–16)

According to Malachi, Israel's sinfulness caused the Lord great distress. In order to remedy such transgression, God has proposed to send his messenger to prepare the way for the Lord's entry into his temple: 'Behold, I send my messenger to prepare the way before me, and the Lord whom you seek will suddenly come to his temple; the messenger of the covenant in whom you delight; behold, he is coming, says the Lord of hosts' (3: 1). Yet because of their iniquity the people will not be able to deal with such a message. The coming of the Lord will thus not bring about Israel's redemption; rather, it will be like a refiner's fire which will purify the nation:

For he is like a refiner's fire and like fullers' soap; he will sit as a refiner and purifier of silver, and he will purify the sons of Levi and refine them like gold and silver, till they present right offerings to the Lord. Then the offering of Judah and Jerusalem will be pleasing to the Lord as in the days of old and as in former years. (3: 2–4).

The prophet insisted that the promise of God's forgiveness and restoration would be fulfilled. Even though Israel has sinned, God will return to his people if they seek him. 'From the days of your fathers you have turned aside from my statutes and have not kept them. Return to me, and I will return to you, says the Lord of hosts' (3: 7). What is required is loyalty to God – the people must bring full tithes as prescribed by the law. If Israel fulfils these commandments, God will open the windows of heaven and pour down an overflowing blessing. Then God will rebuke the devourer so that it will not destroy the fruit of the soil. When this takes place, 'all the nations will call you blessed, for you will be a land of delight' (3: 12).

In the final section of the book, Malachi described the day of the Lord – it will be a time of destruction for the wicked and reward for those who fear his name:

For behold, the day comes, burning like an oven, when all the arrogant and all evildoers will be stubble; the day that comes shall burn them up, says the Lord of hosts, so that it will leave them neither root nor branch. But for you who fear my name the sun of righteousness shall rise, with healing in its wings ... (4: 1–2)

In conclusion Malachi announced that he will send the prophet Elijah before the day of the Lord so that the nation will be reconciled:

Behold, I will send you Elijah the prophet before the great and terrible day of the Lord comes. And he will turn the hearts of fathers to their children and the hearts of children to their fathers, lest I come and smite the land with a curse. (4: 5–6)

WRITINGS

25. Psalms

1. Book 1: Psalms 1–41
2. Book 2: Psalms 42–72
3. Book 3: Psalms 73–89
4. Book 4: Psalms 90–106
5. Book 5: Psalms 107–150

The Book of Psalms is composed of a collection of diverse psalms arranged in five books. The First Book consisting of Psalms 1 to 41 ends with the doxology: 'Blessed be the Lord, the God of Israel, from everlasting to everlasting! Amen and Amen' (41: 13). The Second Book consists of Psalms 42 to 72 concluding with the doxology: 'Blessed be the Lord, the God of Israel, who alone does wondrous things. Blessed be his glorious name for ever; may his glory fill the whole earth! Amen and Amen' (72: 18–19). The Third Book consisting of Psalms 73 to 89 ends with the doxology: 'Blessed be the Lord for ever! Amen and Amen' (89: 52). The Fourth Book consists of Psalms 90 to 106 and concludes with the doxology: 'Blessed be the Lord, the God of Israel, from everlasting to everlasting! And let all the people say "Amen!" Praise be the Lord!' (106: 48). The Fifth Book consists of Psalms 107 to 150.

There are essentially eight categories of Psalms: (1) personal psalms; (2) penitential psalms; (3) psalms of praise; (4) prayer psalms; (5) messianic psalms; (6) historical psalms; (7) liturgical psalms; (8) psalms which ascribe majesty and power to the Lord. The authorship of the psalms is varied, including David, Solomon and Asaph. In all likelihood the Book of Psalms was arranged in its final form in the third century BCE, although much of the material was probably composed from about 1000–500 BCE.

Book 1

Psalm 1 serves as an introduction to the Book of Psalms, describing the joy of the righteous in the study of the law. Here the image of a tree planted by streams of water is used to illustrate the way in which a relationship with God can lead to spiritual nourishment: 'He is like a tree planted by streams of water, that yields its fruit in its season, and its leaf does not wither. In all that he does, he prospers' (1: 3).

Psalm 2 belongs to the category of royal psalms, celebrating the coronation of a new king in Judah as well as the kingship of the Lord over his people. Here the king is depicted as the son of God: 'He said to me, "You are my son, Today I have begotten you. Ask of me, and I will make the nations your heritage, and the ends of the earth your possession"' (2: 7–8).

The title of Psalm 3 indicates that it was written by David when he fled from his son Absalom who had rebelled against him; the psalm emphasizes the Lord's care in the face of his enemies: 'O Lord, how many are my foes! Many are rising against me; many are saying of me, there is no help for him in God. But thou, O Lord, art a shield about me' (3: 1–3).

Psalm 4 is also attributed to David and again speaks of distress: 'There are many who say, "O that we might see some good! Lift up the light of thy countenance upon us, O Lord"' (4: 6).

Psalm 5 is also a prayer for rescue from one's enemies. According to the psalmist, the faithful can be confident in the Lord: 'Give ear to my words, O Lord; give heed to my groaning. Hearken to the sound of my cry, my King and my God, for to thee do I pray' (5: 1–2).

Psalm 6 is again a plea for deliverance; in great distress the psalmist beseeches God to act: 'Turn, O Lord, save my life; deliver me for the sake of thy steadfast love. For in death there is no remembrance of thee; in Sheol who can give thee praise?' (6: 4–5).

The title of Psalm 7 suggests that it was written at the time when David was threatened by Saul. The psalm indicates that David has taken refuge in the face of danger: 'O Lord my God, in thee do I take refuge; save me from all my pursuers, and deliver me, lest like a lion they rend me, dragging me away, with none to rescue' (7: 1–2).

Unlike these previous psalms, Psalm 8 extols God's majesty and humanity's exalted place in creation – human beings, the psalmist asserts, are little lower than the angels: 'Yet thou hast made him little less than God, and dost crown him with glory and honour. Thou hast given him dominion over the works of thy hands; thou hast put all things under his feet' (8: 5–6).

Psalms 9 to 10 may have originally been a single psalm celebrating the Lord's love at times of distress. This theme is continued in Psalms 11 to 14 which stress the need to trust in the Lord. Psalm 15, however, is of different order. Here the psalmist insists on the necessity of holiness and purity on the part of those who wish to be near to God: 'O Lord, who shall sojourn in thy tent? Who shall dwell on thy holy hill? He who walks blamelessly, and does what is right, and speaks truth from his heart' (15: 1–2).

The next three psalms describe the Lord as a place of refuge: he is a rock and fortress in which one can find safety: 'I love thee, O Lord, my strength. The Lord is my rock, and my fortress, and my deliverer, my God, my rock, in whom I take refuge, my shield, and the horn of my salvation, my stronghold' (18: 1–2).

Psalm 19 depicts the glories of the Lord as manifest in the world: his majesty is revealed through nature as well as his law which is sweeter than honey: 'More to be desired are they than gold, even much fine gold; sweeter also than honey and drippings of the honeycomb' (19: 10). Psalms 20 and 21 appear to belong together, expressing the prayer of an army before battle and its thanksgiving after victory. Psalm 22 is of a righteous sufferer; here the psalmist describes his plight and prays for deliverance. Psalm 23 continues the theme of redemption, expressing the psalmist's confidence in God's salvation: 'The Lord is my shepherd, I shall not want; he makes me lie down in green pastures. He leads me beside still waters; he restores my soul. He leads me in paths of righteousness for his name's sake' (23: 1–3).

Psalm 24 is a psalm of celebration, affirming God's kingship; this is followed by three psalms which further reiterate the theme of trust in the Lord: each psalm is a plea for deliverance. Psalm 29 continues with a description of God's lordship over the earth: 'The Lord sits enthroned over the flood; the Lord sits enthroned as king for ever' (29: 10). Psalm 30 is a psalm of dedication which recounts God's saving acts. This is followed by another appeal for God's deliverance. Again God is described as a rock and fortress: 'In thee, O Lord, do I seek refuge; let me never be put to shame; in thy righteousness deliver me! ... Be a rock of refuge for me, a strong fortress to save me!' (31: 1–2). Psalm 32 again emphasizes God's protection, and the next psalm is another psalm of praise recalling God's greatness and abiding presence with his people; this theme is continued in Psalm 34 which stresses God's care for the faithful. The first book concludes with Psalms 34 to 41 which focus on the theme of God's deliverance: he alone is a source of refuge.

Book 2

Psalms 42 and 43 were in all likelihood a single unit – here the psalmist speaks of the absence of God yet he is assured that his presence will be made manifest: 'As a hart longs for flowing streams, so longs my soul for thee, O God. My soul thirsts for God, for the living God' (42: 1–2).

Psalm 44 refers to Israel's defeat in battle which is attributed to the nation's unrighteousness: 'Thou has made us like sheep for slaughter, and has scattered us among the nations' (44: 11).

These psalms are followed by a festive psalm celebrating a royal wedding. Psalm 46 by contrast is a declaration of confidence in God, he is the one who calls upon hearers to trust in him: 'God is our refuge and strength, a very present help in trouble' (46: 1). The theme of protection implicit in this psalm is developed in Psalms 47 and 48 which delight in God's rule over all peoples: 'Clap your hands, all peoples! Shout to God with loud songs of joy! For the Lord, the Most High, is terrible, a great king over all the earth' (47: 1).

Similar ideas are found in the next two psalms which emphasize the need to trust in the Lord rather than in the counsel of the ungodly.

Psalm 51 was allegedly composed by King David after his adulterous affair with Bathsheba – it is a prayer for forgiveness, expressing confidence in God's compassion: 'Have mercy on me, O God, according to thy steadfast love; according to thy abundant mercy blot out my transgressions. Wash me thoroughly from my iniquity, and cleanse me from my sin!' (51: 1–2).

Psalms 52 to 55 constitute a series of psalms, each of which is referred to as a *Maskil*; this term may indicate its meditative character. Psalm 52 asserts confidence in God; Psalm 53 describes the folly of wickedness; Psalm 54 focuses on the significance of trust in the Lord; and Psalm 55 explains the dangers of wickedness and the joy of putting one's confidence in the Lord: 'Cast your burden on the Lord, and he will sustain you; he will never permit the righteous to be moved' (55: 22).

The next collection of psalms, Psalms 56–60, consists of a group of *Miktams* — a term possibly designating prayers of lament. Again the theme of deliverance from evil predominates, repeatedly the psalmist asks for vengeance upon the enemy: 'Thou, Lord God of hosts, art God of Israel. Awake to punish all the nations; spare none of those who treacherously plot evil' (59: 5).

Psalms 61 to 65 are another set of psalms — described as 'psalms of David' — which insist on the Lord's ability to satisfy human needs even in the most difficult circumstances. In various instances poetic imagery is used to convey God's abiding protection: 'for thou hast been my help, as in the shadow of thy wings I sing for joy' (63: 7). The next psalm appears to have been composed to celebrate Jerusalem's deliverance from the Assyrians. Here God's saving acts of the past are rehearsed; a similar notion is contained in Psalm 67. Again in Psalm 68 praise is given for God's wondrous deeds indicating God's providence in the wilderness, the conquest of Canaan, and the establishment of Zion.

Unlike these previous psalms, Psalm 69 again expresses despair in the face of Israel's trials. Frequently the psalmist speaks of his plight at the hands of his enemies:

Save me, O God!
For the waters have come up to my neck.
I sink in deep mire,
Where there is no foothold;
I have come into deep waters,
and the flood sweeps over me.
I am weary with my crying;
my throat is parched.
My eyes grow dim
with waiting for my God. (69: 1–3)

Similar subjects are found in Psalms 70 to 71 in which the psalmist prays for God's help, and the book concludes with a royal psalm associated with King Solomon which prays for proper rule and justice for the nation:

Give the king thy justice, O God,
and thy righteousness to the royal son!
May he judge thy people with righteousness,
and thy poor with justice!
Let the mountains bear prosperity for the people,
and the hills, in righteousness!

May he defend the cause of the poor of the people,
give deliverance to the needy,
and crush the oppressor! (72: 1–4)

Book 3

This book opens with a series of eleven psalms associated with
Asaph, a leader of the choirs established by King David to provide
music in the temple. One of the most important themes of this
collection is God's rule over the nations; this is supplemented by
such topics as the apparent prosperity of the wicked, the expression
of hope that God will redeem his people from oppression, the
acknowledgement that the Lord is saviour over Israel, a recollection
of the mighty acts undertaken by God on behalf of his chosen
people, and the Lord's judgement on all nations. These psalms are
followed by Psalm 84, a meditation on the beauty of the Lord's
house. Here the psalmist utilizes nature imagery to convey his
message:

Even the sparrow finds a home,
and the swallow a nest for herself,
where she may lay her young,
at thy altars, O Lord of hosts,
my King and my God.
Blessed are those who dwell in thy house,
ever singing thy praise! (84: 3–4)

Psalm 85 seems to reflect the circumstances surrounding Ezra and
Nehemiah's return from Babylon to Jerusalem. Here the psalmist
pleas for renewal and restoration so that God's glory may again be
manifest in his holy place:

Let me hear what God the Lord will speak,
for he will speak peace to his people,
to his saints, to those who turn to him in their hearts.
Surely his salvation is at hand for those who fear him,
that glory may dwell in our land. (85: 8–9)

The next psalm again stresses God's help for those who turn to him
in their distress: 'Preserve my life, for I am godly; save thy servant
who trusts in thee. Thou art my God; be gracious to me, O Lord, for
to thee do I cry all the day' (86: 2–3). Psalm 87 is again a celebration

of Zion – the psalmist looks forward to the day when all people shall acknowledge the Lord. The following psalm returns to the theme of Psalm 86: here the psalmist admits his fear in the face of his enemies and questions God's ways: 'But I, O Lord, cry to thee; in the morning my prayer comes before thee. O Lord, why dost thou cast me off? Why dost thou hide thy face from me?' (88: 13–14).

A similar theme is developed in Psalm 89 which possibly dates from the Babylonian attack on Jerusalem; this psalm is a prayer for God's protection in according with his promise to David: 'How long, O Lord? Wilt thou hide thyself for ever? How long will thy wrath burn like fire? ... Lord, where is thy steadfast love of old, which by thy faithfulness, thou didst swear to David?' (89: 46, 49).

Book 4

The fourth book begins with a description of human sinfulness, stressing the brevity of life:

> For a thousand years in thy sight
> are but as yesterday when it is past,
> or as a watch in the night ...
> The years of our life are threescore and ten,
> or even by reason of strength fourscore;
> yet their span is but toil and trouble;
> they are soon gone, and we fly away. (90: 4, 10)

This psalm is followed by the next four psalms (Psalms 91 to 94) which insist on the benefits of knowing God. In Psalm 95 the psalmist calls on his hearers to worship the Lord; here he emphasizes the majesty of God as creator:

> O come, let us sing to the Lord;
> let us make a joyful noise to the rock of our salvation!
> Let us come into his presence with thanksgiving;
> let us make a joyful noise to him with songs of praise!
> For the Lord is a great God,
> and a great King above all gods.
> In his hand are the depths of the earth;
> the heights of the mountains are his also.
> The sea is his, for he made it;
> for his hands formed the dry land. (95: 1–5)

This is followed by a collection of psalms – Psalms 96 to 101 – which describe God's greatness and mighty acts. The next psalm, however, focuses on the psalmist's distress. Yet even in his despair he is confident that the Lord will restore him. Filled with anguish he cries out: 'Hear my prayer, O Lord; let my cry come to thee! Do not hide thy face from me in the day of my distress! Incline thy ear to me; answer me speedily in the day when I call!' (102: 1–2).

Such confidence in God's saving acts continues in the next psalm where the psalmist expresses his trust in the Lord. Despite our frailty, he asserts, God continues to love us: 'But the steadfast love of the Lord is from everlasting to everlasting upon those who fear him' (103: 17). Psalms 104 to 106 reassert such confidence in the Lord – Psalm 104 focuses on God's creative power, and Psalms 105 and 106 list God's previous acts of redemption.

Book 5

The final book begins with Psalm 107, a recitation of God's acts of redemption on behalf of the Israelite nation. Here the psalmist celebrates God's loving concern for his chosen people. In the next psalm the psalmist concentrates on God's love drawing from Psalm 57: 7–11 and 60: 5–12. The next two psalms, 109 to 110, deal with God's trustworthiness. Here the psalmist calls on God to deliver him from false accusation: 'Be not silent, O God of my praise! For wicked and deceitful mouths are opened against me' (109: 1). In Psalm 110 the psalmist describes a messianic king who will be crowned by the Lord: 'The Lord says to my lord: "Sit at my right hand, till I make your enemies your footstool." The Lord sends forth from Zion your mighty sceptre. Rule in the midst of your foes!' (110: 1–2).

Psalms 111 to 118 constitute a collection of psalms which repeatedly use the Hebrew expression 'Hallelujah' (praise the Lord). Here God's goodness is extolled in relation to his past deeds. Thus Psalm 117 declares: 'Praise the Lord, all nations! Extol him, all peoples! For great is his steadfast love toward us; and the faithfulness of the Lord endures for ever. Praise the Lord!' (117: 1–2).

This series of psalms is followed by the longest psalm in the Book of Psalms composed of 176 verses arranged in 22 groups of eight verses. The overarching theme of Psalm 119 is the wonder and greatness of God's word. This is followed by a collection of psalms known as the 'Song of ascents'. These psalms (Psalms 120 to 134) are generally believed to have been used in connection with the ancient pilgrimage festivals. They conclude with a depiction of the entry into the sanctuary: 'Come, bless the Lord, all you servants of the Lord, who stand by night in the house of the Lord! Lift up your hands to the holy place, and bless the Lord!' (134: 1–2).

The next two psalms – Psalms 135 to 136 – again describe God's acts of redemption. Here the theme of Israel's deliverance from bondage is of special significance: 'He it was who smote the first-born of Egypt, both of man and of beast; who in thy midst, O Egypt, sent signs and wonders, against Pharaoh and all his servants' (135: 8–9).

Psalm 137 turns to the nation's exile in Babylon. Here the psalmist stresses the suffering of those exiled from their country:

By the waters of Babylon,
there we sat down and wept,
when we remembered Zion.
On the willows there
we hung up our lyres.
For there our captors
required of us songs,
and our tormentors, mirth, saying
'Sing us one of the songs of Zion!' (137: 1–3)

Psalm 139 is a declaration of God's omnipotence. Even the hidden recesses of the heart are open to him. Here the psalmist states that there is nowhere he can go to flee from God's presence: 'Whither shall I go from thy Spirit? Or whither shall I flee from thy presence? If I ascend to heaven, thou art there! If I make my bed in Sheol, thou art there!' (139: 7–8).

This is followed by a series of psalms – Psalm 140 to 144 – which express the psalmist's distress, calling upon the Lord for deliverance. Here the theme of God's constancy is repeatedly affirmed. The final collection of psalms return to the theme of praise – Psalms 145 to 150 express thanksgiving to the Lord for all his mercies. The book concludes with Psalm 150 which summons all musical instruments to sing praises to the Lord:

Praise him with trumpet sound;
praise him with lute and harp!
Praise him with timbrel and dance;
praise him with strings and pipe!

Praise him with sounding cymbals;
praise him with loud clashing cymbals!
Let everything that breathes praise the Lord!
Praise the Lord! (150: 3–6)

26. Proverbs

According to tradition, King Solomon was the author of the Book of Proverbs, yet such an attribution is unlikely. Some proverbs are referred to as the 'words of the wise' (22: 17; 24: 23); others were copied by scribes during the reign of Hezekiah; and the last two chapters of the book are attributed to Agur and Lemuel – hence the final arrangement of the book could not have taken place before 700 BCE. Unlike other books of the Bible, Proverbs consists of short, pithy sayings designed to provide practical instruction about a variety of topics including knowledge, morality, chastity, laziness and justice. Cast in poetic form, the book consists primarily of couplets.

The prologue to the book (1: 1–7) proclaims the importance of wisdom for everyday life. Such knowledge, the author maintains, is grounded in the fear of the Lord: 'The fear of the Lord is the beginning of knowledge' (1: 7). Following this declaration, Proverbs goes on to explain that not everyone is prepared to accept wisdom; rather, folly and sin blind human beings to what is of true value. According to the Book of Proverbs, the young should keep clear of life's temptations; only in this way can happiness be secured. The reward of seeking wisdom, the author asserts, is more precious than earthly riches:

> Happy is the man who finds wisdom,
> and the man who gets understanding,
> for the gain from it is better than gain from silver
> and its profit better than gold.
> She is more precious than jewels,
> and nothing you desire can compare with her.
> Long life is in her right hand;
> in her left hand are riches and honour.
> Her ways are ways of pleasantness,
> and all her paths are peace.
> She is a tree of life to those who take hold of her. (3: 13–18)

Proverbs 3 continues this theme by stating that wisdom existed before creation and was instrumental in the formation of the universe: 'The Lord by wisdom founded the earth; by understanding he established the heavens; by his knowledge the deeps broke forth, and the clouds drop down the dew' (3: 19–20). Following this declaration the author extolled the benefits of wisdom: the individual who has wisdom will obtain honour and security from the Lord. In this process parents have a significant role – it is they who are capable of imparting the importance of wisdom to their offspring. Reflecting on his own upbringing the author of Proverbs 4 explained:

Hear, O sons, a father's instruction,
and be attentive, that you may gain insight;
for I give you good precepts:
do not forsake my teaching.
When I was a son with my father, tender, the only one in the sight of my mother,
he taught me, and said to me,
'Let your heart hold fast my words; keep my commandments, and live.
(4: 1–4)

The next three proverbs warn against licentiousness. Sexual misconduct is condemned not primarily because it is immoral but because of its consequences:

And now, O sons, listen to me,
and do not depart from the words of my mouth.
Keep your way far from her
and do not go near the door of her house;
lest you give your honour to others
and your years to the merciless;
lest strangers take their fill of your strength,
and your labours go to the house of an alien;
and at the end of your life you groan,
when your flesh and body are consumed. (5: 7–11)

In addition to lustfulness, these proverbs also warn against other forms of waywardness including laziness. 'Go to the ant, O sluggard', the author advises, 'consider her ways, and be wise. Without having any chief, officer or ruler, she prepares her food in summer, and gathers her sustenance in harvest. How long will you lie there, O sluggard?' (6: 6–9).

Here seven sins are also specifically mentioned:

There are six things which the Lord hates,
seven which are an abomination to him:
haughty eyes, a lying tongue,
and hands that shed innocent blood,
a heart that devises wicked plans,
feet that make haste to run to evil,
a false witness who breathes out lies,
and a man who sows discord among brothers. (6: 16–19)

In conclusion, Psalm 7 returns to the theme of sexual indulgence, cautioning against associating with wanton women:

> With much seductive speech she persuades him;
> with her smooth talk she compels him.
> All at once he follows her,
> as an ox goes to the slaughter,
> or as a stag is caught fast
> till an arrow pierces its entrails;
> as a bird rushes into a snare;
> he does not know that it will cost him his life. (7: 21–23)

Chapter 8 continues with a discussion of the nature of wisdom. Here the author personifies wisdom: it is presented as a woman who seeks to give counsel:

> To you, O men, I call,
> and my cry is to the sons of men.
> O simple ones, learn prudence;
> O foolish men, pay attention.
> Hear, for I will speak noble things,
> and from my lips will come what is right;
> for my mouth will utter truth;
> wickedness is an abomination to my lips. (8: 4–7)

This portrayal is followed by a depiction of wisdom as an instrument in creation. As a skilled craftsman, wisdom functions as a servant of the Lord:

> When he established the heavens, I was there,
> when he drew a circle on the face of the deep,
> when he made firm the skies above,
> when he established the fountains of the deep,
> when he assigned to the sea its limit,
> so that the waters might not transgress his command,
> when he marked out the foundations of the earth,
> then I was beside him like a master workman. (8: 27–30)

In the next proverb wisdom and folly are compared – whoever seeks wisdom will prosper, but the man who pursues folly is doomed.

Proverbs 10 to 22 constitute a series of Solomonic proverbs which generally take the form of single statements of a verse in length often containing a contrast. Psalm 14 is a typical example:

Wisdom builds her house,
but folly with her own hands tears it down.
He who walks in uprightness fears the Lord,
but he who is devious in his ways despises him.
The talk of a fool is a rod for his back,
but the lips of the wise will preserve them. (14: 1–3)

In many cases these statements express commands such as the following:

Discipline your son while there is hope;
do not set your heart on his destruction ...
Listen to advice and accept instruction,
that you may gain wisdom for the future ...
Cease, my son, to hear instruction
only to stray from the words of knowledge. (19: 18, 20, 27)

The Book of Proverbs continues with further collections of exhortations. Proverbs 22 to 24 consist of sayings of the wise; these verses are short expressions of worldly wisdom such as Proverbs 23: 6–8:

Do not eat the bread of a man who is stingy;
do not desire his delicacies;
for he is like one who is inwardly reckoning,
'Eat and drink!' he says to you;
but his heart is not with you.
You will vomit up the morsels which you have eaten,
and waste your pleasant words.

Other sayings, however, are more spiritual in character such as the following:

He who has a bountiful eye will be blessed,
for he shares his bread with the poor.
Drive out a scoffer, and strife will go out,
and quarrelling and abuse will cease.
He who loves purity of heart,
and whose speech is gracious,
will have the king as his friend. (22: 9–11)

Proverbs 25 to 29 are a further collection of proverbs attributed to Solomon; they too consist of succinct sayings generally of one verse in length. Many deal with proper government such as 29: 2, 4, 12:

> When the righteous are in authority, the people rejoice;
> but when the wicked rule, the people groan ...
> By justice a king gives stability to the land,
> but one who exacts gifts ruins it ...
> If a ruler listens to falsehood,
> all his officials will be wicked.

Finally, the book concludes with a short collection of 'Sayings of Agur' and 'Sayings of Lemuel' – these were no doubt drawn from collections of material attributed to these writers.

Here the virtues of a noble wife are extolled in a proverb containing twenty-two verses, each of which begin with a consecutive letter of the Hebrew alphabet:

> A good wife who can find?
> She is far more precious than jewels.
> The heart of her husband trusts in her,
> and he will have no lack of gain.
> She does him good, and not harm,
> all the days of her life ...
> Her children rise up and call her blessed;
> her husband also, and he praises her:
> 'Many women have done excellently,
> but you surpass them all.' (31: 10–12; 28–29)

27. Job

      d. Job's reply (19: 1–19: 29)
      e. Zophar's second speech (20: 1–29)
      f. Job's reply (21: 1–34)
  4. Third cycle of speeches (22: 1–31: 40)
      a. Eliphaz's third speech (22: 1–30)
      b. Job's reply (23: 1–24: 25)
      c. Bildad's third speech (25: 1–6)
      d. Job's reply (26: 1–14)
      e. Job's statement to his friends (27: 1–31: 40)

3. Elihu's speeches (32: 1–37: 24)
  1. Anger with Job (32: 1–22)
  2. God uses suffering to chasten people (33: 1–33)
  3. God is not unjust (34: 1–35: 16)
  4. The justice of God (36: 1–37: 24)

4. God's voice (38: 1–42: 6)
  1. God challenges Job (38: 1–3)
  2. Creation (38: 4–15)
  3. Humanity's inability to understand the mystery of creation (38: 16–38)
  4. Humanity's inability to comprehend the mysteries of animals and birds (38: 39–39: 30)
  5. Job's submission (40: 1–5)
  6. God's second speech (40: 6–42: 6)
      a. God challenges Job (40: 6–14)
      b. Behemoth (40: 15–24)
      c. Leviathan (41: 1–34)
      d. Job repentant (42: 1–6)

5. Epilogue (42: 7–17)
  1. Job's prayer (42: 7–9)
  2. Job's fortunes (42: 10–17)

According to tradition, Job was a wealthy man who lived in the land of Uz (possibly in south Edom). The purpose of the Book of Job is to explain the suffering of the righteous; in all likelihood it was written at a later stage in biblical history as Jews became increasingly perplexed about God's justice. As the book opens, Job is portrayed as a person of integrity and faith: 'There was a man in the land of Uz, whose name was Job; and that man was blameless and upright, one who feared God, and turned away from evil' (1: 1). The scene then shifts to a discussion between God and Satan. Convinced that

Job's piety was due to his prosperity, Satan sought to test him:

> Does Job fear God for naught? Hast thou not put a hedge about him and his house and all that he has, on every side? Thou hast blessed the work of his hands, and his possessions have increased in the land. But put forth thy hand now, and touch all that he has, and he will curse thee to thy face. (1: 9–11)

The Lord agreed to Satan's plan, and Job's children, wealth and health were taken from him. Yet despite such misfortune, Job remained faithful to the Lord:

> Then Job arose, and rent his robe, and shaved his head, and fell upon the ground, and worshipped. And he said, 'Naked I came from my mother's womb, and naked shall I return; the Lord gave, and the Lord has taken away; blessed be the name of the Lord.' (1: 20–21)

In the next scene Job suffers physically, yet he remained steadfast in his loyalty to God. At this stage Job was confronted by three friends who wished to help him:

> Now when Job's three friends heard of all this evil that had come upon him, they came each from his own place, Eliphaz the Temanite, Bildad the Shuhite, and Zophar the Naamathite. They made an appointment together to come to condole with him and comfort him. (2: 11)

Initially they sat silently. Job then spoke of his misfortune, expressing the wish that he had never been born: 'Let the day perish wherein I was born, and the night which said, "A man-child is conceived" ' (3: 3). Following Job's recitation of woes, Eliphaz argued that God does not punish the righteous. Hence Job should recognize that his misfortune is due to his own sinfulness. In reply Job rebuked his friends and demanded evidence of his sins:

> Teach me, and I will be silent;
> make me understand how I have erred ...
> But now, be pleased to look at me;
> for I will not lie to your face.
> Turn, I pray, let no wrong be done.
> Turn now, my vindication is at stake.
> Is there any wrong on my tongue?
> Cannot my taste discern calamity? (6: 24, 28–30)

After this speech, Bildad delivered a speech in which he accused Job of being a hypocrite and urged him to seek repentance:

> How long will you say these things,
> and the words of your mouth be a great wind?
> Does God pervert justice?
> Or does the Almighty pervert the right? ...
> if you are pure and upright,
> surely then he will rouse himself for you
> and reward you with a rightful habitation.
> And though your beginning was small,
> your latter days will be very great. (8: 2–3, 6–7)

In reply Job maintained that there is no justice in the world: the strong simply prevail over the weak. Speaking of his own plight, he complained about God's lack of concern for the faithful:

> If I sin, thou dost mark me,
> and dost not acquit me of my iniquity.
> If I am wicked, woe to me!
> If I am righteous, I cannot lift up my head,
> for I am filled with disgrace
> and look upon my affliction.
> And if I lift myself up, thou dost hunt me like a lion. (10: 14–16)

The final comforter, Zophar, then condemned Job; in his eyes, Job is a liar – Job criticized God when he should have condemned himself. What is required, Zophar asserted, is right action. Job must repent and improve his ways:

> If you set your heart aright,
> you will stretch out your hands toward him.
> If iniquity is in your hand, put it far away,
> and let not wickedness dwell in your tents.
> Surely then you will lift up your face without blemish;
> you will be secure and will not fear. (11: 13–15)

In response Job reiterated his belief that justice is not apparent in the world. Beginning with a defence against Zophar's accusations, he went on to express resentment of his friends: 'As for you, you whitewash with lies; worthless physicians are you all. Oh that you would keep silent, and that it would be your wisdom!' (13: 4–5). Here Job defends his own integrity and complains of God's severe dealings: 'How many are my iniquities and my sins? Make me know my transgression and my sin. Why dost thou hide thy face, and count me as thy enemy?' (13: 23–24).

In chapter 15 Eliphaz delivers his second speech. Job's own words condemn him, he argued – Job is deluded, 'Why does your heart carry you away,' he asked, 'and why do your eyes flash, that you turn your spirit against God, and let such words go out of your mouth?' (15: 12–13). Conceding that the wicked do appear to prosper, Eliphaz insisted that they live in fear of divine punishment:

The wicked man writhes in pain all his days,
through all the years that are laid up for the ruthless.
Terrifying sounds are in his ears;
in prosperity the destroyer will come upon him.
He does not believe that he will return out of darkness,
and he is destined for the sword.
He wanders abroad for bread, saying, 'Where is it?'
He knows that a day of darkness is ready at his hand. (15: 20–23)

Again Job replied that the comforters are not the first to offer inadequate answers to the questions he posed: 'I have heard many such things; miserable comforters are you all' (16: 1). He too could have framed their responses. Yet, he is innocent; his conscience is clear. In desperation, Job appealed to God against the verdicts of his friends.

Chapter 18 continues with Bildad's second speech. Emphasizing the plight of the wicked, he reproves Job as haughty and obstinate. In his view, the wicked are destined to suffer:

For he is cast into a net by his own feet,
and he walks on a pitfall.
A trap seizes him by the heel,
a snare lays hold of him.
A rope is hid for him in the ground,
a trap for him in the path.
Terrors frighten him on every side
and chase him at his heels. (18: 8–11)

Replying a second time to Bildad, Job reasserts his perplexity. God is the author of his affliction, and Job pleads for pity from his friends: 'Have pity on me, have pity on me, O you my friends, for the hand of God has touched me!' (19: 21). Even though overcome by desolation, Job still had unshakable confidence in the Lord: 'For I know that my Redeemer lives, and at last he will stand upon the earth; and after my skin has been thus destroyed, then from my flesh I shall see God' (19: 25–26).

Zophar then suggested that it might seem that the wicked go unpunished, but this is an illusion – in the end they will be cut down:

> In the fullness of his sufficiency he will be in straits;
> all the force of misery will come upon him.
> To fill his belly to the full
> God will send his fierce anger into him,
> and rain it upon him as his food.
> He will flee from an iron weapon;
> a bronze arrow will strike him through ...
> Utter darkness is laid up for his treasures;
> a fire not blown upon will devour him. (20: 22–24, 26)

In response Job told his friends to listen carefully. The wicked often prosper in this life – they are not invariably destined to suffer. God does as he pleases, both to the righteous and the wicked:

> Will any teach God knowledge,
> seeing that he judges those that are on high?
> One dies in full prosperity,
> being wholly at ease and secure,
> his body full of fat
> and the marrow of his bones moist.
> Another dies in bitterness of soul,
> never having tasted of good.
> They lie down alike in the dust,
> and the worms cover them. (21: 22–26)

Job, however, replied that this is not the case. The wicked in fact prosper; Zophar has no true understanding of the course of events:

> Why do the wicked live,
> reach old age, and grow mighty in power?
> Their children are established in their presence,
> and their offspring before their eyes,
> Their houses are safe from fear,
> and no rod of God is upon them ...
> How often is it that the lamp of the wicked is put out?

That their calamity comes upon them?
That God distributes pains in his anger? (21: 7–9, 17)

In the third set of speeches Eliphaz and Bildad reiterated their conviction that Job is to blame for what has befallen him. Instead of declaring his innocence, he should submit to God's will; only in this way will he find prosperity: 'Agree with God, and be at peace; thereby good will come to you' (22: 21). In reply Job again describes life's unfairness – the wicked prosper whereas the righteous suffer. Bildad's brief reply is then followed by a series of speeches in which Job rehearsed his previous arguments, recalled his former prosperity, and declared his faithfulness.

Chapters 32 to 37 contain the speeches of Elihu who here makes his appearance. The theme of these discourses is that suffering is a means whereby God exercises judgement. Given God's goodness, Job must have sinned; otherwise his calamities are inexplicable. Elihu's speeches are followed by God's answer to Job, beginning with a series of rhetorical questions. First the Lord asked about Job's understanding of creation:

Where were you when I laid the foundation of the earth?
Tell me, if you have understanding.
Who determined its measurements – surely you know!
Or who stretched the line upon it?
On what were its bases sunk,
or who laid its cornerstone,
when the morning stars sang together,
and all the sons of God shouted for joy? (38: 4–7)

By this catalogue of the wonders of the universe, God demonstrated the range of his wisdom. How can Job hope to comprehend his ways? In response Job recognized that he has no right to question the Lord: 'Then Job answered the Lord: "Behold, I am of small account; What shall I answer thee? I lay my hand on my mouth. I have spoken once, and I will not answer; twice, but I will pretend no further'" (40: 3–5).

In the same chapter God again answered Job out of a whirlwind, challenging his presumption: 'Gird up your loins like a man; I will question you, and you declare to me. Will you even put me in the wrong? Will you condemn me that you may be justified?' (40: 7–8).

Again Job accepted God's judgement:

Then Job answered the Lord:
'I know that thou canst do all things,
and that no purpose of thine can be thwarted.
Who is this that hides counsel without knowledge?
Therefore I have uttered what I did not understand,
things too wonderful for me,
which I did not know. (42: 1–3)

The book concludes with Job's prayer for his friends and an account of the restoration of Job's fortunes.

28. Song of Songs

1. Bride and bridegroom (1: 1–2: 7)
   1. Inscription (1: 1)
   2. Bride and her lover (1: 2–8)
   3. Bride and bridegroom meet (1: 9–2: 7)

2. Praise of her beloved (2: 8–3: 5)
   1. Praise by day (2: 8–17)
   2. Praise by night (3: 1–5)

3. Praise of the bride (3: 6–5: 1)
   1. Bridegroom comes (3: 6–11)
   2. Proposal accepted (4: 1–5: 1)

4. Troubled love (5: 2–7: 9)
   1. Disturbing dream (5: 2–6: 3)
   2. Bridegroom's thoughts (6: 4–7: 9)

5. Love (7: 10–8: 14)
   1. Bride gives her love (7: 10–8: 4)
   2. Beauty of love (8: 5–14)

The Song of Songs is ascribed to King Solomon yet most scholars regard the book as having been written at a later date even though some elements appear to be of an early origin. The book itself consists of a dialogue between a bride, a bridegroom, and the daughters of Jerusalem. Filled with oriental imagery and lavish descriptions of local scenes, the dialogue is a romantic idyll. Various interpretations have been given: according to one theory it is a drama with two main characters (Solomon and the Shulammite); another theory posits three characters (Solomon, the Shulammite, and a country lover). In the Jewish tradition, the Song of Songs has been perceived as an allegory of the love between God and Israel whereas in Christianity it has been understood as representing love between Christ and his Church. In any event, the book focuses on five meetings between the lover and the beloved (1: 2–2: 7; 2: 8–3: 5; 3: 6–5: 1; 5: 2–6: 3; and 6: 4–8: 4).

The book begins with a dialogue between the bride, a country girl and the women of Jerusalem. Here the bride awaits her lover – full of sensual language, this passage depicts her longing: 'O that you would kiss me with the kisses of your mouth! For your love is better than wine' (1: 2). Speaking to the daughters of Jerusalem, she next explained why she has such a dark complexion: 'I am very dark, but comely, O daughters of Jerusalem … Do not gaze at me because I am swarthy, because the sun has scorched me' (1: 5–6).

Now the bride and bridegroom meet, and the bride describes her beloved: 'I compare you, my love, to a mare of Pharaoh's chariots. Your cheeks are comely with ornaments, your neck with strings of jewels' (1: 9–10).

This is followed by the bridegroom's praise of his love: 'Behold, you are beautiful, my love; behold, you are beautiful; your eyes are doves. Behold, you are beautiful, my beloved, truly lovely' (1: 15–16).

Again the bride addresses the daughters of Jerusalem, expressing her longing for her lover: 'Sustain me with raisins, refresh me with apples; for I am sick with love. O that his left hand were under my head, and that his right hand embraced me!' (2: 5–6).

Chapter 2 continues with further praise of the bridegroom. At first the bride described him by day. Here a comparison is drawn between the bridegroom and a gazelle or stag: 'Behold, he comes, leaping upon the mountains, bounding over the hills. My beloved is like a gazelle, or a young stag. Behold, there he stands behind our wall, gazing in at the windows, looking through the lattice' (2: 8–9).

In this daydream the bridegroom beckons his beloved to join him as it is Spring:

Arise, my love, my fair one,
and come away;
for lo, the winter is past,
the rain is over and gone.
The flowers appear on the earth,
the time of singing has come,
and the voice of the turtle dove
is heard in our land. (2: 10–12)

In response the bride expresses her devotion: 'My beloved is mine and I am his, he pastures his flock among the lilies. Until the day breathes and the shadows flee, turn, my beloved, be like a gazelle or a young stag upon rugged mountains' (2: 16–17).

In chapter 3 the bride's longing for her lover is continued in a dream sequence: at night she sought his presence. Unable to find him, she wandered about the city. Encountering the watchmen, she asked if they had seen him. Eventually she found the bridegroom and held him fast: 'I held him, and would not let him go until I had brought him into my mother's house, and into the chamber of her that conceived me' (3: 4).

The scene then changes to a grand procession of King Solomon: from the wilderness, like a column of smoke perfumed with myrrh and frankincense, the king appeared:

Behold, it is the litter of Solomon!
About it are sixty mighty men
of the mighty men of Israel ...
Go forth, O daughters of Zion,
and behold King Solomon
with the crown with which his mother crowned him
on the day of his wedding,
on the day of the gladness of his heart. (3: 7, 11)

The bridegroom then rejoices in the bride's loveliness. Drawing on pastoral imagery, he described her physical beauty:

Your eyes are doves
behind your veil.
Your hair is like a flock of goats,
moving down the slopes of Gilead.
Your teeth are like a flock of shorn ewes
that have come up from washing ...
Your lips are like a scarlet thread,
and your mouth is lovely.
Your cheeks are like halves of a pomegranate
behind your veil ...
Your two breasts are like two fawns,
twins of a gazelle,
that feed upon the lilies. (4: 1–3, 5)

Chapter 5 continues with a depiction of the bride's troubled dream. As she slept, her lover knocked. However, when she opened the door he had fled. She sought him but he was nowhere to be found.

When the watchmen found her wandering about the city, they beat her and took her mantle. This account is followed by the bride's description of her beloved's comeliness. Again, a comparison is made between physical beauty and nature:

> His head is the finest gold;
> his locks are wavy,
> black as a raven.
> His eyes are like doves
> beside springs of water ...
> His cheeks are like beds of spices,
> yielding fragrance.
> His lips are lilies,
> distilling liquid myrrh.
> His arms are rounded gold,
> set with jewels.
> His body is ivory work,
> encrusted with sapphires.
> His legs are alabaster columns
> set upon bases of gold. (5: 11–15)

The next chapter turns to the bridegroom's thoughts about his bride. Here he again describes the bride's beauty – she is a queenly maiden, fair and pleasant. Comparing her to a palm tree, he spoke of his longing:

> You are stately as a palm tree,
> and your breasts are like its clusters.
> I say I will climb the palm tree
> and lay hold of its branches.
> Oh, may your breasts be like clusters of the vine,
> and the scent of your breath like apples,
> and your kisses like the best wine. (7: 7–9)

The bride gives her love: she beckons her beloved to accompany her to the vineyard: 'The mandrakes give forth fragrance, and over our doors are all choice fruits, new as well as old, which I have laid up for you, O my beloved' (7: 13). In the last section the beauty of love is extolled – nothing can quench it:

> Set me as a seal upon your heart,
> as a seal upon your arm;
> for love is strong as death ...

Many waters cannot quench love,
neither can floods drown it.
If a man offered for love
all the wealth of his house,
it would be utterly scorned. (8: 6–7)

29. Ruth

The Book of Ruth is set in the time of the Judges; Boaz, a central character in the story, is described as the great-grandfather of David. Yet, it is likely that the story originated at a much later date. According to tradition, Elimelech of Bethlehem in Judah left his homeland due to a famine and settled in Moab with his wife, Naomi, and his sons Mahlon and Chilion. There these two sons married Moabite women – Orpah and Ruth. When Elimelech and his sons died, Naomi decided to return to her native country. Both daughters-in-law wished to accompany her, but she encouraged them to stay. Orpah agreed, but Ruth wished to leave with her. Arriving in Judah at the beginning of the grain harvest, Ruth gleaned the field owned by her dead husband's kinsman, Boaz. When Naomi discovered that Boaz was kind to Ruth she was pleased, anticipating the possibility of a Levirate marriage between them. Eventually Ruth and Boaz were married, resulting in the redemption of the land of Naomi's deceased husband. The book concludes with a genealogy of King David who was descended from Ruth and Boaz.

The book opens with an account of the famine in Israel. Because of this hardship Elimelech, his wife Naomi, and their two sons set off for Moab. There Mahlon and Chilion married Ruth and Orpah. After the death of her husband and sons, Naomi was left with her daughters-in-law. Hearing that the famine in Judah had ended, Naomi resolved to return home, urging her daughters-in-law to remain in the land of their birth:

> But Naomi said to her two daughters-in-law, 'Go, return each of you to her mother's house. May the Lord deal kindly with you, as you have dealt with the dead and with me. The Lord grant that you may find a home, each of you in the house of her husband!' (1: 8–9)

Although Orpah agreed, Ruth declared her dedication to Naomi. Beseeching her mother-in-law, she pleaded: 'Entreat me not to leave you or to return from following you; for where you go I will go, and where you lodge I will lodge; your people shall be my people, and your God my God' (1: 16).

In consequence both women journeyed together to Bethlehem in time for the barley harvest. There Ruth sought Naomi's permission to go to the land to gather left-over grain which had been set aside for the poor. Without knowing the situation, she began to glean the fields belonging to Boaz, her husband's kinsman. Hearing the account of Ruth's dedication to her mother-in-law, Boaz spoke to her:

> Now, listen, my daughter, do not go to glean in another field or leave this one, but keep close to my maidens. Let your eyes be upon the field which they are reaping, and go after them ... And when you are thirsty, go to the vessels, and drink what the young men have drawn. (2: 8–9)

When she returned to Naomi after labouring in Boaz's fields, Naomi asked where she had been gleaning. Delighted to hear that the land was owned by Boaz, Naomi exclaimed: 'Blessed be he by the Lord, whose kindness has not forsaken the living or the dead! ... The man is a relative of ours, one of our nearest kin' (2: 20). Following

Naomi's advice, Ruth kept close to the maidens of Boaz until the end of the barley and wheat harvests. Naomi then counselled Ruth to wash, anoint herself, put on her best clothes, and go the threshing floor. After Boaz had eaten and drunk, he went to lie down at the end of the heap of grain. In accordance with Naomi's guidance, Ruth uncovered his feet and lay down near him. At midnight Boaz awoke and was startled to find her there. In reply to his queries about her identity, Ruth explained that she was related to him. Although Boaz was moved to marry her and redeem her land, he explained that another individual was a closer kin than he was:

> And now it is true that I am a near kinsman, yet there is a kinsman nearer than I. Remain this night, and in the morning, if he will do the part of the next of kin for you, well; let him do it; but if he is not willing to do the part of the next of kin for you, then, as the Lord lives, I will do the part of the next of kin for you. (3: 12–13)

Chapter 4 relates that Boaz sought the nearest of kin and explained the situation:

> Then he said to the next of kin, 'Naomi, who has come back from the country of Moab, is selling the parcel of land which belonged to our kinsman Elimelech. So I thought I would tell you of it, and say, Buy it in the presence of those sitting here, and in the presence of the elders of my people. If you will redeem it, redeem it; but if you will not, tell me, that I may know, for there is no one besides you to redeem it, and I come after you.' (4: 3–4)

When the kinsman agreed to do this, Boaz pointed out that he would also have to marry Ruth. Alarmed by such a prospect, the kinsman declined because of the legal implications of such a liaison in relation to his own inheritance. Boaz then followed the prescriptions laid down in Scripture: he drew off his sandals and declared to the elders and all the people:

> You are witnesses this day that I have bought from the hand of Naomi all that belonged to Elimelech and all that belonged to Chilion and to Mahlon. Also Ruth the Moabitess, the widow of Mahlon, I have bought to be my wife, to perpetuate the name of the dead in his inheritance. (4: 9–10)

The book concludes with the marriage of Ruth and Boaz and the birth of Obed who became the grandfather of King David.

30. Lamentations

In 587 BCE Jerusalem was destroyed by the Babylonians and Jewish captives were taken into exile. The book of Lamentations is composed of five poems, in all likelihood written in Israel after this event. These laments are acrostics of the twenty-two letters of the Hebrew alphabet and follow an A + B + C + B + A arrangement. Chapters 1 and 5 provide general descriptions of this disaster; chapters 2 and 4 depict death and destruction; chapter 3 contains a confession of sin and trust in the Lord.

The book begins with a portrayal of God's rejection of Jerusalem: the city has become desolate and is now utterly vanquished:

> How lonely sits the city
> that was full of people!
> How like a widow has she become,
> she that was great among the nations! ...
> The roads to Zion mourn,
> for none come to the appointed feasts;
> all her gates are desolate,
> her priests groan. (1: 1, 4)

There is no one to comfort her at the moment of her humiliation – even the Lord appears to have abandoned his people. Such suffering is not an accident of history; rather, the Lord has meted out this affliction as a punishment for sin: 'Her foes have become the head, her enemies prosper, because the Lord has made her suffer for the multitude of her transgressions' (1: 5).

Chapter 1 continues with an acknowledgement of Israel's sinfulness. The Lord is right, the author declares, because of the people's rebellion. Yet he cries out to the Lord for vengeance upon the enemy: 'Bring thou the day thou hast announced, and let them be as I am. Let all their evil doing come before thee; and deal with them as thou hast dealt with me because of all my transgressions' (1: 21–22).

The second lament is a meditation on the Lord's wrath. The destruction of Jerusalem was due to the waywardness of the nation:

> The Lord has become like an enemy,
> he has destroyed Israel;
> he has destroyed all its palaces
> laid in ruins its strongholds;
> and he has multiplied in the daughter of Judah
> mourning and lamentation ...
> The Lord has scorned his altar,
> disowned his sanctuary;
> he has delivered into the hand of the enemy
> the walls of her palaces. (2: 5, 7)

Israel's priests and prophets have failed the Lord – they did not warn the people of their iniquity and the consequences of sin: 'Your prophets have seen for you false and deceptive visions; they have not exposed your iniquity to restore your fortunes, but have seen for you oracles false and misleading' (2: 14). As a result, the city is now waste and rubble, and all those who pass by ridicule the fallen city: 'All who pass along the way clap their hands at you; they hiss and wag their heads at the daughter of Jerusalem; 'Is this the city which was called the perfection of beauty, the joy of all the earth?' (2: 15).

Overwhelmed by this disaster, the author called on the inhabitants to weep for their homeland: 'Cry aloud to the Lord! O daughter of Zion! Let tears stream down like a torrent day and night! Give yourself no rest, your eyes no respite!' (2: 18).

In the third lament the author stresses the importance of repentance and the hope for restoration. Longer than the other chapters, this poem consists of three groups of twenty-two verses: in each group the verses are structured in accordance with the Hebrew alphabet. Speaking on behalf of the people, the author reflected on Zion's tragic condition: 'I am the man who has seen affliction under the rod of his wrath; he has driven and brought me into darkness without any light' (3: 1–2).

Recalling God's mercy, the author expressed his trust in the Lord: 'But this I call to mind, and therefore I have hope: The steadfast love of the Lord never ceases, his mercies never come to an end; they are new every morning; great is thy faithfulness' (3: 21–23).

Given the Lord's compassion, the author pleaded with the nation to turn to God: 'Let us test and examine our ways, and return to the Lord! Let us lift up our hearts and hands to God in heaven' (3: 40–41).

The poem concludes with a cry for vengeance on Israel's enemies: 'Thou wilt requite them, O Lord, according to the work of their hands. Thou wilt give them dullness of heart; thy curse will be on them. Thou wilt pursue them in anger and destroy them from under thy heavens, O Lord' (3: 64–66).

The fourth lament deals with the transgression of the leaders of the nation. Again the author castigated Israel for her sinfulness: the fault, he declared, lies with the priests and prophets: 'This was for the sins of her prophets and the iniquities of her priests, who shed in the midst of her the blood of the righteous' (4: 13). Yet despite such condemnation, the poem ends on a positive note: Zion will suffer, but her torment will not be forever.

The final lament is a prayer for the restoration of the nation; however, the author pointed out that God's anger is justified and he asked whether it has led to the total rejection of his chosen people:

Why dost thou forget us for ever,
why dost thou so long forsake us?
Restore us to thyself, O Lord, that we may be restored!
Renew our days as of old!
Or hast thou utterly rejected us?
Art thou exceedingly angry with us? (5: 20–22)

31. Ecclesiastes

1. First speech (1: 1–2: 26)
   1. Introduction (1: 1–3)
   2. Vanity (1: 4–2: 24)
      a. Vanity of life (1: 4–11)
      b. Vanity of wisdom (1: 12–18)
      c. Vanity of pleasure and wealth (2: 1–11)
      d. The fool and the wise (2: 12–17)
      e. Inheritance (2: 18–23)
      f. Contentment (2: 24–26)

2. Second speech (3: 1–5: 20)
   1. Prudence (3: 1–22)
      a. Time for everything (3: 1–9)
      b. Uselessness of striving (3: 10–15)
      c. Enjoy life (3: 16–22)
   2. Disappointment (4: 1–16)
      a. Oppression (4: 1–3)
      b. Life's trials (4: 4–12)
      c. Political fame (4: 13–16)
   3. Futility of self-seeking (5: 1–20)
      a. Warning against sin (5: 1–7)
      b. The oppressor and the covetous (5: 8–17)
      c. Accepting life (5: 18–20)

3. Third speech (6: 1–8: 17)
   1. Ambition and desire (6: 1–12)
   2. Prudence (7: 1–29)
      a. Choosing the better (7: 1–8)
      b. Wisdom and wealth (7: 9–14)
      c. Asceticism and excess (7: 15–18)
      d. Wisdom and folly (7: 19–25)
      e. Wicked womanhood (7: 26–29)

3. Expediency (8: 1–17)
   a. Acceptance of authority (8: 1–9)
   b. Judgement of the wicked (8: 10–13)
   c. Injustice (8: 14–15)
   d. Ways of God (8: 16–17)

4. Fourth speech (9: 1–12: 8)
   1. Make the best of life (9: 1–18)
      a. Death (9: 1–6)
      b. Enjoy life (9: 7–10)
      c. Chance (9: 11–12)
      d. Wisdom (9: 13–18)
   2. Life's uncertainties and folly (10: 1–20)
      a. Folly and wisdom (10: 1–11)
      b. Empty talk (10: 12–15)
      c. Maxims (10: 16–20)
   3. Life (11: 1–12: 8)
      a. Charity (11: 1–8)
      b. Misspent youth (11: 9–10)
      c. Live for God (12: 1–8)

5. Conclusion (12: 1–14)
   1. Preacher (12: 1–10)
   2. Preacher's message (12: 11–14)

Traditionally the Book of Ecclesiastes was ascribed to King Solomon, but in all likelihood it was written at a much later period in the history of ancient Israel. The word 'Ecclesiastes' is derived from the Septuagint – it is a Greek rendering of the Hebrew word 'Kohelet' (Teacher) by which the author was known. Unlike other books of the Bible, Ecclesiastes propounds a pessimistic philosophy of life. Thus, in the first chapter the author declares that all things are futile: 'Vanity of vanities, says the Preacher, vanity of vanities! All is vanity' (1: 2). Such a view is illustrated by a variety of examples. First, Ecclesiastes emphasizes the meaningless of the cycle of life. A generation comes and passes away, he writes, but the earth remains. This endless flow is full of weariness – 'Is there a thing of which it is said, "See, this is new"? It has been already, in the ages before us. There is no remembrance of former things, nor will there be any remembrance of later things yet to happen' (1: 10–11).

Ecclesiastes then states that he had ruled over Israel, and as king he sought to comprehend all things. He has seen everything – but it is all vanity and a striving after wind. Even wisdom is without purpose: 'For in much wisdom is much vexation, and he who increases knowledge increases sorrow' (1: 18). Similarly pleasure and wealth are futile pursuits:

> So I became great and surpassed all who were before me in Jerusalem; also my wisdom remained with me. And whatever my eyes desired I did not keep from them; I kept my heart from no pleasure, for my heart found pleasure in all my toil, and this was my reward for all my toil. Then I considered all that my hands had done and the toil I had spent in doing it, and behold, all was vanity and a striving after wind, and there was nothing to be gained under the sun. (2: 9–11)

All striving is ultimately meaningless, Ecclesiastes concluded, because death will overtake each person, the wise and the fool alike: 'For of the wise man as of the fool there is no enduring remembrance, seeing that in the days to come all will have been long forgotten' (2: 16).

In the second discourse Ecclesiastes reflects on life's pursuits. Here he appears to advance a fatalistic philosophy:

> For everything there is a season, and a time for every matter under heaven:
> a time to be born, and a time to die;
> a time to plant, and a time to pluck up what is planted;
> a time to kill, and a time to heal;
> a time to break down, and a time to build up;
> a time to weep, and a time to laugh;
> a time to mourn, and a time to dance;
> a time to cast away stones, and a time to gather stones together;
> a time to embrace, and a time to refrain from embracing;
> a time to seek, and a time to lose;
> a time to keep, and a time to cast away;
> a time to rend, and a time to sew;
> a time to keep silence, and a time to speak;
> a time to love, and a time to hate;
> a time for war, and a time for peace. (3: 1–8)

This cycle of human existence is fixed: all things are bound in an unceasing pattern. Both human beings and beasts go to the same place; there is no advantage for one over the other:

> For the fate of the sons of men and the fate of beasts is the same; as one

dies, so dies the other. They all have the same breath, and man has no advantage over the beasts; for all is vanity. All go to one place; all are from the dust, and all turn to dust again. (3: 19–20)

In chapter 4 Ecclesiastes turns to the disappointments of earthly existence. Life is full of oppression – the wicked frequently go unpunished and the innocent suffer. In the face of such injustice, Ecclesiastes concluded that it would be better not to have been born:

And I thought the dead who are already dead more fortunate than the living who are still alive; but better than both is he who has not yet been, and has not seen the evil deeds that are done under the sun. (4: 2)

Despite such pessimism, Ecclesiastes offered advice on how to make the most of one's futile existence. It is best, he argued, to enjoy whatever one is given:

Behold, what I have seen to be good and to be fitting is to eat and drink and find enjoyment in all the toil with which one toils under the sun the few days of his life which God has given him. (5: 18)

Although Ecclesiastes maintained that life is ultimately futile, in chapter 5 he none the less gave warnings against various sins: go to the house of the Lord, he urged; do not be rash with your mouth; when you vow a vow, do not delay fulfilling it; do not let your mouth lead you into sin. Such advice continues in chapter 7 where Ecclesiastes offers further counsel. Here a series of contrasts are made; in all cases, he recommended choosing what is best. Yet Ecclesiastes warned against being overzealous – moderation should be followed in all things:

In my vain life I have seen everything; there is a righteous man who perishes in his righteousness, and there is a wicked man who prolongs his life in evil-doing. Be not righteous overmuch, and do not make yourself overwise; why should you destroy yourself? Be not wicked overmuch, neither be a fool; why should you die before your time? (7: 15–17)

These meditations are followed by a reflection on the fickleness of women. Despairingly Ecclesiastes described their nature:

And I found more bitter than death the woman whose heart is snares and nets, and whose hands are fetters; he who pleases God escapes her, but the sinner is taken by her ... One man among a thousand I found, but a woman among all these I have not found. Behold, this alone I found, that God made man upright, but they have sought out many devices. (7: 26, 28–29)

Such pessimism is also reflected in Ecclesiastes' assessment of the consequences of sin. Unlike the prophets, he was unable to detect divine justice in the fate of the righteous and the wicked: 'there are righteous men to whom it happens according to the deeds of the wicked, and there are wicked men to whom it happens according to the deeds of the righteous' (8: 14). God's ways are inscrutable, and it is impossible to understand life's secrets:

When I applied my mind to know wisdom, and to see the business that is done on earth, how neither day nor night one's eyes see sleep; then I saw all the work of God, that man cannot find out the work that is done under the sun. However much many may toil in seeking, he will not find it out; even though a wise man claims to know, he cannot find it out. (8: 16–17)

The fourth speech returns to the theme of life's futility. Death is inevitable for all – one fate comes to the righteous and the wicked, the good and the evil, the clean and the unclean. Thus it is best to enjoy life:

Go, eat your bread with enjoyment, and drink your wine with a merry heart; for God has already approved what you do. Let your garments be always white; let not oil be lacking on your head. Enjoy life with the wife whom you love, all the days of your vain life which he has given you under the sun, because that is your portion in life and in your toil at which you toil under the sun. Whatever your hand finds to do, do it with your might; for there is no work or thought or knowledge or wisdom in Sheol, to which you are going. (9: 7–10)

Despite such gloomy thoughts, the book concludes in chapters 10 to 12 with a series of admonitions. Here Ecclesiastes emphasizes the importance of wisdom and charity and warns against a misspent youth. What is necessary, he maintains, in the final discourse, is to live according to God's decrees: 'The end of the matter; all has been heard. Fear God, and keep his commandments; for this is the whole duty of man. For God will bring every deed into judgement, with every secret thing, whether good or evil' (12: 13–14).

32. Esther

1. Court at Susa (1: 1–2: 23)
   1. Ahasuerus (1: 1–9)
   2. Queen Vashti (1: 10–22)
      a. Vashti's refusal (1: 10–12)
      b. Vashti's dismissal (1: 13–22)
   3. Esther as queen (2: 1–18)
      a. Search for a queen (2: 1–4)
      b. Esther (2: 5–11)
      c. Ahasuerus and Esther (2: 12–18)
   4. Plot to kill Ahasuerus (2: 19–23)

2. Mordecai and Haman (3: 1–9: 19)
   1. Elevation of Haman and Mordecai's refusal (3: 1–6)
   2. Haman's plot (3: 7–15)
   3. Mordecai and Esther (4: 1–17)
   4. Esther's intervention (5: 1–14)
      a. Appeal to Ahasuerus (5: 1–8)
      b. Haman's plan (5: 9–14)
   5. Deliverance of the Jews (6: 1–9: 19)
      a. Failure of Haman's plot (6: 1–14)
      b. Haman's defeat (7: 1–10)
      c. Mordecai's advancement (8: 1–2)
      d. Esther's request and Ahasuerus' decree (8: 3–14)
      e. Jewish victory (8: 15–9: 15)
      f. Festival of Purim (9: 16–19)

3. Purim (9: 20–10: 3)
   1. Festival of Purim (9: 20–28)
   2. Esther's approval (9: 29–32)
   3. Mordecai's power (10: 1–3)

The Book of Esther deals with the Jewish community in the town of Susa, the Persian capital, during the reign of King Xerxes in the fifth century BCE. The name Esther is derived from the Persian meaning 'star'. According to some scholars the book was written in the second century BCE; other scholars date it much earlier due to the number of Persian loan words contained in the book as well as its oriental atmosphere. Although the book emphasizes God's providential concern with the Jewish people, the name of God is absent. In Jewish practice the Book of Esther is read as part of the Purim festival.

The book opens by setting the scene – here the grandeur of King Ahasuerus is depicted. In the third year of his reign he gave a banquet which lasted for 180 days. When Queen Vashti was ordered to appear before the people, she refused. The king was incensed and his advisers were concerned that Vashti's action would encourage other women to treat their husbands with contempt. At their urging the king resolved to replace Vashti as queen. The king's attendants advised him to gather all beautiful young virgins to his harem in Susa so that he could choose a suitable substitute. Chapter 2 gives an account of Esther's background and selection into the harem:

> Now there was a Jew in Susa the capital whose name was Mordecai ... who had been carried away from Jerusalem among the captives carried away with Jeconiah king of Judah, whom Nebuchadnezzar king of Babylon had carried away. He had brought up Hadassah, that is Esther, the daughter of his uncle, for she had neither father nor mother; the maiden was beautiful and lovely, and when her father and her mother died, Mordecai adopted her as his own daughter. So when the king's order and his edict were proclaimed, and when many maidens were gathered in Susa the capital in custody of Hegai, Esther also was taken into the king's palace and put in custody of Hegai who had charge of the women. And the maiden pleased him and won his favour. (2: 5–9)

Esther, however, refrained from revealing her origins to the king at Mordecai's request. Eventually Esther became the king's favourite taking Vashti's place: 'the king loved Esther more than all the women, and she found grace and favour in his sight more than all the virgins, so that he set the royal crown on her head and made her queen instead of Vashti' (2: 17).

Subsequently Mordecai discovered a plot to overthrow the king which he revealed to Esther; Esther then told this to the king and the men who were guilty of treason were hanged. At this time the king

promoted Haman as chief adviser and all except Mordecai bowed
down to him. When Haman learned that Mordecai disobeyed the
command to pay him homage, he was furious and sought to destroy
all the Jews in the kingdom. Speaking to the king he disclosed his
plan:

> There is a certain people scattered abroad and dispersed among the
> peoples in all the provinces of your kingdom; their laws are different
> from those of every other people, and they do not keep the king's laws,
> so that it is not for the king's profit to tolerate them. If it pleases the
> king, let it be decreed that they be destroyed. (3: 8–9)

King Ahasuerus gave his consent to Haman's scheme, and his
secretaries were summoned to issue an edict giving orders to kill all
Jews on the thirteenth of Adar and confiscate their possessions.
When Mordecai heard of this pronouncement, he appealed to Esther.
The queen then put on her royal robes, stood in the inner court of
the king's palace and entreated her husband to invite Haman to
dinner at the palace. Although Haman bragged to his friends about
this invitation, he was vexed by Mordecai's refusal to pay obeisance
to him. At the urging of his wife and others, he decided to construct
a gallows and request that Mordecai be hanged on them.

Haman's plans, however, were foiled. When the chronicles of the
king's deeds were read out to King Ahasuerus, the king discovered
that Mordecai had uncovered the plot against him. He then asked if
Mordecai had been rewarded – his attendants replied that nothing
had been done. At this stage Haman entered the outer court of the
palace seeking to persuade the king to hang Mordecai on the
gallows that he had constructed. After Haman entered the king's
presence, the king asked him what should be done to someone he
wished to honour. Believing that the king was referring to himself,
he said:

> For the man whom the king delights to honour, let royal robes be
> brought, which the king has worn, and the horse which the king has
> ridden, and on whose head a royal crown is set; and let the robes and
> the horse be handed over to one of the king's most noble princes; let
> him array the man whom the king delights to honour, and let him
> conduct the man on horseback through the open square of the city,
> proclaiming before him: 'Thus shall it be done to the man whom the
> king delights to honour.' (6: 7–9)

While Mordecai was treated in this fashion, Haman went to the banquet at the palace. On the second day as they were drinking wine, the king told Esther that he would grant any request she made. Pleading for her people she declared: 'If I have found favour in your sight, O king, and if it please the king, let my life be given me at my petition, and my people at my request' (7: 3). King Ahasuerus asked Esther who had plotted against the Jews; in reply she declared: 'A foe and enemy! This wicked Haman!' (7: 6). In accord with her wish, Haman was subsequently hanged on the gallows which he had prepared for Mordecai.

Chapters 8 to 10 conclude with an account of the glorification of the Jewish people. At the king's request secretaries wrote to the governors of all the provinces where Jews lived allowing them to defend themselves from attack. To commemorate this victory over the nation's enemies, the festival of Purim was inaugurated:

Therefore they called these days Purim, after the term Pur. And, therefore, because ... of what they had faced in this matter, and of what had befallen them, the Jews ordained and took it upon themselves and their descendants and all who joined them, that without fail they would keep these two days according to what was written and at the time appointed every year, that these days should be remembered and kept throughout every generation, in every family, province, and city, and that these days of Purim should never fall into disuse among the Jews, nor should the commemoration of these days cease among their descendants. (9: 26–28)

33. Daniel

According to tradition Daniel lived in Babylonia in the sixth century BCE during the last days of the Babylonian empire and the emergence of the Medes and the Persians. The first part of the book (chapters 1 to 6) contains six stories about Daniel and his friends; the second part (chapters 7 to 12) relates a series of visions of the four kingdoms under whom the Jews would live from the time of the conquest of Jerusalem until the establishment of their own kingdom. Although some conservative scholars believe the book originated in the sixth century BCE, most scholars contend that it was composed in the second century BCE.

The book commences with an introduction to Daniel and his three companions who were deported to Babylonia during the reign of Nebuchadnezzar. Faithful to the traditions of their ancestors, Daniel and his friends refused to eat the king's food; as a result they were granted wisdom and knowledge. During this period Nebuchadnezzar had a troubling dream which he asked his servants to explain to him. When they failed to do so, Daniel was brought before the king. Daniel then told the king his dream and offered an interpretation:

> This was the dream; now we will tell the king its interpretation. You, O king, the king of kings, to whom the God of heaven has given the kingdom, the power, and the might, and the glory ... After you shall arise another kingdom inferior to you, and yet a third kingdom of bronze, which shall rule over all the earth. And there shall be a fourth kingdom, strong as iron ... it shall break and crush all these. (2: 36–37, 39–40)

After Nebuchadnezzar heard these words, he praised the God of Israel who had revealed the dream and its interpretation to Daniel and he honoured him with high office.

Chapter 3 makes a transition from such tribute to Daniel. Here the king ordered that a gold statue of himself be set up near Babylon, insisting that all his officials bow down to it. Shadrach, Meshach and Abednego, however, refused to do so, and as a punishment they were cast into a fiery furnace. To the king's amazement they did not perish, and he praised the Lord:

> Blessed be the God of Shadrach, Meshach and Abednego, who has sent his angel and delivered his servants, who trusted in him, and set at naught the king's command, and yielded up their bodies rather than serve and worship any god except their own God. (3: 28)

The next two chapters relate events connected with Nebuchadnezzar's dream about a tree that grew to heaven but was subsequently cut down. On hearing the king's words Daniel was dismayed, but at the king's urging he offered an interpretation of the dream's meaning. The tree, he declared, 'it is you, O king, who have grown and become strong' (4: 22). Yet he went on to explain that it was God's decree that the king would be doomed unless he repented of his sins: 'you shall be driven from among men, and your dwelling shall be like the beasts of the field; you shall be made to eat grass like an ox, and you shall be wet with the dew of heaven' (4: 25).

As Daniel predicted, this tragedy befell the king – twelve months later as he surveyed his kingdom from the roof of the palace, a voice from heaven proclaimed; 'O King Nebuchadnezzar, to you it is spoken: The kingdom has departed from you, and you shall be driven from among men, and your dwelling shall be with the beasts of the fields; and you shall be made to eat grass like an ox' (4: 31–

32). Immediately this word was fulfilled, and the king wandered in the field; his body was wet with the dew of heaven, his hair grew as long as eagles' feathers, and his nails were like birds' claws. Eventually, however, the king's reason returned, and he blessed God.

The narrative continues with an account of a feast given by Belshazzar, Nebuchadnezzar's successor. After ordering that the vessels and gold seized from the temple in Jerusalem be brought out, the fingers of a man's hand appeared and wrote on a wall. When the king's wise men failed to interpret the writing, Daniel was summoned to the palace. After reciting the events that had befallen Nebuchadnezzar, Daniel warned the king not to be haughty:

> but you have lifted up yourself against the Lord of heaven; and the vessels of his house have been brought in before you, and you and your lords, your wives, and your concubines have drunk wine from them; and you have praised the gods of silver and gold, of bronze, iron, wood, and stone, which do not see or hear or know, but the God in whose hand is your breath, and whose are all your ways, you have not honoured. (5: 23)

Daniel then explained that the words written on the wall – MENE, MENE, TEKEL and PARSIN – should be understood as indicating the end of the empire: 'MENE, God has numbered the days of your kingdom and brought it to an end; TEKEL, you have been weighed in the balance and found wanting; PERES, your kingdom is divided and given to the Medes and Persians' (5: 26–28). On that night the king was slain and Darius the Mede became king.

Under Darius, Daniel continued to flourish, but his rivals were jealous of his position. With the king's permission, a law was instituted which prohibited anyone from worshipping a god other than Darius. Disregarding this edict Daniel continued to pray to God, and as a consequence was cast into the lion's den. However, when the king went to see him there, he discovered that Daniel had not been devoured. The king then commanded that Daniel be taken out of the lion's den and his enemies and their families be cast there in his place. Impressed by this miraculous event the king wrote to all the peoples in his realm insisting that they should pay homage to the God of the Jews.

Chapters 7 to 12 consist of a series of dreams foretelling future events. The first was a vision of four beasts: a lion, a bear, a leopard, and another beast terrifying in appearance. Each of these beasts represents an empire – the lion corresponds to Babylonia; the bear to the Medo-Persian empire; the leopard to that of Alexander the Great; the fourth to Rome. The theme is that Babylonia will be succeeded by these other empires until God's everlasting reign will be established. Here Daniel refers to one like the Son of Man who will be given dominion over the earth:

> and behold, with the clouds of heaven there came one like a son of man, and he came to the Ancient of Days and was presented before him. And to him was given dominion and glory and kingdom, that all peoples, nations, and languages should serve him. (7: 13–14)

In the next vision a ram representing the Medo-Persian kings is succeeded by a goat, denoting the king of the empire established by Alexander the Great. According to some scholars, 8: 23–25 refers to the coming of the Syrian king Antiochus IV, an enemy of the Jews: 'And at the latter end of their rule, when the transgressors have reached their full measure, a king of bold countenance, one who understands riddles, shall arise. His power shall be great, and he shall cause fearful destruction, and shall succeed in what he does, and destroy mighty men and the people of the saints.'

These visions are followed by Daniel's prayer for deliverance despite the nation's sinfulness:

> O, Lord, the great and terrible God, who keepest covenant and steadfast love with those who love him and keep his commandments, we have sinned and done wrong and acted wickedly and rebelled, turning aside from thy commandments and ordinances; and we have not listened to thy servants the prophets ... O Lord, according to all thy righteous acts, let thy anger and thy wrath turn away from thy city Jerusalem, thy holy hill ... O Lord, hear; O Lord, forgive; O Lord, give heed and act; delay not, for thy own sake, O my God, because thy city and thy people are called by thy name. (9: 4–6, 16, 19)

Daniel's prayer is followed in chapter 10 by a vision of the last days. On the twenty-fourth day of the first month, a man clothed in linen whose loins were girded with rich gold of Uphaz appeared on the Tigris. In several speeches he strengthened and encouraged Daniel, revealing to him later kings who would reign during the period of Greek rule in the region. Of particular importance is the reference in 11: 31 to an abomination that brings desolation: 'Forces from him shall appear and profane the temple and fortress, and shall take away the continual burnt offering. And they shall set up the abomination that makes desolate' — this is widely interpreted as referring to the attack on religious observance that took place during the reign of Antiochus IV in 169 BCE. This passage is followed by prophecies concerning an unknown king, and a final assurance that the Lord will remain faithful to his people:

> And there shall be a time of trouble, such as never has been since there was a nation till that time; but at that time your people shall be delivered, every one whose name shall be found written in the book. And many of those who sleep in the dust of the earth shall awake, some to everlasting life, and some to shame and everlasting contempt. And those who are wise shall shine like the brightness of the firmament; and those who turn many to righteousness, like the stars for ever and ever. (12: 1–3)

34. Ezra

The Book of Ezra concerns the return of Jewish exiles from Babylon to Jerusalem. Named after its principal character, Ezra, the book contains several different sources: (1) Hebrew documents relating to Zerubbabel; (2) extracts from Aramaic documents (4: 8–6: 18); and (3) Ezra's personal writing (7: 27–9: 15). The book covers two major periods: the return of the exiles under Zerubbabel (1–6) and the return under Ezra (7–10). According to 7: 7, Ezra's return took place in the seventh year of the reign of Artaxerxes. This has been variously interpreted as occurring in 458 BCE during the reign of Artaxerxes I (465–424 BCE), assuming that a scribe erroneously changed the thirty-seventh year to the seventh year of Artaxerxes' reign; or in 397 during the reign of Artaxerxes II (404–358 BCE).

The book opens with an account of the exiles' return from Babylonia – the first verses appear to follow on from 2 Chronicles. Chapter 1 records Cyrus' decree:

> The Lord, the God of heaven, has given me all the kingdoms of the earth, and he has charged me to build him a house at Jerusalem, which is in Judah. Whoever is among you of all his people, may his God be with him, and let him go up to Jerusalem, which is in Judah, and rebuild the

house of the Lord, the God of Israel – he is the God who is in Jerusalem; and let each survivor, in whatever place he sojourns, be assisted by the men of his place with silver and gold, with goods and with beasts, besides freewill offerings for the house of God which is in Jerusalem. (1: 2–4)

In response to this edict, the leaders of the Jewish nation made extensive preparations for this journey. The returning exiles were given vessels of silver and gold as well as goods and beasts, and Cyrus also brought out the vessels of the temple which Nebuchadnezzar had carried away from Jerusalem.

Chapter 2 continues with a depiction of the first return under Zerubbabel – here a long list of the exiles is presented in 2: 1–70. Chapter 3 continues with a description of the rebuilding of the altar by Jeshua with his fellow priests and Zerubbabel with his kinsmen. They set up the altar and offered burnt offerings to God; in addition, they kept the Festival of Booths and offered daily sacrifices as well as burnt offerings for the new moon and at all the appointed feasts. At this stage there was no temple in Jerusalem, but in the second year after their return Zerubbabel and Jeshua with the priests and the Levites and all who had come to Jerusalem began the process of reconstruction accompanied by music and song:

And when the builders laid the foundation of the temple of the Lord, the priests in their vestments came forward with trumpets, and the Levites, the sons of Asaph, with their cymbals, to praise the Lord, according to the directions of David king of Israel; and they sang responsively, praising and giving thanks to the Lord, 'For he is good, for his steadfast love endures for ever toward Israel.' And the people shouted with a great shout, when they praised the Lord, because the foundation of the house of the Lord was laid. (3: 10–11)

Many of the old men who had seen the first temple wept as they saw the foundation of the temple being laid: 'so that the people could not distinguish the sound of the joyful shout from the sound of the people's weeping, for the people shouted with a great shout, and the sound was heard afar' (3: 13).

When those who remained in the northern part of the country heard that the exiles were rebuilding the temple, they offered their assistance. But Zerubbabel, Jeshua and the leaders of the nation refused their help because they were viewed as having been contaminated by pagan practices. As a result, these northerners attempted to frustrate their plans by appealing to the king of Persia:

> To Artaxerxes the king: Your servants, the men of the province Beyond the River, send greeting. And now be it known to the king that the Jews who came up from you to us have gone to Jerusalem. They are rebuilding that rebellious and wicked city; they are finishing the walls and repairing the foundations. Now be it known to the king that, if this city is rebuilt and the walls finished, they will not pay tribute, custom or toll, and the royal revenue will be impaired. Now because we eat the salt of the palace and it is not fitting for us to witness the king's dishonour, therefore we send and inform the king. (4: 11–14)

In reply the king decreed that a letter should be written forbidding the exiles to continue:

> And I made a decree, and search has been made, and it has been found that this city from of old has risen against kings, and that rebellion and sedition have been made in it ... Therefore make a decree that these men be made to cease, and that this city be not rebuilt, until a decree is made by me. (4: 19, 21)

Despite this setback, the prophets Haggai and Zechariah prophesied to the Jews in Judah and Jerusalem encouraging them in their efforts, and work on the temple began again under Zerubbabel and Jeshua. Although an official investigation was undertaken to determine the extent of this rebuilding, King Darius discovered Cyrus' original decree and gave his permission that the temple be rebuilt. In addition, he stated that whatever provisions were needed to complete this project should be supplied:

> And whatever is needed – young bulls, rams, or sheep for burnt offerings to the God of heaven, wheat, salt, wine, or oil as the priests at Jerusalem require – let that be given to them day by day without fail, that they may offer pleasing sacrifices to the God of heaven, and pray for the life of the king and his sons. (6: 9–10)

In the sixth year of the reign of Darius the king the project was finished, and the people dedicated the temple to God:

> And the people of Israel, the priests and the Levites, and the rest of the returned exiles, celebrated the dedication of this house of God with joy. They offered at the dedication of this house of God one hundred bulls, two hundred rams, four hundred lambs, and as a sin offering for all Israel

twelve he-goats, according to the number of the tribes of Israel. (6: 16–17)

Chapter 7 continues with an account of Ezra's return to the land. In the seventh year of Artaxerxes' reign, Ezra went to Jerusalem accompanied by priests, Levites, singers, gatekeepers and temple servants. Chapters 7 to 8 record Artaxerxes' commission to Ezra to return to the land as well as a list of the returning remnant. On his arrival, however, Ezra was dismayed by the extent of the mixed marriages that had taken place. In despair he rent his garments and mantle, pulled hair from his head, and sat appalled. Eventually he prayed to God:

> O my God, I am ashamed and blush to lift my face to thee, my God, for our iniquities have risen higher than our heads, and our guilt has mounted up to the heavens. From the days of our fathers to this day we have been in great guilt; and for our iniquities we, our kings, and our priests have been given into the hand of the kings of the lands, to the sword, to captivity, to plundering, and to utter shame, as at this day ... And now, O our God, what shall we say after this? For we have forsaken thy commandments, which though didst command by thy servants the prophets, saying, 'The land which you are entering, to take possession of it, is a land unclean with the pollutions of the peoples of the lands, with their abominations which have filled it from end to end with their uncleanness. (9: 6–7, 10–11)

Determined to reform the nation, Ezra compelled all of Israel to put away their foreign wives:

> And Ezra the priest stood up and said to them, 'You have trespassed and married foreign women, and so increased the guilt of Israel. Now then make confession to the Lord the God of your fathers, and do his will; separate yourselves from the peoples of the land and from the foreign wives. (10: 10–11)

The book concludes with a list of offending priests who had married foreign wives whom they agreed to put away along with their children.

35. Nehemiah

1. Nehemiah's reforms (1: 1–7: 73)
   1. Introduction (1: 1–2: 20)
      a. Nehemiah's sorrow (1: 1–11)
      b. Nehemiah's request to go to Jerusalem (2: 1–8)
      c. Journey to Jerusalem (2: 9–16)
      d. Rebuilding the temple (2: 17–20)
   2. Rebuilding the walls (3: 1–6: 19)
      a. Workers (3: 1–32)
      b. Opposition to work (4: 1–6: 19)
         i.   Sanballat and Tobiah (4: 1–23)
         ii. Disaffection among the Jewish community (5: 1–19)
         iii. Further difficulties (6: 1–19)
   3. New order in Jerusalem (7: 1–73)
      a. Hanai and Hananiah (7: 1–4)
      b. Returning exiles (7: 5–73)

2. Reading of the law and renewing of the covenant (8: 1–10: 39)
   1. Reading and explanation of the law (8: 1–12)
   2. Feast of Tabernacles (8: 13–18)
   3. Covenant renewed (9: 1–10: 39)
      a. Separation from unbelievers (9: 1–5)
      b. Penitential psalm (9: 6–38)
      c. Those who signed the covenant (10: 1–27)
      d. Covenant (10: 28–39)
         i.   Mixed marriages (10: 28–30)
         ii. Sabbath (10: 31)
         iii. Covenantal obligations (10: 32–39)

3. Reconstitution of Jerusalem (11: 1–13: 31)
   1. Reopening of Jerusalem (11: 1–2)
   2. Leaders of the people (11: 3–24)
   3. Villages outside Jerusalem (11: 25–36)

4. Priests and Levites (12: 1–26)
5. City walls (12: 27–43)
6. Collectors, singers and gatekeepers (12: 44–47)
7. Final reforms (13: 1–31)
   a. People separated (13: 1–3)
   b. Tobiah's furniture (13: 4–9)
   c. Support of the priesthood (13: 10–14)
   d. Sabbath reforms (13: 15–22)
   e. Marriage reforms (13: 23–29)
   f. Conclusion (13: 31)

According to modern scholarship, the Book of Nehemiah and the Book of Ezra form a single unit based on two separate sources: (1) material which concludes the Chronicler's history (Ezra 1–10; Nehemiah 8–10), and (2) the memoirs of Nehemiah (1–7, 11–13). In all likelihood these sources were put together by the same author, but it is difficult to determine when this occurred. There is also considerable uncertainty about whether Nehemiah followed Ezra or vice versa. In any event, Nehemiah was a cupbearer of Artaxerxes, the Persian king. His call came as a result of a disturbing report about the conditions in Jerusalem brought to him by a kinsman Hanani. With Artaxerxes' permission, he travelled to Judah. The first part of the book of Nehemiah is autobiographical in character – this material and the book of Ezra provide most of our knowledge of the history of the Jewish nation from 538–430 BCE.

The Book of Nehemiah opens with an account of Nehemiah's sorrow on hearing a report about the desperate conditions in Jerusalem: 'The survivors there in the province who escaped exile are in great trouble and shame; the wall of Jerusalem is broken down, and its gates are destroyed by fire' (1: 3). When Nehemiah heard these words, he wept and mourned for his people. Recounting the sinfulness of the nation, he prayed to God for forgiveness. In chapter 2, Nehemiah approaches the king and requests that he be allowed to return to Jerusalem: 'If it pleases the king, and if your servant has found favour in your sight, that you send me to Judah, to the city of my father's sepulchres, that I may rebuild it' (2: 5).

With the king's permission, Nehemiah set out for Judah, but when news of this reached Sanballat and Tobiah they were displeased. Secretly Nehemiah inspected the temple walls and resolved to begin the task of rebuilding them; despite Sanballat and Tobiah's opposition, work commenced on the walls and gates of the city. In chapter 3 each of the city's ten gates are identified along with those who embarked on the task of reconstruction. None the less Nehemiah's opponents rallied together in an attempt to disrupt this work. Sanballat ridiculed Nehemiah's efforts in the presence of his brethren and all of those in Samaria: 'What are these feeble Jews doing? Will they restore things? Will they sacrifice? Will they finish up in a day? Will they revive the stones out of the heaps of rubbish, and burned up ones at that?' (4: 2).

Tobiah, too, denounced such aspirations: 'Yes, what they are building – if a fox goes up on it he will break down their stone wall!' (4: 3).

As time passed, the efforts involved in rebuilding and protecting the walls became overwhelming – public discontent, financial difficulties and a food shortage all combined to create disenchantment with the project. Eventually Nehemiah was unable to ignore the situation; he demanded that those who benefited financially from this work pay back interest charges and restore property that had been mortgaged to secure loans. In addition he declared that he would join in the suffering endured by the population by refusing his food allowance as governor. As work progressed, Sanballat continued to oppose the rebuilding by spreading a rumour that Nehemiah intended to use Jerusalem as a base for launching an attack on Artaxerxes: 'It is reported among the nations, and Geshem also says it, that you and the Jews intend to rebel; that is why you are building the wall; and you wish to become their king, according to this report' (6: 6).

Undeterred Nehemiah pressed ahead with the programme of rebuilding, and on the twenty-fifth of Elul the wall was finished. The doors were put in place; the governors, singers and Levites appointed; and Hanani and Hananiah installed as governors of Jerusalem. Nehemiah then decreed:

> Let not the gates of Jerusalem be opened until the sun is hot; and while they are still standing guard let them shut and bar the doors. Appoint guards from among the inhabitants of Jerusalem, each to his station and each opposite his own house. (7: 3)

Chapter 7 continues with a list of those who had returned from exile paralleling the list in Ezra 2: 1–70.

Following this catalogue of names, there is a description of the reading of the law: in the seventh month, the people gathered at the

Water Gate and told Ezra to bring the book of the law before the assembly. There he read it from early morning to midday in the presence of the men and women who had gathered there:

And Ezra opened the book in the sight of all the people, for he was above the people; and when he opened it all the people stood. And Ezra blessed the Lord, the great God; and all the people answered, 'Amen, Amen,' lifting up their hands; and they bowed their heads and worshipped the Lord with their faces to the ground. (8: 5–6)

Ezra and the Levites explained the meaning of what was read to the people. Then Ezra, Nehemiah who was governor, and the Levites declared that the day was holy to the Lord, and that the nation should not be grieved: as a result the people departed, rejoicing that they had understood what had been read to them. After this the Feast of Tabernacles was celebrated in accordance with the commandments contained in Scripture – during this period Ezra read again from the book of the law.

Due to these events, the people confessed their sins; they assembled with fasting and in sackcloth and prayed to God. Ezra, too, recited a penitential psalm recalling God's dealings with the Israelites from the time of Abraham to the Exodus from Egypt, the wandering in the desert, and the conquest of the land. Yet despite God's graciousness, his chosen people rebelled against him. On this day, however, they resolved to reform their ways:

They did not serve thee in their kingdom, and in thy great goodness which thou gavest them, and in the large and rich land which thou didst set before them; and they did not turn from their wicked works … Because of all this we make a firm covenant and write it, and our princes, our Levites, and our priests set their seal to it. (9: 35, 38)

Those who signed this covenant made a series of promises – not to intermarry, to observe the Sabbath, and to carry out specific covenantal obligations including temple worship.

Chapter 11 continues with Nehemiah's determination to repopulate Jerusalem. Once the walls and gates had been rebuilt, it was imperative that the Jewish community be re-established in the city – hence the leaders of the people agreed to reside there as well as families chosen by lot. There follows a list of the leading Jews who settled in Jerusalem along with the priests and Levites. At the end of chapter 12 there is a description of the dedication of the city walls, apparently from Nehemiah's memoirs:

> And at the dedication of the wall of Jerusalem they sought the Levites
> in all their places, to bring them to Jerusalem to celebrate the dedication
> with gladness, with thanksgivings and with singing, with cymbals,
> harps and lyres ... Then I brought up the princes of Judah upon the
> wall, and appointed two great companies which gave thanks and went
> in procession ... The other company of those who gave thanks went to
> the left, and I followed them with half of the people, upon the wall ...
> And they offered great sacrifices that day and rejoiced, for God had
> made them rejoice with great joy; the women and children also rejoiced.
> And the joy of Jerusalem was heard afar off. (12: 27, 31, 38, 43)

At this event the Book of Moses was read in the hearing of the
people which included a reference to the exclusion of the
Ammonites and Moabites from the assembly of God. Having
accomplished the task of rebuilding the city, Nehemiah returned to
the court of Artaxerxes but subsequently requested permission to
return to Jerusalem. On his arrival he discovered that one of the
storerooms which had been set aside for tithes and temple offerings
had been taken by Tobiah for his personal use. This, however, was
not the only infraction that had taken place – the portions reserved
from the Levites had not been given to them, forcing them to labour
in the fields. Nehemiah rectified this situation, thereby insuring the
proper administration of the temple. Even so, other abuses were
uncovered: Sabbath regulations were not being followed, and
intermarriage remained a serious problem. Thus the Book of
Nehemiah ends on a ominous note; despite Nehemiah's energetic
rebuilding of the city, the people had again turned away from God's
commandments.

36. 1 and 2 Chronicles

b. David's plans (22: 2–19)
c. Levites (23: 1 27: 34)
d. David's abdication (28: 1–29: 30)

3. Solomon (2 Chronicles 1: 1–9: 31)
1. Inauguration (1: 1–17)
2. Temple (2: 1–7: 22)
    a. Contracts and building work (2: 1–3: 17)
    b. Minor furnishings (4: 1–22)
    c. The ark (5: 1–7: 22)
3. Solomon's rule (8: 1–9: 31)
    a. Commerce and urban restoration (8: 1–16)
    b. Benefits (8: 17–9: 31)

4. Kings of Judah (2 Chronicles 10: 1–36: 23)
1. Israelite dynasty (10: 1–16: 14)
    a. Rehoboam (10: 1–12: 16)
    b. Jeroboam (13: 1–22)
    c. Asa (14: 1–16: 14)
2. Social unrest (17: 1–25: 28)
    a. Jehoshaphat (17: 1–20: 37)
    b. Athaliah (21: 1–23: 31)
    c. Joash and Amaziah (24: 1–25: 28)
3. Book of prophecy (26: 1–32: 33)
    a. Uzziah (26: 1–23)
    b. Isaiah (27: 1–28: 27)
    c. Hezekiah (29: 1–32: 33)
4. Judah's disillusionment (33: 1–36: 23)
    a. Manasseh (33: 1–25)
    b. Josiah (34: 1–35: 27)
    c. Babylonian officials (36: 1–23)

The Hebrew title of the book of Chronicles means 'Words of the Days'. 1 and 2 Chronicles were originally one book, but it was separated into two units by the Septuagint translators. In the Jewish Bible it is the last book, whereas in the Septuagint and Vulgate it is placed after the Book of Kings. According to some scholars it was written about 300 BCE on the basis of genealogies in 1 Chronicles 3: 17–24 and Nehemiah 12: 10, 11, 22. Other scholars, however, have pointed out the similarity in language between the Book of Chronicles and Ezra's memoirs in 7: 27–29: 15, suggesting that Ezra was the author of Chronicles. In any event, it is clear that a number of older sources were utilized in the composition of these books including genealogies, court records of Israel and Judah, and the writings of the prophets, Samuel, Nathan, Gad, Ahijah, Shemaiah, Iddo, Jehu and Isaiah. In common with the Books of Samuel and Kings, the author of Chronicles used similar material, yet there are important differences: the northern kingdom is generally ignored; references to the deficiencies of David and Solomon are eliminated; and the numbers of Israelites are rounded off and usually larger than those given in other books. Further, the Chronicler pays particular attention to the temple and to the rule of David – his intention was most likely to assure post-exilic Jews of the continuity of their traditions from Davidic times.

1 Chronicles commences with an account of the genealogies of Israel – here there is no attempt to provide a setting for the early history of the nation. The purpose of this long list of individuals is to demonstrate that there is an unbroken continuity until the time of the monarchy. Chapter 10, however, affirms a detailed account of the reign of David, beginning with a narrative of Saul's closing days and death. No background information is offered; instead there is simply a brief depiction of Saul's suicide. According to 1 Chronicles, Saul

> died for his unfaithfulness; he was unfaithful to the Lord in that he did not keep the command of the Lord, and also consulted a medium, seeking guidance, and did not seek guidance from the Lord. Therefore the Lord slew him, and turned the kingdom over to David the son of Jesse. (10: 13–14)

David was then acclaimed king and captured Jerusalem. In the recital of David's glorious deeds, prominence is given to his capture of the ark:

> And David and all Israel went up to Ba-alah, that is, to Kiriath-jearim which belongs to Judah, to bring up from there the ark of God, which is called by the name of the Lord who sits enthroned above the cherubim ... And David and all Israel were making merry before God with all their might, with song and lyres and harps and tambourines and cymbals and trumpets. (13: 6, 8)

In the chapters which follow the events of David's kingship are developed in detail including the construction of his palace, his defeat of the Philistines, and the transfer of the ark to Jerusalem – as a result of God's favour, David gave thanks to the Lord in chapter 16 with a psalm of gratitude. Now that the ark was in Jerusalem, David was convinced that a house of worship should be built. The Lord, however, declared that the temple should be constructed by his successor: 'When your days are fulfilled to go to be with your fathers, I will raise up your offspring after you, one of your own sons, and I will establish his kingdom. He shall build a house for me, and I will establish his throne for ever' (17: 11–12). Chapters 18 to 20 continue this narrative with a series of military victories which were attributed to God's providence This is followed by an account of the census, paralleled in 2 Samuel 24: 1–25. In the Book of Samuel the desire for a census is attributed to the Lord, but here it is due to Satan. Because the Lord was displeased with this action, he smote Israel with a pestilence resulting in the death of 70,000 men.

After these occurrences, the scene shifts to preparations for the building of the temple. David was unable to complete this project himself because his hands were stained with blood on account of his involvement in warfare: here he explains to his son Solomon why he must undertake this task:

> My son, I had it in my heart to build a house to the name of the Lord my God. But the word of the Lord came to me saying, 'You have shed much blood and have waged great wars; you shall not build a house to my name, because you have shed so much blood before me upon the earth. Behold, a son shall be born to you; he shall be a man of peace ... He shall build a house for my name (22: 7–9, 10).

The instructions for this task are set out in chapters 23 to 27 dealing with the Levites, the division of the priests, the arrangements for music, the divisions of the gatekeepers, the nature of the treasuries, the appointment of officers and judges, and the designation of military and civil officials.

In the next section the transition from the reign of David to Solomon is described. Here David explains that he had intended to build a house for the ark, but that it was God's intention that this labour be entrusted to his son. In chapter 29 Solomon is recognized as David's successor and enthroned as king:

> And they made Solomon the son of David king ... and they anointed him as prince for the Lord, and Zadok as priest. Then Solomon sat on the throne of the Lord as king instead of David his father; and he prospered, and all Israel obeyed him. (29: 22–23)

2 Chronicles continues this account of the early monarchy by focusing on the construction of the temple. In chapter 1 Solomon prays for wisdom from the Lord; the next chapter outlines the preparations for the construction of the temple, and in chapter 3 the building of the temple is described in detail, concentrating on its site, dimensions, and furnishing as well as the material used in its creation. When all the work was finished, the ark was brought to the temple and Solomon delivered an address on its dedication:

> Blessed be the Lord, the God of Israel, who with his hand has fulfilled what he promised with his mouth to David my father, saying. 'Since the day that I brought my people out of the land of Egypt, I chose no city in all the tribes of Israel in which to build a house, that my name might be there, and I chose no man as prince over my people Israel; but I have chosen Jerusalem that my name may be there and I have chosen David to be over my people Israel ... Now the Lord has fulfilled his promise which he made; for I have risen in the place of David my father, and sit on the throne of Israel, as the Lord promised, and I have built the house for the name of the Lord, the God of Israel.' (6: 4–6, 10)

Standing before the altar in the presence of the assembly of Israel, Solomon knelt and prayed to the Lord; in response God sent down fire from heaven which consumed the burnt offerings and sacrifices that had been placed on the altar. The concluding chapters of this section depict the grandeur of Solomon's reign and his wisdom.

Chapters 10 to 36 continue the narrative of Israel's history with a chronicle of events from the time of Solomon to the exile – here there are parallels with the account in 1 Kings 12 to 2 Kings 25. None the less, there are important differences: 2 Chronicles draws on additional material and focuses solely on the southern kingdom. In all likelihood the intention of the Chronicler was to enable the community in Judah which had returned from exile to gain an understanding of its previous history. The first section opens with a discussion of the division between the northern and southern kingdoms: the feud between Rehoboam and Jeroboam led to the division of the country into two nations. This survey continues in chapter 11 with the history of Rehoboam and his descendants.

The narrative continues in chapters 11 to 27 with the history of Rehoboam and his successors, paralleling the Book of Kings: chapter 13 records the reign of Abijah; chapters 14 to 16 of Asa; chapter 17 of Jehosophat; chapter 21 of Jehoram; chapters 22 to 23 of Ahaziah and Athaliah; chapter 24 of Joash; chapter 25 of Amaziah; chapter 26 of Uzziah. This is followed in chapter 28 by a presentation of the apostasy of Ahaz who is depicted as a wholly corrupt king who lapsed into paganism and thereby threatened the future of the kingdom:

> Ahaz was twenty years old when he began to reign, and he reigned sixteen years in Jerusalem. And he did not do what was right in the eyes of the Lord, like his father David, but walked in the ways of the kings of Israel. He even made molten images for the Baals; and he burned incense in the valley of the son of Hinnom, and he burned his sons as an offering, according to the abominable practices of the nations whom the Lord drove out before the people of Israel. (28: 1–3)

In chapters 29 to 32 Ahaz's successor, Hezekiah, is depicted as a righteous reformer who attempted to reverse the policies of his predecessors. Here the establishment of the Passover festival was of particular importance, symbolizing the return of the people to ancient ways:

> Hezekiah sent to all Israel and Judah, and wrote letters also to Ephraim and Manasseh, that they should come to the house of the Lord at Jerusalem, to keep the passover to the Lord the God of Israel ... So couriers went throughout all Israel and Judah with letters from the king and his princes, as the king had commanded, saying, 'O people of Israel, return to the Lord, the God of Abraham, Isaac and Israel, that he may turn again to the remnant of you who have escaped from the hand of the kings of Assyria.' (30: 1, 6)

Hezekiah was succeeded by Manasseh. Although 2 Kings 21: 1–18 portrays him in negative terms, the Chronicler in chapter 33 stresses his attempt to eliminate pagan practices from the cult. His successor, Amon, however, continued with the evil practices of previous kings and was assassinated.

In chapters 34 to 35 the reforming rule of Josiah is described at length, emphasizing the discovery of the book of the law and its effect on the people:

> Then the king sent and gathered together all the elders of Judah and Jerusalem. And the king went up to the house of the Lord, with all the men of Judah and the inhabitants of Jerusalem and the priests and the Levites, all the people both great and small; and he read in their hearing all the words of the book of the covenant which had been found in the house of the Lord. And the king stood in his place and made a covenant

before the Lord, to walk after the Lord and to keep his commandments and his testimonies and his statutes, with all his heart and all his soul, to perform the words of the covenant that were written in this book. (34: 29–31)

In chapters 35 to 36 Josiah's successors are briefly mentioned; this is followed by a fuller account of the final days of Jerusalem. Here the Chronicler stresses that the exile to Babylonia was God's punishment upon his people for forsaking the covenant, yet the Book of Chronicles ends on a note of hope for the future:

Now in the first year of Cyrus king of Persia, that the word of the Lord by the mouth of Jeremiah might be accomplished, the Lord stirred up the spirit of Cyrus king of Persia so that he made a proclamation throughout all his kingdom and also put it in writing: 'Thus says Cyrus king of Persia, "The Lord, the God of heaven, has given me all the kingdoms of the earth, and he has charged me to build him a house at Jerusalem, which is in Judah. Whoever is among you of all his people, may the Lord his God be with him. Let him go up."' (36: 22–23)

Further Reading

Genesis

Commentaries

Brueggemann, W. (1982) *Genesis*, John Knox.
Sarna, N.M. (1989) *Genesis*, The JPS Torah Commentary; Jewish Publication Society.
Speiser, E. (1964) *Genesis*, Doubleday.
von Rad, G. (1961) *Genesis*, Westminster.
Westermann, C. (1984–86) *Genesis: A Commentary*, trans. J. J. Scullian, Augsburg.

Studies

Alter, R. (1981) *The Art of Biblical Narrative*, Basic Books.
Barton, J. (1984) *Reading the Old Testament*, Westminster.
Bloom, H. with Rosenberg, D. (1990) *The Book of J*, Grove Weidenfeld.
Cassuto, U. (1961; Hebrew edn. 1941) *The Documentary Hypothesis*, trans. I. Abrahams, Magnes Press.
Clines, D.J. (1978) *The Theme of the Pentateuch*, Sheffield.
Kikawada, I.M. and Quinn, A. (1985) *Before Abraham Was: The Unity of Genesis 1–11*, Abingdon.
Millard, A.R. and Wiseman, D.J. (eds) (1980) *Essays on the Patriarchal Narratives*, Inter-Varsity.
Ross, A.P. (1988) *Creation and Blessing: A Guide to the Study and Exposition of Genesis*, Baker.
van Seters, J. (1975) *Abraham in History and Tradition*, Yale University Press.
Whybray, R.N. (1987) *The Making of the Pentateuch: A Methodological Study*, Sheffield.

Exodus

Commentaries

Cassuto, U. (1967) *Commentary on Exodus*, trans. I. Abrahams, Magnes Press.
Childs, B.S. (1974) *The Book of Exodus*, Westminster.
Durham, J.I. (1987) *Exodus*, Word.
Kaiser, W. (1990) 'Exodus', *The Expositor's Bible Commentary*, Zondervan.
Noth, M. (1962) *Exodus*, Westminster.

Studies

Bimson, J.J. (1978) *Redating the Exodus and Conquest*, Sheffield.
Dozeman, T.B. (1989) *God on the Mountain*, Scholars Press.
Gooding, D.W. (1959) *The Account of the Tabernacle*, Cambridge.
Haran, M. (1978) *Temples and Temple-Service in Ancient Israel*, Oxford.
Kitchen, K.A. (1966) *Ancient Orient and the Old Testament*, Inter-Varsity.
Longman III, T. and Reid, D. (1995) *God Is a Warrior: Studies in Old Testament Biblical Theology*, Zondervan.
Miller, P.D., Jr. (1973) *The Divine Warrior in Early Israel*, Harvard University Press.
Moberly, R. (1983) *At the Mountain of God: Story and Theology in Exodus 32–34*, Sheffield.
Soltau, H.W. (1865) *The Holy Vessels and Furniture of the Tabernacle of Israel*, London.
Sternberg, M. (1985) *The Poetics of Biblical Narrative*, Indiana University Press.
Stock, A. (1969) *The Way in the Wilderness*, Liturgical Press.

Leviticus

Commentaries

Harrison, R.K. (1980) *Leviticus*, Inter-Varsity.
Knight, G.A.F. (1981) *Leviticus*, Westminster.
Levine, B.A. (1989) *Leviticus*, Jewish Publication Society.
Snaith, N.H. (1967) *Leviticus and Numbers*, Eerdmans.
Wenham, G.J. (1979) *The Book of Leviticus*, Eerdmans.

Studies

Cody, A. (1969) *A History of Old Testament Priesthood*, Pontifical Biblical Institute.
Douglas, M. (1966) *Purity and Danger*, Routledge.

Haran, M. (1978) *Temples and Temple-Service in Ancient Israel*, Oxford.
Kaufmann, Y. (1960) *The Religion of Israel*, University of Chicago Press.
Kline, M.G. (1980) *Images of the Spirit*, Baker.
Levine, B.A. (1974) *In the Presence of the Lord*, Brill.
Milgrom, J. (1976) *Cult and Conscience: The 'Asham' and the Priestly Doctrine of Repentance*, Brill.
Neusner, J. (1973) *The Idea of Purity in Ancient Judaism*, Brill.
Wenham, G.J. (1981) 'The Theology of Unclean Food', *Evangelical Quarterly*, 53: 6–15.

Numbers

Commentaries

Milgrom, J. (1990) *Numbers*, Jewish Publication Society.
Noordtzij, A. (1983) *Numbers*, Zondervan.
Riggans, W. (1983) *Numbers*, Westminster.
Snaith, N.H. (1967) *Leviticus and Numbers*, Eerdmans.
Wenham, G.J. (1981) *Numbers*, Inter-Varsity.

Studies

Baroody, W. (1993) 'Exodus, Leviticus, Numbers and Deuteronomy', in *A Complete Literary Guide to the Bible*, Zondervan, pp. 121–36.
Clines, D.J. (1978) *The Theme of the Pentateuch*, Sheffield.
Coats, G.W. (1968) *Rebellion in the Wildnerness*, Abingdon.
Davies, G.I. (1979) *The Way of the Wilderness*, Cambridge University Press.
Hackett, J. (1984) *The Balaam Text from Deir'Alla*, Scholars Press.

Deuteronomy

Commentaries

Craigie, P.C. (1976) *The Book of Deuteronomy*, Eerdmans.
Cuncliffe-Jones, G. (1951) *Deuteronomy*, SCM Press.
Driver, S.R. (1895) *A Critical and Exegetical Commentary on Deuteronomy*, Scribner.
Miller, P.D., Jr. (1990) *Deuteronomy*, John Knox.
von Rad, G. (1966) *Deuteronomy*, Westminster.

Studies

Carmichael, C.M. (1974) *The Laws of Deuteronomy*, Cornell University Press.
Clements, R.E. (1989) *Deuteronomy*, Sheffield.
Gold, J. (1982) 'Deuteronomy and the World: The Beginning and the End', in *The Biblical Mosaic*, R. Polzin and E. Rothman (eds), Fortress, pp. 45–59.
Kitchen, K.A. (1966) *Ancient Orient and Old Testament*, Inter-Varsity.
Kline, M.G. (1963) *Treaty of the Great King*, Eerdmans.
McCarthy, D.J. (1978; 2nd edn) *Old Testament Covenant: A Survey of Current Opinions*, Pontifical Biblical Institute.
Nicholson, E.W. (1967) *Deuteronomy and Tradition*, Fortress.
von Rad, G. (1953) *Studies in Deuteronomy*, Westminster.
Weinfeld, M. (1972) *Deuteronomy and the Deuteronomic School*, Clarendon.

Joshua

Commentaries

Auld, A.G. (1984) *Joshua, Judges, and Ruth*, Westminster.
Goslinga, C.J. (1986) *Joshua, Judges, Ruth*, Zondervan.
Soggin, J. (1972) *Joshua*, Westminster.
Woudstra, M. (1981) *The Book of Joshua*, Eerdmans.

Studies

Alt, A. (1966) *Essays on Old Testament History and Religion*, Blackwell.
Diepold, P. (1972) *Israel's Lane*, Kohlhammer.
Greenspoon, L.J. (1983) *Textual Studies in the Book of Joshua*, Scholars Press.
Kaufmann, Y. (1985; 2nd edn) *The Biblical Account of the Conquest of Palestine*, Magnes Press.
Polzin, R. (1980) *Moses and the Deuteronomist*, Seabury.
Weippert, M. (1971) *The Settlement of the Israelite Tribes in Palestine*, Allenson.
Younger, K.L., Jr. (1990) *Ancient Conquest Accounts: A Study in Ancient Near Eastern and Biblical History Writing*, Sheffield.

Judges

Commentaries

Auld, A.G. (1984) *Joshua, Judges and Ruth*, Westminster.
Goslinga, C.J. (1986) *Joshua, Judges, Ruth*, Zondervan.

Hamlin, E.J. (1990) *Judges: At Risk in the Promised Land*, Eerdmans.
Martin, J.D. (1975) *The Book of Judges*, Cambridge University Press.
Soggin, J.A. (1981) *Judges*, Westminster.

Studies

Bodine, W.R. (1980) *The Greek Text of Judges: Recensional Developments*, Scholars Press.
Buber, Martin (1967) *Kingship of God*, trans. R. Scheimann, Harper & Row.
Halpern, B. (1988) *The First Historians*, Harper & Row.
Klein, L.R. (1988) *The Triumph of Irony in the Book of Judges*, Almond.
Mayes, A.D.H. (1974) *Israel in the Period of the Judges*, Allenson.
Polzin, R. (1980) *Moses and the Deuteronomist*, Seabury.
Webb, B.G. (1987) *The Book of the Judges: An Integrated Reading*, Sheffield.

Samuel

Commentaries

Ackroyd, P.R. (1971) *The First Book of Samuel* and *The Second Book of Samuel*, Cambridge University Press.
Brueggemann, W. (1990) *First and Second Samuel*, John Knox.
Gordon, R.P. (1988) *1 and 2 Samuel*, Zondervan.
McCarter, P.K., Jr. (1980 and 1984) *I Samuel and II Samuel*, Doubleday.
Payne, D.F. (1982) *I and II Samuel*, Westminster.

Studies

Birch, B.C. (1976) *The Rise of the Israelite Monarchy: The Growth and Development of Samuel 7–15*, Scholars Press.
Campbell, A.F. (1975) *The Ark Narrative*, Scholars Press.
Carlson, R.A. (1964) *David the Chosen King*, Almquist and Wiksell.
Cross, F.M. (1973) *Canaanite Myth and Hebrew Epic*, Harvard University Press.
Eslinger, L. (1985) *Kingship of God in Crisis: A Close Reading of 1 Samuel 7–12*, Almond.
Gunn, D.M. (1980) *The Fate of King Saul*, Sheffield.
Halpern, B. (1981) *The Constitution of the Monarchy in Israel*, Scholars Press.
Miscall, P. (1986) *1 Samuel: A Literary Reading*, Indiana University Press.
Polzin, R. (1989) *Samuel and the Deuteronomist*, Harper and Row.
Whybray, R.N. (1968) *The Succession Narrative: A Study of II Samuel 9–20 and I Kings 1 and 2*, Allenson.

Kings

Commentaries

Auld, A.G. (1986) *I and II Kings*, Westminster.
Cogan, M. and Tadmor, H. (1988) *II Kings*, Doubleday.
Jones, G.H. (1984) *1 and 2 Kings*, vols 1–2, Eerdmans.
Vos, H.F. (1989) *1, 2 Kings*, Zondervan.
Wiseman, D. (1993) *1 and 2 Kings*, Inter-Varsity.

Studies

Bright, J. (1981) *A History of Israel*, Westminster.
Cogan, M. (1974) *Imperialism and Religion: Assyria, Judah, and Israel in the Eighth and Seventh Centuries BC*, Scholars Press.
Cross, F.M. (1973) *Canaanite Myth and Hebrew Epic*, Harvard University Press.
Ellul, J. (1972) *The Politics of God and the Politics of Man*, Eerdmans.
McKay, J. (1973) *Religion in Judah under the Assyrians*, Allenson.
McKenzie, S.L. (1991) *The Trouble with Kings*, Brill.
Peckham, B. (1985) *The Composition of the Deuteronomistic History*, Scholars Press.
Thompson, M.W. (1982) *Situation and Theology: Old Testament Interpretations of the Syro-Ephraimite War*, Almond.
Wallace, R.S. (1957) *Elijah and Elisha*, Eerdmans.
Weinfeld, M. (1972) *Deuteronomy and the Deuteronomic School*, Oxford University Press.

Isaiah

Commentaries

Clements, R.E. (1980) *Isaiah 1–39*, Eerdmans.
Gray, G.B. (1912) *A Critical and Exegetical Commentary on the Book of Isaiah 1–27*, T & T Clark.
Kaiser, O. (1972) *Isaiah 1–39*, Westminster.
Westermann, C. (1969) *Isaiah 40–46*, Westminster.
Whybray, R.N. (1980) *Isaiah 40–66*, Eerdmans.
Young, E.J. (1965, 1969, 1972) *The Book of Isaiah*, vols 1–3, Eerdmans.

Studies

Allis, O.T. (1950) *The Unity of Isaiah*, Presbyterian and Reformed.
Childs, B. (1967) *Isaiah and the Assyrian Crisis*, SCM Press.
Clines, D.J. (1976) *I, He, We, and They: A Literary Approach to Isaiah 53*, Sheffield.

Margalioth, R. (1964) *The Indivisible Isaiah*, Yeshiva University.
Odendaal, D. (1970) *The Eschatological Expectation of Isaiah 40–66*, Presbyterian and Reformed.
Radday, Y.T. (1973) *The Unity of Isaiah in the Light of Statistical Linguistics*, Gerstenberg.
Seitz, C. (ed.) (1988) *Reading and Preaching the Book of Isaiah*, Fortress.
Sweeney, M. (1988) *Isaiah 1–4 and the Post-Exilic Understanding of the Isaianic Tradition*, BZAW 171, De Gruyter.
Whybray, R.N. (1978) *Thanksgiving for a Liberated Prophet*, Sheffield.
Young, E.J. (1952) *Isaiah Fifty-three*, Eerdmans.
Young, E.J. (1954) *Studies in Isaiah*, Eerdmans.
Young, E.J. (1958) *Who Wrote Isaiah?*, Eerdmans.
Young, E.J. (1961) *Isaiah's Message for Today*, Cincinnati Bible Seminary.

Jeremiah

Commentaries

Bright, J. (1962) *Jeremiah*, Doubleday.
Carroll, R.P. (1986) *The Book of Jeremiah*, Westminster.
Clements, R.E. (1988) *Jeremiah*, John Knox.
Davidson, R. (1983, 1985) *Jeremiah and Lamentations*, vols 1–2, Westminster.
McKane, W.A. (1986) *A Critical and Exegetical Commentary on Jeremiah*, vol. 1, T & T Clark.
Nicholson, E.W. (1973, 1975) *Jeremiah*, vols 1–2, Cambridge.
Thompson, J.A. (1979) *The Book of Jeremiah*, Eerdmans.

Studies

Blank, S.H. (1961) *Jeremiah – Man and Prophet*, Hebrew Union College.
Carroll, R.P. (1981) *From Chaos to Covenant: Uses of Prophecy in the Book of Jeremiah*, SCM Press.
Hyatt, J.P. (1958) *Jeremiah, Prophet of Courage and Hope*, Abingdon.
Janzen, J.G. (1973) *Studies in the Text of Jeremiah*, Harvard University Press.
Nicholson, E.W. (1970) *Preaching to the Exiles: A Study of the Prose Tradition in the Book of Jeremiah*, Blackwell.
O'Connor, K. (1988) *The Confessions of Jeremiah: Their Interpretation and Role in Chapters 1–25*, Scholars Press.
Raitt, T.M. (1977) *A Theology of Exile: Judgement and Deliverance in Jeremiah and Ezekiel*, Fortress.
Robinson, H.W. (1955) *The Cross in the Old Testament*, SCM Press.
Skinner, J. (1922) *Prophecy and Religion*, Cambridge University Press.
Stulman, L. (1986) *The Prose Sermons of the Book of Jeremiah*, Scholars Press.
Unterman, J. (1987) *From Repentance to Redemption*, Sheffield.

Ezekiel

Commentaries

Allen, L.C. (1990) *Ezekiel 20–48*, Word.
Brownlee, W.H. (1986) *Ezekiel 1–19*, Word.
Eichrodt, W. (1970) *Ezekiel*, Westminster.
Gowan, D.E. (1985) *Ezekiel*, John Knox.
Greenberg, M. (1983) *Ezekiel 1–20*, Doubleday.
Hals, R.M. (1989) *Ezekiel*, Eerdmans.
Zimmerli, W. (1979, 1983) *Ezekiel*, vols 1–2, Fortress.

Studies

Ackroyd, P. (1968) *Exile and Restoration*, Westminster.
Carley, K.W. (1974) *Ezekiel Among the Prophets*, Allenson.
Fishbane, M. (1984) 'Sin and Judgement in the Prophecies of Ezekiel', *Interpretation*, 38: 131–50.
Fox, M.V. (1980) 'The Rhetoric of Ezekiel's Vision of the Valley of the Bones', *Hebrew Union College Annual*, 51: 1–15.
Greenberg, M. (1980) 'The Vision of Jerusalem in Ezekiel 8–11: A Holistic Interpretation,' in *The Divine Helmsman*, J. Crenshaw (ed), KTAV, 143–64.
Greenberg, M. (1983) 'Ezekiel 17: A Holistic Interpretation,' *Journal of the American Oriental Society* 3: 149–54.
Greenberg, M. (1984) 'The Design and Themes of Ezekiel's Program of Restoration,' *Int* 38: 181–208.
Haran, M. (1979) 'The Law Code of Ezekiel XL–XLVIII and Its Relation to the Priestly School', *Hebrew Union College Annual*, 50: 45–71.
Irwin, W.A. (1943) *The Problem of Ezekiel*, University of Chicago Press.
Levenson, J.D. (1976) *Theology of the Program of Restoration of Ezekiel 40–48*, Scholars Press.
Rowley, H.H. (1953) 'The Book of Ezekiel in Modern Study', *Bulletin of the John Rylands Library*, 36: 146–90.
Talmon, S. and Fishbane, M. (1976) 'The Structuring of Biblical Books: Studies in the Book of Ezekiel', *Annual of the Swedish Theological Institute*, 10: 129–53.
Wilson, R.R. (1984) 'Prophecy in Crisis: The Call of Ezekiel', *Interpretation*, 38: 117–30.

Hosea

Commentaries

Andersen, F.I. and Freedman, D.N. (1980) *Hosea*, Doubleday.

Davies, G.I. (1992) *Hosea*, Eerdmans.
Hubbard, D.A. (1989) *Hosea*, Inter-Varsity.
Mays, J.L. (1969) *Hosea*, Westminster.
Stuart, D.K. (1987) *Hosea-Jonah*, Word.
Wolff, H.W. (1965) *Hosea*, Fortress.

Studies

Brueggemann, W. (1968) *Tradition for Crisis: A Study in Hosea*, John Knox.
Daniels, D.R. (1990) *Hosea and Salvation History*, De Gruyter.
Emmerson, G.I. (1984) 'Hosea: An Israelite Prophet in Judean Perspective', *Journal for the Society of the Old Testament*.
Fensham, F.C. (1984) 'The Marriage Metaphor in Hosea for the Covenant Relationship Between the Lord and His People (Hos. 1: 2–9)', *Journal of North West Semitic Languages*, 12: 71–8.
Kaiser, W.C., Jr. (1985) 'Inner Biblical Exegesis as a Model for Bridging the "Then" and the "Now" Gap: Hos. 12: 1–6', *Journal of the Evangelical Theological Society*, 28: 33–46.
Kruger, P.A. (1988) 'Prophetic Imagery: On Metaphors and Similes in the Book of Hosea', *Journal of North West Semitic Languages*, 14: 143–51.
Weems, R.J. (1989) 'Gomer: Victim of Violence or Victim of Metaphor?' *Semeia*, 47: 87–104.
Wyrtzen, D.B. (1984) 'The Theological Center of the Book of Hosea', *Bibliotheca Sacra*, 141: 315–29.
Yee, G.A. (1987) *Composition and Tradition in the Book of Hosea: A Redaction Critical Investigation*, Scholars Press.

Joel

Commentaries

Allen, L.L. (1976) *The Books of Joel, Obadiah, Jonah, and Micah*, Eerdmans.
Craigie, P. (1984) *Twelve Prophets*, vol 1, Westminster.
Dillard, R.B. (1992) *Joel*, Baker Commentary on the Minor Prophets, Baker.
Jones, D.R. (1972) *Isaiah 56–66 and Joel*, SCM Press.

Studies

Ahlström, G.W. (1971) *Joel and the Temple Cult of Jerusalem*, Brill.
Baron, S. (1971) *The Desert Locust*, Scribner.
Myers, J.M. (1962) 'Some Considerations Bearing on the Date of Joel', *Zeitschrift für die alttestamentliche Wissenschaft*, 74: 177–95.
Ogden, G. (1983) 'Joel 4 and Prophetic Response to National Laments', *Journal for the Study of the Old Testament* 26: 97–106.
Prinsloo, W.S. (1985) *The Theology of the Book of Joel*, De Gruyter.

Stephenson, F.R. (1969) 'The Date of the Book of Joel', *Vetus Testamentum* 19: 224–9.

Thompson, J.A. (1974) 'The Date of Joel', in *A Light Unto My Path*, Fs. J.M. Myers; A. Bream *et al.* (eds), Temple University Press.

Treves, M. (1957) 'The Date of Joel', in *Vetus Testamentum* 7: 149–56.

Amos

Commentaries

Amsler, S. (1982) *Amos*, Delachaux & Niestlé.

Anderson, F.I. and Freedman, D.N. (1989) *Amos*, Doubleday.

Auld, A.G. (1986) *Amos*, Sheffield.

Mays, J.L. (1979) *Amos*, Westminster.

Paul, S.M. (1991) *Amos: A Commentary on the Book of Amos*, Fortress.

Smith, G.V. (1988) *Amos, A Commentary*, Zondervan.

Soggin, R. (1987) *The Prophet Amos: A Translation and Commentary*, SCM Press.

Studies

Barstad, H.M. (1984) *The Religious Polemics of Amos*, Brill.

Barton, J. (1980) *Amos's Oracles Against the Nations: A Study of Amos 1: 3–2: 5*, Cambridge University Press.

Coote, R. (1981) *Amos Among the Prophets: Composition and Theology*, Fortress.

Doorly, W.J. (1989) *Prophet of Justice: Understanding the Book of Amos*, Paulist.

Hayes, J.H. (1988) *Amos, His Time and His Preaching: The Eighth-Century Prophet*, Abingdon.

Petersen, D.L. (1981) *The Social Roles of Israel's Prophet*, Sheffield.

Polley, M.E. (1989) *Amos and the Davidic Empire: A Socio-Historical Approach*, Oxford University Press.

Rosenbaum, S.N. (1990) *Amos of Israel: A New Interpretation*, Mercer University Press.

Routtenberg, H.J. (1971) *Amos of Tekoa: A Study in Interpretation*, Vantage.

Thorogood, B.A. (1971) *A Guide to the Book of Amos, with Thema Discussions on Judgement, Social Justice, Priest and Prophet*, SPCK.

van der Wal, A. (1983) 'The Structure of Amos', *Journal for the Study of the Old Testament*, 26.

van der Wal, A. (1986; 3rd edn.) *Amos: A Classified Bibliography*, Free University Press.

Williamson, H.G.M. (1990) 'The Prophet and the Plumb-line', in *In Quest of the Past*, A. van der Woude (ed.), Leiden, Brill.

Obadiah

Commentaries

Allen, L.C. (1976) *The Books of Joel, Obadiah, Jonah, and Micah*, Eerdmans.
Baker, D.W., Alexander, T.D. and Waltke, B.K. (1988) *Obadiah, Jonah, and Micah*, Leicester, Inter-Varsity.
Coggins, R.J. and Re'emi, S.P. (1985) *Nahum, Obadiah, Esther: Israel Among the Nations*, Eerdmans.
Eaton, J.H. (1961) *Obadiah, Nahum, Habakkuk, Zephaniah*, SCM Press.
Limburg, J. (1988) *Hosea-Micah*, Knox.
Stuart, D. (1987) *Hosea-Jonah*, Word.

Studies

Lillie, J.R. (1979) 'Obadiah – A Celebration of God's Kingdom', *Currents in Theology and Missions 6*.
Ogden, G.S. (1982) 'Prophetic Oracles Against Foreign Nations and Psalms of Communal Lament: the Relationship of Jeremiah 49: 7–22 and Obadiah', *Journal for the Study of the Old Testament* 24: 89–97.
Robinson, R.B. (1988) 'Levels of Naturalization in Obadiah', *Journal for the Study of the Old Testament* 40: 83–97.
Snyman, S.D. (1987) 'Cohesion in the Book of Obadiah', *Zeitschrift für die alttestamentliche Wissenschaft* 101: 59–71.

Jonah

Commentaries

Allen, L.C. (1976) *The Books of Joel, Obadiah, Jonah and Micah*, Eerdmans.
Baker, D.W., Alexander, T.D. and Waltke, B.K. (1988) *Obadiah, Jonah, Micah*, Inter-Varsity.
Berlin, A. (1983) *Poetics and Interpretation of Biblican Narrative*, Almond.
Craigie, P.C. (1985) *Twelve Prophets*, Westminster.
Rudolph, W. (1971) *Joel, Amos, Obadiah, Jonah*, Mohn.
Stuart, D. (1987) *Hosea-Jonah*, Word.

Studies

Aalders, G. Ch. (1948) *The Problem of Jonah*, Tyndale.
Hart-Davies, D.E. (1937) 'The Book of Jonah in the Light of Assyrian Archaeology', *Journal of the Transactions of the Victoria Institute* 69: 230–47.
Magonet, J.D. (1976) *Form and Meaning: Studies in the Literary Techniques in the Book of Jonah*, Herbert Lang.

Micah

Commentaries

Allen, L.C. (1976) *The Books of Obadiah, Jonah, and Micah*, Eerdmans.
Baker, D.W., Alexander, T.D. and Waltke, B.K. (1988) *Obadiah, Jonah, Micah*, Inter-Varsity.
Hillers, D. (1984) *Micah*, Fortress.
Mays, J.L. (1976) *Micah*, Westminster.
Smith, R.L. (1984) *Micah-Malachi*, Word.

Studies

Dawes, S. (1988) 'Walking Humbly: Micah 6: 8 Revisited', *Scottish Journal of Theology* 41: 331–9.
Jeppesen, K. (1978) 'New Aspects of Micah Research,' *Journal for the Study of the Old Testament* 8: 3–32.
Jeppesen, K. (1979) 'How the book of Micah Lost Its Integrity: Outline of the History of the Criticism of the Book of Micah with Emphasis on the 19th Century', *StTh* 33: 101–31.
Kapelrud, A.S. (1961) 'Eschatology in the Book of Micah', *Vetus Testamentum* 11: 392–405.
Smith, L.P. (1952) 'The Book of Micah', *Interpretation* 6: 210–27.
Van der Woude, A.S. (1969) 'Micah and the Pseudo-Prophets', *Vetus Testamentum* 19: 244–60.

Nahum

Commentaries

Achtemeier, E. (1986) *Nahum-Malachi*, John Knox.
Longman III, T. (1993) 'Nahum', in *Commentary on the Minor Prophets*, T. McComiskey (ed.), Baker.
Maier, W.A. (1959; reprint 1980) *The Book of Nahum: A Commentary*, Concordia and Baker.
Smith, J.M.P. (1912) *A Critical and Exegetical Commentary on the Book of Nahum*, T & T Clark.
Smith, R.L. (1984) *Micah-Malachi*, Word.

Studies

Cathcart, K.J. (1973) *Nahum in the Light of Northwest Semitic Philology*, Pontifical Biblical Institute.
Haldar, A. (1947) *Studies in the Book of Nahum*, Uppsala.
Janzen, W. (1972) *Mourning Cry and Woe Oracle*, De Gruyter.

Longman III, T. (1982) 'The Divine Warrior: The New Testament Use of an Old Testament Motif', *WJT* 44: 290–307.

Longman III, T. (1985) 'The Form and Message of Nahum: Preaching from a Prophet of Doom', *Reformed Theological Journal* 1: 13–24.

Longman III, T. (1985) 'Psalm 98: A Divine Warrior Victory Song,' *JETS* 27: 267–74.

Longman III, T. and Reid, D. (1995) *God is a Warrior*, Zondervan.

Zawadzki, S. (1988) *The Fall of Assyria and Median-Babylonian Relations in Light of the Nabopolassar Chronicle*, Eburon.

Habakkuk

Commentaries

Baker, D.W. (1988) *Nahum, Habakkuk, and Zephaniah*, Inter-Varsity.

Bruce, F.F. (1993) 'Habakkuk', in *Commentary on the Minor Prophets*, T. McComiskey (ed.), Baker.

Eaton, J.H. (1961) *Obadiah, Nahum, Habakkuk, and Zephaniah*, SCM Press.

Gowan, D.E. (1976) *The Triumph of Faith in Habakkuk*, John Knox.

Robertson, O.P. (1990) *The Books of Nahum, Habakkuk, and Zephaniah*, Eerdmans.

Smith, R.L. (1984) *Micah-Malachi*, Word.

Watts, J.D.W. (1975) *Joel, Obadiah, Jonah, Micah, Nahum, Habakkuk, Zephaniah*, Cambridge University Press.

Studies

Albright, W.F. (1950–1) 'The Psalm of Habakkuk', in *Studies in Old Testament Prophecy Dedicated to T. H. Robinson*, H.H. Rowley (ed.), T & T Clark, pp. 1–18.

Gunneweg, A.H.J. (1986) 'Habakkuk and the Problem of the Suffering Just', in *Proceedings of the Ninth World Congress of Jewish Studies*, World Union of Jewish Studies, A: 85–90.

Peckham, B. (1986) 'The Vision of Habakkuk', *CBQ* 48: 617–36.

Rast, W. (1983) 'Habakkuk and Justification by Faith', *Currents in Theology and Mission* 10: 169–75.

Sanders, J.A. (1959) 'Habakkuk in Qumran, Paul and the Old Testament', *JR* 38: 232–44.

Zephaniah

Commentaries

Baker, D.W. (1988) *Nahum, Habakkuk, and Zephaniah*, Inter-Varsity.

Eaton, J.H. (1961) *Obadiah, Nahum, Habakkuk, and Zephaniah*, SCM Press.

Robertson, O.P. (1990) *The Books of Nahum, Habakkuk, and Zephaniah*, Eerdmans.

Smith, R.L. (1984) *Micah-Malachi*, Word.

Watts, J.D.W. (1975) *Joel, Obadiah, Jonah, Micah, Nahum, Habakkuk, Zephaniah*, Cambridge University Press.

Studies

Anderson, G.W. (1977/8) 'The Idea of the Remnant in the Book of Zephaniah', *Annual of the Swedish Theological Institute* 11: 11–14.

Ball, I.J. (1987) 'The Rhetorical Shape of Zephaniah', in *Perspectives on Language and Text*, E. Conrad and E. Newing (eds), Eisenbrauns.

House, P.R. (1988) *Zephaniah: A Prophetic Drama*, Almond.

Williams, D.L. (1963) 'The Date of Zephaniah', *JBL* 82: 77–88.

Haggai

Commentaries

Baldwin, J.G. (1972) *Haggai, Zechariah, Malachi*, Tyndale.

Jones, D.R. (1964) *Haggai, Zechariah, and Malachi*, SCM Press.

Petersen, D. (1984) *Haggai and Zechariah 1–8*, Westminster.

Smith, R.L. (1984) *Micah-Malachi*, Word.

Verhoef, P. (1987) *The Books of Haggai and Malachi*, Eerdmans.

Studies

Ackroyd, P.R. (1968) *Exile and Restoration*, Westminster.

Gelston, A. (1966) 'The Foundation of the Second Temple', *Vetus Testamentum* 16: 232–5.

Verhoef, P. (1988) 'Notes on the Dates in the Book of Haggai', in *Text and Context*, W. Classen (ed), JSOT.

Wessels, W. J. (1988) 'Haggai from a Historian's Point of View', *OTE* 1, 2: 47–61.

Wolf, H. (1976) ' "The Desire of All Nations" in Haggai 2: 7: Messianic or Not?', *JETS* 9: 97–102.

Zechariah

Commentaries

Baldwin, J.G. (1972) *Haggai, Zechariah, Malachi*, Tyndale.

Jones, D.R. (1964) *Haggai, Zechariah, and Malachi*, SCM Press.

Petersen, D. (1984) *Haggai and Zechariah 1–8*, Westminster.

Studies

Ackroyd, P.R. (1968) *Exile and Restoration*, Westminster.
Bruce, F.F. (1961) 'The Book of Zechariah and the Passion Narrative', *BJRL* 43: 336–53.
Hanson, P. (1987) 'In Defiance of Death: Zechariah's Symbolic Universe', *Love and Death in the Ancient Near East*, J. Marks and R. Good (eds), Four Quarters.
Johnson, A.R. (1955) *Sacral Kingship in Ancient Israel*, University of Wales Press.
Petersen, D. (1984) 'Zechariah's Visions: A Theological Perspective', *Vetus Testamentum* 34: 195–206.
Portnoy, S. and Petersen, D. (1984) 'Biblical Texts and Statistical Analysis: Zechariah and Beyond', *JBL* 103: 11–21.

Malachi

Commentaries

Achtemeier, E. (1986) *Nahum-Malachi*, John Knox.
Baldwin, J.G. (1972) *Haggai, Zechariah, Malachi*, Inter-Varsity.
Craigie, P.C. (1985) *Twelve Prophets*, Westminster.
Isbell, C.D. (1980) *Malachi*, Zondervan.
Kaiser, W.C. (1984) *Malachi: God's Unchanging Love*, Baker.
Mitchell, H.G., Smith, J.M.P. and Bewer, J.A. (1912) *Haggai, Zechariah, Malachi, and Jonah*, T & T Clark.
Ogden, G.S. and Deutsch, R.R. (1987) *Joel and Malachi: A Promise of Hope, a Call to Obedience*, Eerdmans.
Smith, R.L. (1984) *Micah-Malachi*, Word.
Verhoef, P.A. (1987) *The Books of Haggai and Malachi*, Eerdmans.

Studies

Allison, D.C., Jr. (1984) 'Elijah Must Come First', *JBL* 103: 256–8.
Baldwin, J.G. (1972) 'Malachi 1: 11 and the Worship of the Nations in the Old Testament', *Tyn Bul* 23: 117–24.
Berquist, J.L. (1989) 'The Social Setting of Malachi', *BibThBul* 19: 121–6.
Blomberg, C.L. (1987) *Criswell Theological Review* 2: 99–117.
Clendenen, E.R. (1987) 'The Structure of Malachi: A Textlinguistic Study', *Criswell Theological Review* 2: 3–17.
Fishbane, M. (1983) 'Form and Reformulation of the Biblical Priestly Blessing', *JAOS* 103: 115–21.
Fitzmeyer, J.A. (1987) *Malachi: The Divine Messenger*, Scholars Press.
Klein, G.L. (1987) 'An Introduction to Malachi', *Criswell Theological Review* 2: 19–37.

McKenzie, S.L. and Wallace, H.N. (1983) 'Covenant Themes in Malachi', *CBQ* 45: 549–63.
Torrey, C.C. (1898) 'The Prophecy of Malachi', *JBL* 17: 1–17.

Psalms

Commentaries

Allen, L.C. (1983) *Psalms 100–150*, Word.
Anderson, A.A. (1972) *Psalms*, Eerdmans.
Briggs, C.A. and E.G.A. (1909) *A Critical and Exegetical Commentary on the Book of Psalms*, T & T Clark.
Craigie, P.C. (1983) *Psalms 1–50*, Word.
Dahood, M.J. (1965–70) *Psalms*, Doubleday.
Gerstenberger, E.S. (1989) *Psalms*, Eerdmans.
Kidner, D. (1973–6) *Psalms*, Inter-Varsity.
Knight, G.A.F. (1982) *Psalms*, Westminster.
Weiser, A. (1962) *The Psalms*, Westminster.

Studies

Allen, R.B. (1983) *When the Son Is New: Understanding the Kingdom in the Psalms*, Thomas Nelson.
Anderson, B.W. (1983) *Out of the Depths: The Psalms Speak to Us Today*, Westminster.
Beckwith, R. (1983) *The Old Testament Canon of the New Testament Church*, SPCK.
Eaton, J.H. (1976) *Kingship and the Psalms*, Allenson.
Kraus, H-J (1986) *Theology of the Psalms*, trans. K. Crim, Augsburg.
Miller, P.D., Jr. (1986) *Interpreting the Psalms*, Fortress.
Mowinckel, S. (1962) *The Psalms in Israel's Worship*, vols 1–2, Abingdon.
Westermann, C. (1980) *The Psalms: Structure, Content, and Message*, Augsburg.

Proverbs

Commentaries

Kidner, D. (1964) *Proverbs*, Inter-Varsity.
McKane, W. (1970) *Proverbs: A New Approach*, Westminster.
Scott, R.B.Y. (1965) *Proverbs, Ecclesiastes*, Doubleday.
Toy, C.H. (1916) *The Book of Proverbs*, Scribner.

Studies

Bryce, G.E. (1979) *A Legacy of Wisdom: The Egyptian Contribution to the Wisdom of Israel*, Bucknell University Press.

Bullock, C.H. (1979) *An Introduction to the Old Testament Poetic Books*, Moody.

Lang, B. (1986) *Wisdom and the Book of Proverbs: An Israelite Goddess Redefined*, Pilgrim.

Oesterley, W.O.E. (1927) *The Wisdom of Egypt and the Old Testament in the Light of the Newly Discovered 'Teaching of Amenem-ope'*, SPCK.

Skehan, P.W. (1971) *Studies in Israelite Poetry and Wisdom*, CBQMS 1: The Catholic Biblical Association of America.

von Rad, G. (1972) *Wisdom in Israel*, Abingdon.

Whybray, R.N. (1968) *Wisdom in Proverbs: The Concept of Wisdom in Proverbs*, vols 1–9, Allenson.

Williams, J.G. (1981) *Those Who Ponder Proverbs: Aphoristic Thinking and Biblical Literature*, Almond.

Job

Commentaries

Andersen, F.I. (1976) *Job*, Inter-Varsity.

Clines, D.J. (1975, reprint) *Job*, Eerdmans.

Dhorme, E. (1984; orig. 1926) *A Commentary on the Book of Job*, Thomas Nelson.

Driver, S.R., and Gray, G.B. (1921) *The Book of Job*, T & T Clark.

Gordis, R. (1978) *The Book of Job: Commentary, New Translation, Special Studies*, Jewish Theological Seminary.

Janzen, J.G. (1990) *Job*, John Knox.

Murphy, R.E. (1970) *Wisdom Literature: Job, Proverbs, Ruth, Canticles, Ecclesiastes, Esther*, Eerdmans.

Pope, M.H. (1965) *Job*, Doubleday.

Rowley, H.H. (1970) *Job*, Eerdmans.

Studies

Barr, J. (1971–2) 'The Book of Job and Its Modern Interpreters', *BJRL* 54: 28–46.

Clines, D.J.A. (1982) 'The Arguments of Job's Three Friends', in *Art and Meaning: Rhetoric in Biblical Literature*, D.J.A. Clines et al. (eds), *JSOTS* 19: 215–29.

Curtis, J. (1979) 'On Job's Response to Yahweh', *JBL* 98: 497–511.

Lambert, W.G. (1960) *Babylonian Wisdom Literature*, Oxford.

Robertson, D.A. (1972) *Linguistic Evidence in Dating Early Hebrew Poetry*,

SBL Dissertation Series 3.

Westermann, C (1981) *The Structure of the Book of Job*, trans. C. Muenchow, Fortress.

Zerafa, P. (1978) *The Wisdom of God in the Book of Job*, Herder.

Song of Songs

Commentaries

Caird, G.B. (1980) *The Language and Imagery of the Bible*, Westminster.
Carr, G. Lloyd (1984) *Song of Solomon*, Inter-Varsity.
Ginsburg, C.D. (197; orig. 1857) *The Song of Songs and Coheleth*, KTAV.
Glickman, S.C. (1976) *A Song for Lovers*, Inter-Varsity.
Gordis, R. (1974; rev. edn.) *The Song of Songs and Lamentations*, ? Schocken.
Pope, M.H. (1977) *Song of Songs*, Doubleday.
Seerveld, C. (1967) *The Greatest Song*, Trinity Pennyasheet Press.
Snaith, J.G. (1993) *The Song of Songs*, Eerdmans.

Studies

Davidson, R.M. (1989) 'Theology of Sexuality in the Song of Songs: Return to Eden', *AUSS* 27: 1–19.
Falk, M. (1982) *Love Lyrics from the Bible*, Almond.
Godet, F. (1894; 9th edn; reprinted 1972) *Studies in the Old Testament* in *Classical Evangelical Essays*, W.C.Kaiser, Jr. (ed.), Hodder and Stoughton; Baker.
Goulder, M.D. (1986) *The Song of Fourteen Songs*, JSOTS 36, Almond.
Mariaselvan, A. (1989) *The Song of Songs and Ancient Tamil Love Poems: Poetry and Symbolism*, Editrice Pontificio Istituto Biblico.
Segal, M.H. (1973) 'The Song of Songs', *Vetus Testamentum* 12: 470–90.
Trible, P. (1978) *God and the Rhetoric of Sexuality*, Fortress.
White, J.B. (1978) *A Study of the Language of Love in the Song of Songs and Ancient Egyptian Poetry*, Scholars Press.

Ruth

Commentaries

Atkinson, D. (1983) *The Message of Ruth*, Inter-Varsity.
Auld, A.G. (1984) *Joshua, Judges, and Ruth*, Westminster.
Campbell, E.F., Jr. (1975) *Ruth*, Doubleday.
Cundall, A.E. and Morris, L. (1968) *Judges and Ruth*, Inter-Varsity.
Goslinga, J. (1967) *Joshua, Judges and Ruth*, Eerdmans.
Hubbard, R.L., Jr. (1988) *The Book of Ruth*, Eerdmans.

Sasson, J.M. (1989) *Ruth: A New Translation with Philological Commentary and a Formalist-Folklorist Interpretation*, JSOT.

Studies

Fewell, D.N. and Gunn, D.M. (1990) *Compromising Redemption: Relating Characters in the Book of Ruth*, Westminster/John Knox.
Hals, R.M. (1969) *The Theology of the Book of Ruth*, Fortress.
Howard, D.M., Jr. (1993) *An Introduction to the Old Testament Historical Books*, Moody.
Ryken, L. (1992) 'Ruth,' in *A Dictionary of Biblical Tradition in English Literature*, D.L. Jeffrey (ed.), Eerdmans: pp. 669–780.
Tischler, N.M. (1993) 'Ruth,' in *A Complete Literary Guide to the Bible*, L. Ryken and T. Longman III (eds), Zondervan: pp. 151–64.

Lamentations

Commentaries

Davidson, R. (1985) *Jeremiah* (vol 2) *and Lamentations*, Westminster.
Harrison, R.K. (1973) *Jeremiah and Lamentations*, Inter-Varsity.
Hillers, D.R. (1972) *Lamentations*, Doubleday.
Martin-Achard, R. and Re'emi, S. Paul (1984) *Amos and Lamentations*, Eerdmans.
Provan, I. (1991) *Lamentations*, Eerdmans.

Studies

Albrektson, B. (1963) *Studies in the Text and Theology of Lamentations*, Gleerup.
Gordis, R. (1974) 'The Conclusion of the Book of Lamentations (5: 22)', *JBL* 93: 289–93.
Gottwald, N.K. (1954) *Studies in the Book of Lamentations*, SCM Press.
Grossberg, D. (1989) *Centripetal and Centrifugal Structures in Biblical Poetry*, Scholars Press.
Kaiser, W.C., Jr. (1982) *A Biblical Approach to Personal Suffering*, Moody.
Longman III, T. and Reid, D. (1995) *God Is a Warrior*, Zondervan.
Mintz, A. (1982) 'The Rhetoric of Lamentations and the Representation of Catastrophe', *Prooftexts* 2: 1–7.
Moore, M.S. (1983) 'Human Suffering in Lamentations', *RB* 90: 534–55.

Ecclesiastes

Commentaries

Barton, G.A. (1908) *Ecclesiastes*, T & T Clark.
Crenshaw, J.L. (1987) *Ecclesiastes*, Westminster.
Delitzsch, F. (1975; orig. 1872) *Proverbs, Ecclesiastes, Song of Solomon,* Eerdmans.
Eaton, M.A. (1983) *Ecclesiastes*, Inter-Varsity.
Ginsburg, D.D. (1970; orig. 1957) *The Song of Songs and Coheleth*, KTAV.
Scott, R.B.Y. (1965) *Proverbs, Ecclesiastes*, Doubleday.
Whybray, R.N. (1989) *Ecclesiastes*, Eerdmans.

Studies

Fox, M. (1968) 'Frame-Narrative and Composition in the Book of Qohelet', *HUCA* 48: 83–106.
Fredericks, D.C. (1988) *Qoheleth's Language: Re-evaluating Its Nature and Date*, ANETS 3; Edwin Mellen.
Gordis, R. (1951) *Koheleth: The Man and His World*, Schocken.
Isaksson, B. (1857) *Studies in the Language of Qoheleth*, Uppsala.
Kaiser, W.C., Jr. (1989) *Ecclesiastes: Total Life*, Moody.
Whybray, R.N. (1982) 'Qohelet: Preacher of Joy', *JSOT* 23: 87–92.

Esther

Commentaries

Baldwin, J.G. (1984) *Esther: An Introduction and Commentary*, Inter-Varsity.
Moore, C.A. (1971) *Esther*, Doubleday.
Paton, L.B. (1908) *A Critical and Exegetical Commentary on the Book of Esther*, T & T Clark.
Vischer, W. (1937) *Esther*, Chr. Kaiser Verlag.

Studies

Bickerman, E. (1967) *Four Strange Books of the Bible*, Schocken.
Gordis, R. (1976) 'Studies in the Esther Narrative', *JBL* 95: 43–58.
Gordis, R. (1981) 'Religion, Wisdom and History in the book of Esther', *JBL* 100: 359–88.
Moore, C.A. (1975) 'Archaeology and the Book of Esther', *BA* 38: 62–79.
Talmon, S. (1963) ' "Wisdom" in the Book of Esther', in *Vetus Testamentum* 13: 419–55.
Thornton, T.C.G. (1986) 'The Crucifixion of Haman and the Scandal of the Cross', *JTS* 37: 419–26.

Wright, J.S. 'The Historicity of the Book of Esther', in *New Perspectives on the Old Testament*, J.B. Payne (ed.), Word: 37–47.

Yamauchi, E. (1980) 'The Archaeological Background of Esther', *BibSac* 137: 99–117.

Zadok, R. (1984) 'On the Historical Background of the Book of Esther', *BibNot* 24: 18–23.

Daniel

Commentaries

Baldwin, J.G. (1978) *Daniel: An Introduction and Commentary*, Inter-Varsity.

Collins, J.J. (1984) *Daniel with an Introduction to Apocalyptic Literature*, Eerdmans.

Goldingay, J.E. (1989) *Daniel*, Word.

Hartman, L.P. and DiLella, A.A. (1978) *The Book of Daniel*, Doubleday.

Lacocque, A. (1979) *The Book of Daniel*, John Knox.

Montgomery, J.A. (1927) *A Critical and Exegetical Commentary on the Book of Daniel*, T & T Clark.

Porteous, N.W. (1965) *Daniel: A Commentary*, Westminster.

Preminger, A. and Greenstein, E.L. (1968) *The Hebrew Bible in Literary Criticism*, Ungar.

Towner, W.S. (1984) *Daniel*, John Knox.

Studies

Charlesworth, J.H. (1983) *The Old Testament Pseudepigrapha: Apocalyptic Literature and Testaments*, vol 1, Doubleday.

Fewell, D.N. (1988) *Circle of Sovereignty: A Story of Stories in Daniel 1–6*, BLS 20, Almond.

Grayson, A.K. (1975) *Babylonian Historical-Literary Texts*, University of Toronto Press.

Hanson, P.D. (1975) *The Dawn of Apocalyptic*, Fortress.

Hayes, J.H. and Miller, J.M. (1977) *Israelite and Judaean History*, Westminster.

Kugel, J. (1981) *The Idea of Biblical Poetry*, Yale University Press.

Mickelsen, A.B. (1984) *Daniel and Revelation: Riddles or Realities?*, Thomas Nelson.

Rowley, H.H. (1935) *Darius the Mede and the Four World Empires in the Book of Daniel*, The University of Wales Press Board.

Ezra-Nehemiah

Commentaries

Batten, L.W. (1913) *Ezra and Nehemiah*, T & T Clark.
Blenkinsopp, J. (1988) *Ezra-Nehemiah*, Westminster.
Clines, D.J.A. (1984) *Ezra, Nehemiah, Esther*, Eerdmans.
Coggins, R.J. (1976) *The Books of Ezra and Nehemiah*, Cambridge.
Fensham, F.C. (1982) *The Books of Ezra and Nehemiah*, Eerdmans.
Kidner, D. (1979) *Ezra and Nehemiah*, Inter-Varsity.
McConville, J.G. (1985) *Ezra, Nehemiah and Esther*, Westminster.
Myers, J.M. (1965) *Ezra, Nehemiah*, Doubleday.
Williamson, H.G.M. (1985) *Ezra-Nehemiah*, Word.

Studies

Ackroyd, P.R. (1972) 'The Temple Vessels – A Continuity Theme', in *Studies in the Religion of Ancient Israel*, VTSup 23: 166–81.
Ackroyd, P.R. (1985) 'The Historical Literature', in *The Hebrew Bible and Its Modern Interpreters*, D.A. Knight and G.M. Tucker (eds), Fortress/Scholars: pp. 297–323.
Braun, R.L. (1979) 'Chronicles, Ezra, and Nehemiah', in *Studies in the Historical Books of the Old Testament*, VTSup 30: 52–64.
Emerton, J.A. (1966) 'Did Ezra Go to Jerusalem in 428 BC?' *JTS* 17: 1–19.
Eskenazi, T.C. (1986) 'The Chronicler and the Composition of 1 Esdras', *CBQ* 48: 39–61.
Eskenazi, T.C. (1988) *In an Age of Prose: A Literary Approach to Ezra-Nehemiah*, Scholars.
Hoglund, K.G. (1992) *Achaemenid Imperial Administration in Syria-Palestine and the Missions of Ezra and Nehemiah*, Scholars.
Howard, D.M., Jr. (1993) 'Ezra-Nehemiah', in *An Introduction to the Old Testament Historical Books*, Moody, pp. 273–313.
Japhet, S. (1968) 'The Supposed Common Authorship of Chronicles and Ezra-Nehemiah Investigated Anew', *Vetus Testamentum* 18: 330–71.
Japhet, S. (1982) 'Sheshbazzar and Zerubbabel – Against the Background of the Historical and Religious Tendencies of Ezra-Nehemiah', *ZAW* 94: 66–98.
Williamson, H.G.M. (1977) *Israel in the Books of Chronicles*, Cambridge University Press.
Williamson, H.G.M. (1983) 'The Composition of Ezra i–vi', *JTS* 34: 1–30.

Chronicles

Commentaries

Ackroyd, P. (1973) *I and II Chronicles, Ezra, Nehemiah*, SCM Press.
Allen, L. 1, (1987) *2 Chronicles*, Word.
Coggins, R.J. (1976) *The First and Second Books of the Chronicles*, Cambridge University Press.
Curtis, E.L. and Madsen, A. (1910) *A Critical and Exegetical Commentary on the Books of Chronicles*, T & T Clark.
Dillard, R.B. (1987) *2 Chronicles*, Word.
Williamson, H.G.M. (1982) *1 and 2 Chronicles*, Marshall, Morgan, and Scott.

Studies

Allen, L. (1974) *The Greek Chronicles*, vols 1–2, VTSup 25, 27, Brill.
Dillard, R.B. (1980) 'The Chronicler's Solomon', *WTJ* 43: 289–300.
Dillard, R.B. (1984) 'The Literary Structure of the Chronicler's Solomon Narrative', *JSOT* 30: 85–93.
Dillard, R.B. (1984) 'Reward and Punishment in Chronicles: The Theology of Immediate Retribution', *WTJ* 46: 164–72.
Dillar, R.B. (1986) 'The Reign of Asa (2 Chr 14–16) An Example of the Chronicler and the Composition of 1 Esdras', *CBQ* 48: 39–61.
Newsome, J.D. (1975) 'Toward a New Understanding of the Chronicler and His Purposes', *JBL* 94: 204–17.
North, R. (1963) 'The Theology of the Chronicler', *JBL* 82: 369–81.
Petersen, D.L. (1977) *Late Israelite Prophecy*, SBLMS 23, Scholars Press.

Index

k is due for return on or before the last date shown below.

DG 02242/71